CHILDREN AND FAMILY IN LATE ANTIQUE EGYPTIAN MONASTICISM

This is the first book-length study of children in one of the birthplaces of early Christian monasticism, Egypt. Although comprised of men and women who had renounced sex and family, the monasteries of late antiquity raised children, educated them, and expected them to carry on their monastic lineage and legacies into the future. Children within monasteries existed in a liminal space, simultaneously vulnerable to the whims and abuses of adults and cherished as potential future monastic prodigies. Caroline T. Schroeder examines diverse sources – letters, rules, saints' lives, art, and documentary evidence – to probe these paradoxes. In doing so, she demonstrates how early Egyptian monasteries provided an intergenerational continuity of social, cultural, and economic capital while also contesting the traditional family's claims to these forms of social continuity.

CAROLINE T. SCHROEDER is Professor of Classics and Letters at the University of Oklahoma. She is the author of *Monastic Bodies* (2007), coeditor of *Melania* (2016), and cofounder of the groundbreaking digital project Coptic Scriptorium.

CHILDREN AND FAMILY IN LATE ANTIQUE EGYPTIAN MONASTICISM

CAROLINE T. SCHROEDER

University of Oklahoma

CAMBRIDGE
UNIVERSITY PRESS

CAMBRIDGE
UNIVERSITY PRESS

University Printing House, Cambridge CB2 8BS, United Kingdom

One Liberty Plaza, 20th Floor, New York, NY 10006, USA

477 Williamstown Road, Port Melbourne, VIC 3207, Australia

314–321, 3rd Floor, Plot 3, Splendor Forum, Jasola District Centre, New Delhi – 110025, India

79 Anson Road, #06–04/06, Singapore 079906

Cambridge University Press is part of the University of Cambridge.

It furthers the University's mission by disseminating knowledge in the pursuit of education, learning, and research at the highest international levels of excellence.

www.cambridge.org
Information on this title: www.cambridge.org/9781107156876
DOI: 10.1017/9781316661642

First published 2021

A catalogue record for this publication is available from the British Library.

Library of Congress Cataloging-in-Publication Data
NAMES: Schroeder, Caroline T., 1971– author.
TITLE: Children and family in late antique Egyptian monasticism / Caroline T. Schroeder, University of Oklahoma.
DESCRIPTION: Cambridge, United Kingdom ; New York, NY, USA : Cambridge University Press, 2020. | Includes bibliographical references and index.
IDENTIFIERS: LCCN 2020012174 (print) | LCCN 2020012175 (ebook) | ISBN 9781107156876 (hardback) | ISBN 9781316661642 (ebook)
SUBJECTS: LCSH: Christian children – Religious life – History – To 1500. | Children – Egypt – History – To 1500. | Families – Egypt – History – To 1500. | Church history – Primitive and early church, ca. 30–600.
CLASSIFICATION: LCC BR195.C46 S37 2020 (print) | LCC BR195.C46 (ebook) | DDC 276.2/02–dc23
LC record available at https://lccn.loc.gov/2020012174
LC ebook record available at https://lccn.loc.gov/2020012175

ISBN 978-1-107-15687-6 Hardback

For David Brakke

Contents

Figures

Acknowledgments

Many people and institutions have helped me bring this project to fruition. I conducted early research during a postdoctoral fellowship in the Introduction to the Humanities Program at Stanford University, during research terms funded by the Mellon Foundation. Additional support from internal grants at the University of the Pacific and a Graves Award in the Humanities allowed me to continue the early phases of research and write the chapters in Part II. A fellowship from the Alexander von Humboldt Foundation and a summer stipend from the National Endowment for the Humanities allowed me to write additional chapters. I am deeply grateful to the Seminar for Egyptology and Coptology at Georg-August University, Goettingen, and my host, Heike Behlmer. This book could not have been completed without the extensive resources at their library, the help of research assistant Frederic Krueger, and feedback from faculty, including Heike and Jürgen Horn. A fellowship from the American Council of Learned Societies provided the release time necessary to write the final pages and revise the full manuscript.

Some chapters contain material I previously published elsewhere. Content originally published in the chapter "Children in Early Egyptian Monasticism" in *Children in Late Antique Christianity*, ed. Cornelia B. Horn and Robert R. Phenix (Tübingen: Mohr Siebeck, 2009), 317–38, has been revised and now appears throughout the book. Chapter 3 is an edited version of "Queer Eye for the Ascetic Guy?" from the *Journal of the American Academy of Religion* 77 (2009): 333–47. Chapter 4 has been revised from its original appearance as "Child Sacrifice in Egyptian Monastic Culture" in the *Journal of Early Christian Studies* 20 (2012): 269–302. Chapter 5 has been edited and expanded from its original publication as "Monastic Family Values" in *Coptica* 10 (2011): 21–28. Some material in the section "Reading Early Christian Emotions" of Chapter 8 is a revised version of a section on Stoicism and affect theory in "The Perfect Monk," published in *Copts in Context*, ed. Nellie van Doorn-Harder

(Columbia: University of South Carolina Press, 2017), 181–93. I also thank the American Research Center in Egypt for permission to print images from the Red Monastery and the Monastery of Saint Antony in the book and on the cover, and the University of Michigan Visual Resources Collections for permission to print images from Saint Catherine's Monastery in Sinai, Egypt.

The wisdom and generosity of colleagues and friends were boundless. I appreciate comments and advice from the many people who read drafts of various chapters: Mattias Brand, Malcolm Choat, Jennifer Cromwell, Stephen Davis, Andrew Jacobs, Tina Sessa, and most especially Janet Timbie. Many colleagues suggested sources and avenues of research along the way, and I wish to thank Susan Ashbrook Harvey, Alain Delattre, Andrew Crislip, and the late William Harmless especially. Elizabeth Bolman, William Lyster, Stephen Davis, Marcus Mueller, and the monks of the Red and White Monasteries hosted me on trips to the sites of the men's and women's communities in the White Monastery Federation, site visits that immeasurably affected my work; Elizabeth and William's insights and conversations at the Red Monastery with Agnes Szymańska, Malcolm Choat, David Brakke, and Eugene Rogers also provided an experience of a lifetime. I thank Jonathan Farr and Anna Cwikla for their careful editing. Audiences at many academic lectures, workshops, and conference presentations asked questions and gave feedback that shaped the book for the better. Any remaining errors are solely my own. Elizabeth A. Clark, Elizabeth Castelli, Christopher Goff, Rebecca Krawiec, Andrew Jacobs, Tina Shepardson, C. Mike Chin, Michael Penn, Hany Takla, and Amir Zeldes encouraged me even when I feared failure. Eric E. Johnson's unshakable faith in my work and my vision sustained me over the many years of research, writing, and revision.

I dedicate this book to David Brakke. David's work has been for me an academic north star, guiding my research and inspiring my writing since early in my graduate training. David has since become a mentor and friend who has championed my work during challenging times, shared the hard truths when I needed them, and nourished my intellect and broadened my world. I know he has been such a figure for many. This book is for you, David.

Abbreviations

All papyri are cited using the sigla at http://papyri.info/docs/checklist.
Many are available at http://papyri.info/ or www.trismegistos.org/.

AJR	*Ancient Jew Review*
AP	*Apophthegmata Patrum*
AP Anon.	*Apophthegmata Patrum, Anonymous Collection*
AP Syst.	*Apophthegmata Patrum, Systematic Collection*
A22	*Acephalous Work 22* (by Shenoute)
BMCR	*Bryn Mawr Classical Review*
BSAC	*Bulletin de la Société d'archéologie copte*
BZ	*Byzantinische Zeitschrift*
CCSL	Corpus Christianorum Series Latina
CSCO	Corpus Scriptorum Christianorum Orientalium
CSEL	Corpus Scriptorum Ecclesiasticorum Latinorum
DOP	*Dumbarton Oaks Papers*
JECS	*Journal of Early Christian Studies*
JJP	*Journal of Juristic Papyrology*
Mus	*Muséon: Revue d'études orientales*
NPNF	*A Select Library of Nicene and Post-Nicene Fathers of the Christian Church*. Edited by Philip Schaff and Henry Wace. 28 vols. in 2 series. 1886–89.
OLA	Orientalia Lovaniensia Analecta
PG	*Patrologia Graeca*
PL	*Patrologia Latina*
PO	*Patrologia Orientalis*
SAC	Studies in Antiquity and Christianity
SC	Scriptores Coptici

Vit. Patr.	*Vitae Patrum*
V. Pach. Bo	Bohairic *Life of Pachomius*
V. Pach. G^I	First Greek *Life of Pachomius*
V. Pach. S^{10}	Tenth Sahidic *Life of Pachomius*
WZKM	*Wiener Zeitschrift für die Kunde des Morgenlandes*

Introduction

Do not bring young boys here. Four congregations in Scetis are deserted because of boys.[1]

> *Sayings of the Desert Fathers*, attributed to Isaac of Kellia

[As for boys] or girls or old men or women among us, and it is the case that they eat twice a day, the order shall be given to them by the male Elder to eat at the hour that he has told the server to feed them.[2]

> Shenoute, *Canons*, vol. 5

Medieval and Byzantine monasteries and convents were teeming with children. From orphans deposited on their doorsteps to become monastics, to pupils studying in their schools before moving on to an uncloistered adult life, to sick children seeking care from church hospitals, monastic institutions for men and women across the East and West sheltered scores of children during the period we call the "Middle Ages."[3] What, however, of the formative period of Christian monasticism? Where were the children?

This book interrogates the narratives in ascetic and monastic literature about children – narratives in which the views articulated in the epigraph attributed to a certain Abba Isaac dominate. Such views have informed our historical imaginings of the earliest monasteries as child-free zones. I argue instead that late antique monastic textual sources (particularly those from Egypt in the fourth through sixth centuries) serve a different purpose, not to exclude children from monastic and ascetic life but rather to position the monastery as both rival and heir to the ancient institutions of the family and household. Moreover,

---

[1] *AP* Isaac of Kellia 5, in *PG* 65:225; trans. Ward, *Sayings of the Desert Fathers*, 100, mod.
[2] Shenoute, *Canons*, vol. 5, MONB.XS 319, in Leipoldt, *Vita et Opera Omnia*, vol. 4, 53–54; trans. Layton, *Canons of Our Fathers*, 159, mod.
[3] See the classic Boswell, *The Kindness of Strangers*. On children in the Byzantine era including monasticism with a postscript on the Latin West, see Miller, *Orphans of Byzantium*.

even narratives that exhibit disdain for children do their work in a space, a place, and a time when children indeed roamed the monastery. The presence of monastic children, commonplace in medieval and Byzantine institutions, originates with the very beginnings of monasticism in Egypt, even though later authors lauded the region as home to some of the most rigorous monastic practices.

Sources for Egyptian asceticism document the presence of children among adult monks, as the epigraph from Shenoute attests. Certainly, minor children living in their parents' households formed a crucial wing of the ascetic movement from its beginnings in the wider Mediterranean world. Girls on the cusp of adolescence, as they approached the appropriate age for marriage as early as twelve years old, soon became the standard-bearers for a religion that prized moral and sexual virtue.[4] Male clerics extolled female martyrs, whom the men wrote into history as dying rather than risking losing their virginity to rape.[5] As early as the second and third centuries, male ecclesiastics held up virgin girls who shunned marriage to become brides of Christ as symbols of the church.[6] By the fourth century in Egypt, and particularly in Alexandria, "house virgins" and their families comprised an important religious and political constituency with whom Athanasius, bishop of the city, had to contend.[7]

But what of the emerging institutions we now call monasteries? What roles did children play in them? What role did they have in the monastic imagination?

Children Count

In accounting for children in monasteries, we must also ask who counts as a child. The field of childhood studies has long noted the socially and historically constructed character of "childhood" and the group of people we call "children," going back as far as Philip Ariès's argument in 1960 that "childhood" as a life phase distinct from infancy or adulthood emerged as a concept only in the thirteenth century, taking full form in the

---

[4] On marriage and betrothal, see Grubbs, *Law and Family in Late Antiquity*, 141–202; Caldwell, *Roman Girlhood*, 48, 116–19.

[5] Burrus, "Reading Agnes."

[6] E.g., Cyprian on the virgin as "flower" of the church in *De habitu virginum* 3 in *CSEL* 3.1:189; trans. Deferrari et al., *St. Cyprian: Treatises*, 33–34. See also Tertullian, *De exhortatione castitatis* and *De virginibus velandis* in *CCSL* 2:1015–35, 1209–26.

[7] See Brakke's translations and analyses of Athanasius' *Letters to Virgins* and *On Virginity* in *Athanasius and Asceticism*, 17–79 and 274–309.

seventeenth century.[8] While Ariès's particular framing of childhood no longer dominates scholarship, most would agree with him that the *modern* idea of childhood did not hold sway in antiquity.[9] The very definition of a "child" – including the age range of who counts as a child – is historically contingent.[10] In Western societies today, many psychologists posit either the extension of childhood or youth into the late teens and early twenties or the existence of a transition period before adulthood ("emerging adulthood") for all genders.[11] Such a life phase, however, may not exist across the globe, much less in different historical periods; even its contours in the contemporary West are contested.[12]

Accounting for children by following a strictly philological approach of examining terminology for children and youth is not practical. This book draws on sources in Greek, Latin, and Coptic, all of which use vocabularies that possess ambiguities or fluidity. The classic example in Greek is *pais*, which can mean "child" or "enslaved person," and the challenges of terminology do not end there.[13] (Throughout this book, I follow the work of Gabrielle Foreman and use the language of "enslaved person" rather than "slave" as much as possible.[14])

This book follows a standard classification of life stages in late antiquity and attempts to be mindful of the fluidity of these phases and of the intersectionality of gender, economic status, and enslaved/free status. Infants typically are three or younger, with childhood ending at twelve for free girls and fourteen for free boys, and "youth" continuing into the late teens or early twenties

---

[8] Ariès, *Centuries of Childhood*, 33–34, 61, 128–29; see esp. 128: "In medieval society the idea of childhood did not exist."

[9] Christian Laes assesses scholarship on childhood in antiquity in the aftermath of Ariès's work in *Children in the Roman Empire*, 13–18.

[10] See Ariès's survey of life stages in antiquity and the Middle Ages in *Centuries of Childhood*, 15–32; for more recent work on childhood in antiquity and late antiquity, see (among other studies): Beaumont, *Childhood in Ancient Athens*; Laes, *Children in the Roman Empire*; Grubbs, Parkin, and Bell, *The Oxford Handbook of Childhood and Education*; Vuolanto, *Children and Asceticism*; Horn and Martens, *"Let the Little Children Come to Me"*; Horn and Phenix, *Children in Late Ancient Christianity*; Laes and Vuolanto, *Children and Everyday Life*.

[11] Arnett, "Emerging Adulthood"; Tanner, "Recentering during Emerging Adulthood"; Kuper, Wright, and Mustanski, "Gender Identity Development."

[12] Compare to the life stage of "youth" in late antiquity: Laes and Strubbe, *Youth in the Roman Empire*, 1–3, 23–30. On complicating the contemporary category of "emerging adulthood," see Ruddick, "Politics of Aging"; Arnett et al., *Debating Emerging Adulthood*.

[13] Surveys of the terminology in Greek and Latin appear in Laes and Strubbe, *Youth in the Roman Empire*, 41–60; Grubbs, Parkin, and Bell, *The Oxford Handbook of Childhood and Education*, 6–7; for Coptic, see Chapter 2 of this volume and Cromwell, "From Village to Monastery."

[14] Foreman et al., "Writing about 'Slavery'?"

for men.[15] For free girls, the end of childhood corresponded to the minimum legal age of marriage (twelve) and the expected age of menarche.[16] Yet typically only elite women married at twelve; women from lower classes married later. In Roman Egypt, women married in their mid- or late teens, and men around age twenty-five.[17] For most girls, womanhood began upon marriage. Technically, adulthood for free males involved legal rights; however, such maturity often did not fully begin until seventeen years of age or even twenty or twenty-five (the legal age of majority in the Empire and the typical age at which free, propertied men could hold office).[18] The concept of youth or adolescence applied to free males who had reached puberty but not full adulthood. These classifications reflect late antique understandings of biology as well as legal and social concerns. One question, for example, was whether males under twenty-five could be responsible for making wise financial decisions.[19] For free and primarily elite men in the early Western Empire, the transition out of childhood was marked with a ceremonial donning of an adult toga. The ritual seems to have continued even into late antiquity.[20] In Egypt, we have some evidence for a festival celebrating "cutting the hair lock" (a traditional boy's hairstyle).[21] Typically, enslaved and free boys and girls began apprenticeships at twelve to fourteen years of age, another indication of the significance of this age as a period of transition.[22] In Egypt, boys were considered of age and paid the poll tax beginning at fourteen.[23] Nonetheless, "youth" in adolescence and the early twenties, even for males, did not automatically confer all the privileges of adulthood; a young man could be appointed a *curator* to make financial and legal decisions for him, rendering boys minors up to the age of twenty-five. Under Constantine, men twenty years old could be considered legal adults with the support of character

---

[15] Laes and Strubbe, *Youth in the Roman Empire*, 31; Prinzing, "Observations on the Legal Status of Children," 16–20; Laes, *Children in the Roman Empire*, chs. 3 and 4; Wiedemann, *Adults and Children in the Roman Empire*, 113–39.

[16] Caldwell, *Roman Girlhood*, 125.

[17] Huebner, *Family in Roman Egypt*, 49–50. Also see Laes, *Children in the Roman Empire*, 252–56.

[18] Laes and Strubbe, *Youth in the Roman Empire*, 31–34.

[19] Laes and Strubbe, *Youth in the Roman Empire*, 33–34; Prinzing, "Observations on the Legal Status of Children," 17–19.

[20] Laes and Strubbe, *Youth in the Roman Empire*, 55–58.

[21] Legras, "Mallokouria et mallocourètes"; Laes and Strubbe, *Youth in the Roman Empire*, 54.

[22] Laes, *Children in the Roman Empire*, 191–95; Pudsey, "Children in Roman Egypt," 503–04.

[23] Huebner, *Family in Roman Egypt*, 18.

witnesses.[24] Thus, for men, childhood might end at fourteen but adulthood might not begin until their twenties. Early monastic sources in particular rarely mention people's ages. Additionally, throughout the Empire, other factors besides strict biological age affected a person's stage in the life cycle: perceived wisdom or physical maturity, marital status, economic class, and gender.[25] Many people likely did not even know their specific age.

Sexuality did not mark the boundary between childhood and adulthood in late antiquity, since minor children were not regarded as "presexual." Enslaved children of all genders could be compelled to have sex with the people who owned them.[26] Judith Evans Grubbs has posited that for children who survived abandonment (exposure) as infants, "slavery, including sex slavery," was their most likely fate.[27] Children, enslaved or free, worked as prostitutes.[28] Adult men had sex with children and adolescent boys in late antiquity, despite Roman sensibilities that disapproved of such practices more often than ancient Greek sensibilities did.[29] Elite girls at times moved in with their intended fiancés at age ten or eleven, before their legal age of marriage.[30]

Likewise, neither did labor mark a boundary between childhood and adulthood. Outside of the elite classes, free children worked within the household (whether in urban or rural settings) and were often sent to be apprentices, living in other households.[31] Despite twelve to fourteen being a common age to begin apprenticeships, we know that boys especially apprenticed for a trade at a younger age.[32] In first-century Oxyrhynchus, for example, young Dioskus, while still "underage," went to live with and

---

[24] Laes and Strubbe, *Youth in the Roman Empire*, 33–34.

[25] Hence, Huebner's assertion: "In general, it is, however, more helpful . . . to define the individual by their status in a specific life-cycle position" (*Family in Roman Egypt*, 18). Laes and Strubbe also emphasize the fluidity of the category of "youth" and the impossibility of applying specific age boundaries to the life stages of childhood and adulthood (*Youth in the Roman Empire*, chs. 2–4 throughout).

[26] Laes, *Children in the Roman Empire*, 256–58.

[27] Grubbs, "Infant Exposure and Infanticide," 95.

[28] Canon 12 of the Canons of the Synod of Elvira (306) condemns parents who prostitute their children: von Hefele, *Histoire des conciles* 1.1, 228–29; Leyerle, "Children and 'the Child' in Early Christianity," 566.

[29] On sexuality, boys, and adolescent males in ancient Greece, much has been written; see especially Beaumont, "Shifting Gender," 203–04. On Roman practices, especially the distinctions of free status and citizenship, see Laes, *Children in the Roman Empire*, 242–52.

[30] Caldwell, *Roman Girlhood*, 107–16.

[31] Sigismund-Nielsen, "Slave and Lower-Class Roman Children," 296–97; Laes, *Children in the Roman Empire*, 148–221.

[32] See Laes, *Children in the Roman Empire*, 191, on apprenticeship contracts, including the mention of children as "underage."

learn from the weaver Apollonios; Dioskus' father, Pausiris (also a weaver), pledged money for the boy's food and clothing.[33] Even when they are not specified as "underage," male apprentices are often called children and boys, and they cannot represent themselves legally, as in one contract from Tebtunis negotiated by a woman and her guardian for the apprenticeship of her son, a "child" (*pais*).[34]

Though demographic information, vocabulary, and knowledge about social norms can help us sketch some of the parameters of late antique childhood, we will never know for certain the precise age of most people under examination in this book. Our sources do not always use existing vocabulary to differentiate between infants (up to age three in the ancient world), adolescents, and children who fall between infancy and adolescence. Thus, throughout this book, the age of fourteen roughly marks the end of "childhood" per se, but references to "minor children" include persons under the age of twenty. While such terminology may seem imprecise and messy, it reflects our sources, which are equally imprecise and messy.

As this discussion of the definition of "childhood" has progressed, we can also see how much other status and identity markers affect who counts as a child. From education to sexual history to nourishment, enslaved girls under the age of fourteen lived very different lives from their wealthy counterparts; enslaved girls rarely even receive mention in our sources and so often do not count as "children" in the same sense as free girls. Similarly, working-class and elite boys would have experienced differing labor histories, healthcare, and educations.

Contested Childhoods

One aspect of late antique childhood that crosses different class and gender boundaries is childhood as the site of adult aspirations. And when those aspirations conflict or fail to materialize as expected, children become sites of contestation for adults, which is especially evident in both Christian literature and late antique papyri. In seventh-century Thebes, an outraged husband called upon Bishop Pisentius to resolve a dispute with his wife, who had left him for another man and had since given birth to a baby girl. The new lover insisted that the estranged husband bore responsibility for the infant, since she had been born only six months after the beginning of

---

[33] *P. Wisc. 1* 4.   [34] *P. Tebt 2* 385.

the affair.[35] Other petitions preserved in papyri position children as evidence in grievances between disputing parents – for example, a father complaining that his wife has run off with some of his property and left him to fend for their son,[36] and a sick woman charging that her husband abandoned her and their four sons.[37] One surviving papyrus from the early Roman period documents a widow who successfully petitioned to abandon her infant, presumably to increase her chances of marrying again, since the petition also addresses her dowry and potential remarriage.[38] A sixth-century petition even records an adult man complaining about his father's abandonment of him as a child, when the man left his career and family to become a monk.[39] In each of these cases, the interests of the children are subordinated to or placed in service of the objectives of the adults.

Of course, affect and aspiration were not mutually exclusive; children could be loved while also serving as projections of adult ambitions. In Oxyrhynchus, a woman named Thermouthian (possibly with no children, or at least no living sons) wrote of her "despair" upon the traumatic injury of Peina, an enslaved girl. Thermouthian described Peina as like her "own little daughter," which meant a relationship of economics and affection. Thermouthian intended for Peina to care for her as she aged, since she had no one else, and "loved" her. While walking to a singing lesson, Peina collided with (or was run down by?) a donkey driven by an enslaved man owned by someone else, resulting in a disabling and potentially deadly accident; she lost most of her hand. Thermouthian's concern – recorded in a petition to an official seeking redress for this injury – arises from her feelings for the girl, the economic loss of her property, and the future loss of a caregiver in her old age.[40] For all elderly free Egyptians, but especially widowed or divorced women, care in old age was of paramount concern; this need motivated childbirth as well as adoptions.[41] Free people also kept enslaved persons in their households to care for them until death, sometimes manumitting them in their wills.[42]

This understanding of children and childhood as the site of adult (and contested) aspirations is not merely an artifact of the genre of the sources.

---

[35] *P.Pisentius 17* (unpublished, Louvre Museum) as discussed in Cromwell, "Potential Paternity Problem."

[36] *P.Heid.* III 237 (*BL* V 43, IX 103).

[37] *SB Kopt.* IV 1709. See also discussion in Cromwell, "An Abandoned Wife and Unpaid Alimony."

[38] *BGU* IV 1104. On infanticide and exposure, see Grubbs, "Infant Exposure and Infanticide"; Grubbs, "Church, State and Children."

[39] *P.Lond.* V 1676. See also translation and discussion in Ruffini, *Life in an Egyptian Village*, 135.

[40] *P.Oxy.* L 3555; trans. Rowlandson, *Women and Society*, 92–93.

[41] Huebner, *Family in Roman Egypt*, 175–87.   [42] Huebner, *Family in Roman Egypt*, 172–74.

The examples listed here come primarily from documentary sources such as wills, petitions, contracts, and letters documenting a dispute – texts often deriving from confrontational circumstances. Literary sources, however, also testify to the construction of children as the embodiment of adult aspirations. Part II of the book addresses this theme's expression in multiple motifs in ascetic literature in more detail, but for now, two examples suffice. According to the Greek *Life of Pachomius*, of his own volition the young Theodore (eventual father of the whole monastic federation) joined a monastery of Pachomius at *around* fourteen years of age, meaning he may have been legally of age but still a youth potentially requiring guardianship, or he may have been just under fourteen and thus underage. His mother came looking for him, with letters in hand from bishops demanding his return to the family household. After telling Pachomius of his desire to remain, he went to meet his mother (who was staying at the women's monastery while awaiting his return). Seeing his dedication, she decided not only not to fight his decision but also to join the women's monastery herself.[43] Thus, Theodore's story is not only an account of a child forging his own path in life, distinct from his parents' aspirations, but also a narration of adult expectations, disappointment, and ultimately conversion.[44] The *Apophthegmata Patrum* narrates the choice of asceticism of another remarkable monk, Zacharias. According to the story, Zacharias became a monk only as a result of the choices and actions of his parents. His father, Carion, had abandoned his wife and two children (Zacharias and an unnamed sister) to join the monastic community at Scetis. During a famine, the unnamed woman came to the edge of Scetis and publicly shamed Carion with his hungry children. Carion called for both children to come to live with him, but the girl turned back to be with her mother. The boy, Zacharias, lived with Carion, eventually becoming a more accomplished monk than his father.[45] In the narrative, the parents drive the plotline of Zacharias' monastic vocation: Carion's failings as an absentee father, his mother's fortitude in demanding he support his children, and his father's decision to take physical custody of the child. Even the vignette about the boy's entry to Scetis appears in sayings classified under his father's name in the Alphabetical Collection of *Apophthegmata*. In neither of these instances do I posit that children named Theodore and

---

[43] *V. Pach. G¹* 37, in Halkin, *Sancti Pachomii Vitae Graecae*, 22; ed. and trans. Veilleux, *Pachomian Koinonia One*, 323–24.

[44] Vuolanto argues that intrafamilial disputes were not as common as the hagiography would lead us to believe in *Children and Asceticism*.

[45] *AP* Carion 1–3, in *PG* 65:249–52.

Zacharias lived the lives these narratives describe. Rather, I argue that these literary accounts share with our documentary sources a profound ideological construction of "the child" as the embodiment of adult ambitions, which also presents us with a methodological conundrum: late antique accounts of children, including monastic sources, are written by and for adults and foreground adult concerns.

Trauma, Abuse, and Social Norms

In the 600s in upper Egypt, a girl ran away from her husband and took refuge in the home of another Christian couple, Elisabeth and Papnoute. We know little about her circumstances: Did she not love her husband? Did he hurt her? Did she simply not want to marry? We do not even know her name. All we know is that she was a "young girl" who fled her marriage in defiance of church regulations and social norms yet was supported in this decision by two other Christians. This girl was likely in her teens (and thus a girl by modern American standards). Even though the letter describes her as a "young girl," vocabulary was fluid when referencing teenagers; possibly she was in her early teens. We know of her situation thanks to a sternly worded letter from a prominent local priest ordering Elisabeth and Papnoute to instruct the girl to return to her husband and "obey him" or face excommunication.[46]

This one small story of an unhappily married girl opens a window to a number of aspects of late antique girlhood. The priest's letter articulates the widespread policy of the ancient church in Egypt, that leaving a marriage was forbidden except in cases of adultery. Even a girl who experienced domestic violence or extreme poverty could not divorce her husband and expect to remain in good standing with the church. A girl who wished to leave her husband needed a supportive social network outside her marital household – parents, friends, or other relatives.

And thus, we see quite clearly implemented the social norms of the time: child brides, church policy on divorce, expectations for wifely obedience. We also see quite clearly *resistance* to such norms. For whatever reason, this girl has taken hold of her own future and left her husband, flouting convention. Moreover, two other Christians have supported her disobedience.

Throughout this book, it is important to keep in mind these moments of resistance, because they speak to the cultural historian

---

[46] *O.Lips.Copt.* 24; see also the discussion in Cromwell, "Runaway Child Bride."

of religion faced with the challenge of analyzing social norms that we might consider violent. Child marriage, enslavement, corporal punishment, food deprivation – these are but a few of the *normative* and *traumatic* conditions of childhood we encounter in this book. Despite their normativity, views that diverge from or even challenge these norms existed. This fits with other examples in history in which an abusive social practice, such as the enslavement of people of African descent in Europe and the United States, was legal and widespread yet opposed by some. Proslavery views were normative among white free people, and many in the Northern "free" states of antebellum America acquiesced to slavery in the South.[47] Nonetheless, antislavery and abolitionist writing and activism were widespread in America and England when slavery was legal in each nation. In particular, people of African descent opposed slavery and the slave trade publicly, such as authors and speakers, including Olaudah Equiano in the late 1700s and Sojourner Truth and Fredrick Douglass in the 1800s.[48]

To understand the life of a child in late antiquity is to understand a life likely marked by violence – violence experienced structurally and personally, imparted by social systems and individuals. We need to name and analyze that violence, neither overlooking nor dismissing it because of its normativity. Likewise, we must not allow the normativity of violence against children in the ancient world to overwhelm our interpretive and methodological frameworks so that we overlook the evidence of both children and adults who questioned, challenged, or transgressed these social norms.

Evidence for violence against children comes in many forms, some documentary or legal, others literary or artistic. As Laura Nasrallah cautions historians of religion, setting aside violence in art and literature as symbolic and representational (and as such, not "real") brackets from our view significant cultural and historical justifications or motivations for violence: "The concern underlying the phrase 'representations of violence' . . . may be that representations of violence in image and word are ephemeral, hard to prove violent, even 'merely' rhetorical violence. Instead, we should be thinking about representations of violence as

---

[47] E.g., Dabney, *Life and Compaigns of Lieut.-Gen. Thomas J. Jackson*; Wheaton, *Discourse on St. Paul's Epistle to Philemon*; see also Boles, "Dabney, Robert Lewis (1820–1898)."

[48] Equiano, *Interesting Narrative and Other Writings*; for a history of black women using biblical interpretation to challenge social norms in the United States regarding gender and race, see Junior, *Introduction to Womanist Biblical Interpretation*.

instantiations of violence, as possibly producing and constituting present and future violence."[49]

Missing Children

Children, as this book shows, lived in early monasteries, received health-care and education in these communities, and experienced physical abuse there. Yet children are missing in the historiography of early Egyptian monasticism. Few modern books, even exemplary books, include studies of children in communal monastic settings. Prior to 2007, when I first began publishing on the topic, the field of the history of early monasticism had itself neglected children.

In historical imagination, the era of the earliest ascetics, particularly those in Egypt, signified a golden age of monasticism, one in which rigorous askesis and deep devotion combined to produce exemplars for later monks, but exemplars whose holy achievements could never be fully replicated by succeeding generations.[50] The most popular literature consumed and distributed in the West that documents asceticism and monasticism in Egypt (e.g., hagiography, *Sayings of the Desert Fathers*, the writings of Cassian and Jerome) conveys this view. In this vision of monastic origins, children are to be eschewed, not welcomed into the monastic communities. They represent emotional and social attachments (to parents, siblings, spouses, and offspring), displaced labor (caring for children rather than the soul and God), and temptation (primarily sexual).

Despite the dismantling of the golden age historiographical trope in recent decades, much of twentieth- and early twenty-first-century scholarship in the field replicates a worldview shaped by predominantly hagiographical and gnomic sources – a worldview that neglects, overlooks, and ignores children except when they represent a problem for monastics. Late antique children *outside* the early monastery appear in scholarship as problems for monks to solve; we find ill and possessed offspring of lay Christians who require healing or exorcism from a holy person, and a monk preaching to protect lay infants at risk of exposure by Christian parents.[51] At times the "problem child" constitutes an obstacle to the ascetic's holiness or reputation, as when a monk fathers a child or faces

---

[49] Nasrallah, "What Violence Does"; see also Castelli, "Researching and Responding to Violence."

[50] Goehring, "Dark Side of Landscape"; Goehring, "Encroaching Desert"; Larsen, "*Apophthegmata Patrum*."

[51] Burton-Christie, *Word in the Desert*, 257; Harmless, *Desert Christians*, 61; Brakke, *Demons*, 83, 197, 256n31; Chitty, *Desert a City*, 127.

a false accusation of impregnating a woman.[52] Scholarship also attends to children in literary anecdotes or ascetic invectives that imitate biblical narratives or herald biblical models of piety: the near sacrifice of children by monks mirroring Abraham and Isaac in Genesis; the patriarch Jacob's loss of his son Joseph; childless Elisha and Jeremiah; 1 Timothy's injunction to bear children (creatively exegeted in support of asceticism).[53] David Brakke's work has demonstrated that metaphors of the child serve genealogical and ethnographic purposes as well – to map people of piety in contrast to those beyond the pale of orthodox Christianity: heretics as children of the Greeks, children of God opposed to children of Satan, a demon as the daughter of the devil, virgins as daughters of Jerusalem, and so on.[54]

Commonly, scholarship notices children situated *within* the Egyptian monastery who trigger, and thus symbolize, temptation and anxiety over status.[55] Derwas Chitty's *Desert a City* is particularly influential for this historiographical trope. Chitty's book discusses children primarily in the context of sexual temptation. The admission of children into monasteries also introduced a new temptation. In this historiographic narrative, the ensuing corruption tarnished what had been a golden age of monasticism.[56]

Children figure as pious and virtuous in histories of early Egyptian monasticism primarily when examples are sifted from hagiography. According to their *vitae*, the great monks Pachomius and Antony were exceptional children, demonstrating virtue and holiness at an early age.[57] Such portraits of the saint as an "exceptional child" would become a trope imitated in later hagiography.[58] Children who will go on to become not-so-famous monks also receive mention.[59] Virtuous younger monks also appear in hagiography as "children" of their more established superiors, although these figures are not necessarily *minor* children.[60] Occasionally

---

[52] Harmless, *Desert Christians*, 194, 206, 239.

[53] Two of many examples are Burton-Christie, *Word in the Desert*, 114, 169; Brakke, *Athanasius and Asceticism*, 55, 279, 283.

[54] Brakke, *Demons*, 99, 107, 111, 166, 203; Brakke, *Athanasius and Asceticism*, 41, 139–40.

[55] Gould, *Desert Fathers on Monastic Community*, 125 (what seems to be the only reference to children is in a section on sex); Harmless, *Desert Christians*, 233–34; Brakke, *Demons*, 164, 176; Chitty, *Desert a City*, 66–67; see also Chitty's discussion of "beardless youth" admitted only to one particular *lavra* in Palestine with its undercurrent of sexual problematics, on 94, 108, 115.

[56] Chitty, *Desert a City*, 66–67.

[57] Chitty, *Desert a City*, 123, 128; Rousseau, *Pachomius*, 129; Harmless, *Desert Christians*, 60; Brakke, *Demons*, 37, 84, 95; Brakke, *Athanasius and Asceticism*, 230.

[58] Caseau, "Childhood in Byzantine Saints' Lives."   [59] Chitty, *Desert a City*, 65–66, 87.

[60] Rousseau, *Pachomius*, 178, 185; Harmless, *Desert Christians*, 121; Brakke, *Demons*, 190.

historians will mention parent-child (or grandparent-grandchild) ascetic pairs, such as Carion and Zacharias of *Sayings of the Desert Fathers*, little Paula and her grandmother Paula (founder of a double monastery in Palestine with Jerome), and the mother-daughter monks of the *Lausiac History*.[61] In historical works, citations of papyri referencing children in monastic environments are exceptionally rare, with the primary exception being analysis of documents of child donations at the Phoibammon monastery in Western Thebes (across the Nile from modern Luxor).[62] Some research discusses the changing parent-child relationship as a result of monastic familial renunciation.[63]

Until recently, children's meaning in most relevant scholarship has been molded by adult concerns, young people's lives refracted through the lenses of adult experiences and priorities. Moreover, these adult perspectives are often filtered as well, either due to over-sampling from hagiography and *Sayings of the Desert Fathers* or by presenting and interpreting evidence from late ancient sources through the lens of the idealized literature itself.

Monks and Their Children

Children and Family in Late Antique Egyptian Monasticism interrogates the assumption that children were neither present nor welcome in the earliest forms of Christian asceticism and monasticism. This book simultaneously analyzes the religious and cultural construction of children and childhood in early monastic literature written by adults and writes a social history of early Egyptian monastic children centering the child. My research focuses primarily on sources from and about early Christianity in Egypt such as rules and other writings by the monastic leaders Shenoute, Besa, Pachomius, and Pachomius' successors; documentary papyri and ostraca; monastic art and archaeological remains; and some hagiography and other literary texts. The book also contextualizes the experiences of monastic children and parents with comparisons to other sources by writers such as

---

[61] Harmless, *Desert Christians*, 233; Rousseau, *Ascetics, Authority, and the Church*, 120–21; Brakke, *Athanasius and Asceticism*, 27; Elm, *Virgins of God*, 239, 374.

[62] Brakke, *Athanasius and Asceticism*, 27; Goehring, "Origins of Monasticism," 25; Goehring, "Monastic Diversity," 202–03. In her monumental books on Egyptian monasticism, Wipszycka almost never mentions children, except in her work on the rule at the Naqlun monastery: Wipszycka, *Études sur le christianisme*; Wipszycka, *Moines et communautés monastiques*. On the monastery of Phoibammon, see Papaconstantinou, "Notes sur les actes de donation d'enfants"; MacCoull, "Child Donations and Child Saints"; Richter, "What's in a Story?"; Schenke, "Healing Shrines."

[63] Elm, *Virgins of God*, 110–11; Vuolanto, *Children and Asceticism*.

Jerome and John Cassian, whose asceticism was shaped in part by their time in Egypt.

The book's methodology is interdisciplinary. Social historical methods reconstruct the lives and environments of monastic children. Art history and literary analysis contribute to an understanding of how children are represented in monastic culture. Approaches from religious and theological history illuminate the ways religious systems (including interpretation of scripture) inform the development of the place and role of children in the church and monasticism as institutions. Archaeological remains are examined for evidence of children's material presence in monastic spaces in late antiquity. Philological analyses of vocabulary in textual sources seek to understand the age and nature of this population. This interdisciplinary approach allows for an appraisal of monastic childhood from diverse perspectives.

In Part I of the book, two chapters assess our evidence for children, arguing that they were a consistent presence in even the very earliest monastic communities. Chapter 1 systematically examines papyri, inscriptions, rules, and literary texts from monasteries in Egypt from the 300s to the 600s to document the presence of minor children and reconstruct how and why they came to live in these communities. Chapter 2 explores the methodological and linguistic challenges in constructing a history of monastic children, especially young children. The terms for "boys" and "girls" are used as markers of status, essentially as titles for monastic novices. This chapter explains the language and vocabulary of childhood in monastic written sources in order to discern whether the sources indeed refer to underage children.

Part II examines the literary representations of children in our early monastic sources and their significance for adult ascetics' identity and social roles. Chapter 3 examines the construction of male sexuality through writings about children and sexuality. It analyzes stories about children in the collection of literary texts known as *Sayings of the Desert Fathers* alongside references to children in monastic rules prohibiting sex. This chapter interrogates the representation of the masculine ascetic ideal, which is built upon certain classical ideals of masculinity, especially the control of the passions, while purporting to eschew classical models of eroticism in which the adolescent male represented an ideal erotic partner. Chapter 4 examines accounts of child killings in various textual and visual sources: *Sayings of the Desert Fathers*, paintings of the sacrifice of Jephthah's daughter and the averted sacrifice of Isaac at the monasteries of Saint Antony on the Red Sea and Saint Catherine at Sinai, and exegesis of the same biblical narratives in the writings of various ascetic authors. The literature and art present the sacrifice of children as a model for the monastic renunciation of family, even including stories of monks who attempt to kill their own children for their asceticism. Simultaneously, these materials are theologically, politically, and even socially generative and affirm an ascetic reproduction of monastic communities. Chapter 5 examines accounts of monks healing children, arguing that they position the child as a symbol of society's future potential, including familial legacy and inheritance. In these stories of people bringing their children to monks for healing, these communities of respected ascetics ensured the survival of the next generation of Christian families through their acts of healing and exorcising.

Part III of the book turns from the ways monastic texts "think through" children to a social history of children in these communities. Chapter 6 analyzes accounts of children and monastic rules pertaining to children in order to reconstruct how and why children were cared for and educated in the monasteries, including literacy, discipline, and responsibilities of caregivers. Many children were not simply temporary residents in the communities until adulthood but were reared by adult monks with the expectation that these youths would become ascetics themselves. Chapter 7 examines the daily lives of children in the monasteries. The monastery offered a fairly stable home with food, healthcare, and educational opportunities for a lifetime. Yet children were regarded as a challenge, even a danger, to adult monks, who often prioritized their own needs and power over children's well-being. This chapter looks at these complexities with respect to sexuality, food, labor, health and disability, and even death and burial. Chapter 8 examines the social and emotional bonds between children and parents. Despite the ascetic imperative to renounce family upon taking up the ascetic life, monks joined communities with their own children or monasteries in which other children were present. Be they entire ascetic families, or lay parents with monastic children, or even monastic parents with lay children, family ties bound kin together, even in the face of competing imperatives to replace their legal or biological families with monastic ones.[64] While Christian figures around the Mediterranean preached the virtues of new monastic families over against traditional configurations of family, they also drew upon familial bonds

---

[64] On ascetic family, see especially Jacobs and Krawiec, "Fathers Know Best?"; Krawiec, "From the Womb of the Church"; Jacobs, "Let Him Guard Pietas"; Vuolanto, "Choosing Asceticism"; Vuolanto, "Early Christian Communities As Family Networks"; Vuolanto, "Children and Asceticism."

latent in their audiences, at times to persuade their own relatives or relatives of their students and followers to become ascetics, or to instruct monastics and lay Christians alike in the ways of ascetic life.

The concluding chapter ends by looking at the roles of children and family in the legacies early monasteries created for themselves. In both Egypt and southern Gaul, where John Cassian founded communities based on his years living with the monks of Egypt, the monastery as an institution challenged the ancient household's status as the cornerstone of society's political and economic apparatuses. The monastery positioned itself as a rival to the household, and in doing so, defined itself institutionally as both a kinship network and much more than a replacement for traditional kinship networks. Monastic authors envisioned their communities as part of an eternal and eschatological genealogy of prophets, saints, and monks stretching from biblical times into the future.

PART I

Finding Children

CHAPTER I

Documenting the Undocumented
Children in the Earliest Egyptian Monasteries

In the 300s, Christians in Egypt and all over the Roman Empire came to the Nile Valley and outlying deserts to become monks, men as well as women. The rhetoric of this movement emphasized a retreat into the wilderness, a retreat away from the city, family, and property – everything one had. Perhaps the most famous passage in monastic hagiography evokes this renunciation of family. Athanasius, author of the *Life of Antony*, declares that so many people had come to Egypt to become monks that the desert had transformed into a well-populated community:

> And so, from then on, there were monasteries in the mountains, and the desert was made a city by monks, who left their own people and registered themselves for the citizenship in the heavens.[1]

The desert was no longer a "retreat" from the city but was instead itself speckled with small monastic cities. Nonetheless, the rhetoric of retreat and withdrawal remained in monastic literature, especially the urgency of withdrawal from family. Athanasius here defines monks as people who "left behind their own" – their friends, family, property. Thus, from its very beginnings, monasticism was often described and envisioned as a movement in opposition to the traditional family and social structures.

Yet, despite a traditional discourse opposing family and children, children lived in early Egyptian monasteries or were cared for by monks as early as the fourth century. We know this without a doubt. They were not numerous, and our sources often remain circumspect, but children dwelled inside these communities or lived within their networks under the economic or social protection of monks.

This chapter serves to document the previously undocumented – to map out the places and spaces where children lived with monks or where monks

---

[1] Athanasius, *Vita Antonii* 14, in *PG* 26:865; trans. Gregg in Athanasius, *Life of Antony and the Letter to Marcellinus*, 42–43.

cared for children's basic welfare within their social networks. Papyri, inscriptions, rules, and literary texts from or about monasteries in Egypt from the 300s to the 600s document the presence of minor children in and around monasteries. When I told people, including other historians of Christianity, that I was working on a book about children in early Egyptian monasteries, I frequently received the response: "But there weren't any, were there?" This chapter documents the historical presence of children in monastic communities and charts the circumstances surrounding or driving their affiliations where such circumstances can be determined. In many cases, evidence for children's history is fleeting, providing only the barest witness to a population. Sometimes, the evidence is more expansive, providing details of monastic children's daily lives. This chapter documents both the fleeting and the expansive in order to sketch in broad but unmistakable strokes the realities of monastic children, but it does not provide in-depth analysis of the details. Part III of this book unspools some of the implications of this evidence for crafting a history of children and childhood in early monasteries. Consequently, some sources mentioned here receive fuller treatment in later chapters. This chapter reconstructs how and why children came to live in or under the social or economic canopy of individual monks or communities. Up and down the Nile river valley, children lived with monks or were legally or economically dependent on monks and monasteries for their basic survival. Often, they came to live in or in the orbit of these communities because of poverty, illness, or orphanhood; at other times, they resided in monasteries due to their parents' ascetic ambitions for their children or for the family.

On the relationship between the very earliest Egyptian monasteries and their local or regional communities and economies, two models prevail in current scholarship. In one, monasteries' boundaries were economically, physically, and theologically porous. James Goehring's research on the Pachomian monastic federation has demonstrated that Pachomian communities were dependent on their local villages and the wider Egyptian economy for trade, resulting in monks regularly traveling outside of their communities to sell and purchase goods.[2] Moreover, monks who professed different theologies or who were members of different ecclesial groups even resided next to each other.[3] Although monasticism required a set of commitments differentiating the monk from the lay Christian, coenobitics did *not* necessarily "reject the world"; significant modes of exchange

[2] Goehring, "World Engaged"; Goehring, "Dark Side of Landscape."
[3] Goehring, "Monastic Diversity."

between the monastery and the outside world existed. Papyrologists such as Ewa Wipszycka concur with this model.[4] In contrast, in his research on the monastic federation of Shenoute (also known as the White Monastery Federation), Bentley Layton has argued for fairly rigid boundaries between that community and the outside world, proposing a model of ascetic formation in which monks break down their former identities and rebuild new subjectivities according to the monastery's rules and expectations.[5] I have argued for a different interpretation of boundaries and identity formation in the White Monastery, positing that while the rules of Shenoute's federation resulted in an ascetic subjectivity particular to that community, borders between the inside and outside worlds were regularly crossed, and individual monks did not abandon their previous identities upon joining the community, despite pressure to do so.[6]

Our adherence to one or the other of these two models, one of more rigid boundaries and the other of more porous boundaries, can affect our ability to see children in and around early monasteries, since the sources are frequently minimal, partial, or opaque. In what follows, I begin by examining the evidence for children who lived within monasteries or in their near orbits, and from that evidence I argue for a more porous understanding of early monastic boundaries, as well as a model of early monasticism that transforms the ancient family rather than rejecting family, property, and reproduction. Texts from and about early *lavra*s and coenobitic monasteries provide a patchwork of evidence about the presence of children. This material expresses deep ambivalence about allowing children to reside in monasteries, as Part II of this book explores. Yet it also documents that even during this formative stage of Christianity, children lived in ascetic communities, many in training to become adult monks.[7]

An Assumption of Children's Presence

Historical sources – rules, inscriptions, letters – from monastic communities from the fourth through seventh centuries often document the presence of children about whom we know very little, especially their reasons for being there. The most famous coenobitic community in Egypt was comprised of a series of monasteries originally founded by the

[4] Wipszycka, "Le monachisme égyptien et les villes"; Wipszycka, "Les aspects économiques."
[5] Layton, *Canons of Our Fathers*, 77–85; Layton, "Rules, Patterns, and the Exercise of Power."
[6] Schroeder, "In the Footsteps of Shenoute"; Schroeder, *Monastic Bodies*, 13, 116–17.
[7] Some of the material in this chapter also appears in Schroeder, "Children in Early Egyptian Monasticism."

fourth-century monk Pachomius. Several versions of Pachomius' *Vita* exist, along with some of his letters (which he composed in difficult-to-decipher alphanumeric and biblical codes) as well as monastic rules and instructional addresses (some authored by him, others written by subsequent leaders of his monastic federation).[8] The most extensive version of the rules currently exists in the form of a Latin translation by Jerome, but some Coptic and Greek excerpts have survived. The rules outline a number of prohibited behaviors as well as required practices, with some mentions of children.[9] Anecdotes involving children living in the Pachomian *koinonia* also appear in the Greek *Vita* of Pachomius, the *Letter of Ammon*, the fragmentary Tenth Sahidic Coptic *Vita* of Pachomius, and the fragments known as the Pachomian *Paralipomena*.[10] Hagiography's idealizing tendencies make *vitae* unreliable witnesses for events in the time periods they purport to narrate, and Pachomius' Greek *Vita*, in particular, is known for its tendency to shape Pachomius' history to favor the political and theological landscape of the time of its writing in the 390s, some five decades after Pachomius' death.[11] Despite these difficulties, when read carefully and only alongside other more reliable supporting evidence, these sources can contribute to our evidence for children's presence in late fourth-century monasteries, if not during Pachomius' own lifetime.

The rules and letters penned by Shenoute, who directed a federation of coenobia that were home to several thousand men and women in the fourth and fifth centuries, provide more insight into the lives of children in coenobitic monasticism. Known as Shenoute's Monastery (despite having existed before and well after his tenure) or as the White Monastery Federation (on account of a central basilica constructed of white stone), the community consisted of three monastic residences plus affiliated hermits who lived in the nearby desert caves. Shenoute became the leader of the White Monastery Federation in or around the year 385 and remained in that position until his death in 465.[12] His writings are contemporaneous with or slightly later than the Pachomian *Vitae* and Latin translations of the Pachomian rules. His letters and rules are filled with the Coptic terms

[8] Harmless, *Desert Christians*, 115–59; Rousseau, *Pachomius*.   [9] See Chapters 6 and 7.
[10] V. Pach. G¹ 49, in Halkin, *Sancti Pachomii Vitae Graecae*, 32; ed. and trans. Veilleux, *Pachomian Koinonia, Volume One*, 331. V. Pach. Sᵗᵒ Fragment 2, in Lefort, *S. Pachomii Vitae Sahidice Scriptae*, 33–34; ed. and trans. Veilleux, *Pachomian Koinonia, Volume One*, 451–52. Goehring, *Letter of Ammon and Pachomian Monasticism*. Pachomian *Paralipomena* 15, in Halkin, *Sancti Pachomii Vitae Graecae*, 138–39; ed. and trans. Veilleux, *Pachomian Koinonia, Volume Two*, 36–38.
[11] Goehring, "Pachomius's Vision of Heresy"; Goehring, "Monastic Diversity."
[12] Emmel, "Shenoute the Monk"; Schroeder, *Monastic Bodies*, 30–49; Schroeder, "Early Monastic Rule," 20–25.

for "boys," "girls," and "little ones," providing information on their healthcare and meals as well as guidance for the monks responsible for raising them.[13] The references demonstrate that the monastic community included many young people, and that their presence was considered neither an aberration nor suboptimal. Both the Pachomian and Shenoutean sources take the children's presence for granted. Unfortunately for us, they do not typically provide details about how children came to enter the monastery.

By the sixth through eighth centuries, documentary sources preserved on papyri and ostraca provide anecdotal evidence of children living in monastic settlements, particularly in the Theban region, again often without a sense of how they came to live there. An eighth-century ostracon mentions some "lesser brethren" (*nelaue šēm*),[14] which some Coptologists have interpreted to mean children.[15] In the same region and employing similar terminology, a letter requesting prayers for sick young people (*nlelaue šēm*) seems to refer to children.[16] One ostracon from the seventh or eighth century mentions orphans in a letter to a monk at an unnamed community.[17] At the Theban Monastery of Epiphanius, a piece of correspondence also preserved on a pottery shard encourages the recipient not to inform the "lesser" or "little" "brothers" (*ncnēu šēm*) that the writer of the letter is ill.[18] This letter seems to provide evidence for minors at the Monastery of Epiphanius. Another papyrus from the same community, however, suggests that children were forbidden at some point in the seventh century; in a testament, the legal owner and monastic superior of the Monastery of Epiphanius (Jacob) and his appointed successor (Elias) designate a third monk (Stephen) as their heir and also forbid males under the age of twenty to live in the settlement. (Apa Jacob had inherited the monastery from Apa Psan, who inherited it from Apa Epiphanius.)[19] This evidence presents us with at least three possible scenarios: (1) the ban on boys occurred *after* the letter mentioning the "little brothers" was written; (2) the ban was in effect and the "little brothers" are junior or novice monks over the age of twenty; or (3) the ban was ineffective or short-lived.

We find scattered documentary evidence elsewhere in Egypt as well. Much further north, at the Monastery of Apa Jeremias in Saqqara, an

---

[13] The Coptic terms for boy and girl pose some interpretive challenges for the social historian; see Chapter 2 and Cromwell, "From Village to Monastery," 24.
[14] *O.Brit.Mus.Copt.* I XX/4.   [15] Winlock and Crum, *Monastery of Epiphanius I*, 139n7.
[16] *P.Mon.Epiph.* 359.   [17] *O.Brit.Mus.Copt.* I XX/4.   [18] *P.Mon.Epiph.* 297.
[19] *P.KRU* 75. Also see discussion in O'Connell, "Transforming Monumental Landscapes," and Dekker, "Chronology of the *Topos* of Epiphanius," 756, 760–61.

inscription on a stela memorializes "David, the little Apa" (*pkoui napa*), possibly referencing a child or adolescent.[20] In Middle Egypt, at the monastery of Bawit, we have firmer evidence. Graffiti and at least one contract mention a cell of children ("little ones," *tri nekoui*). One graffito identifies a certain Victor (*Biktōr*) along with an unnamed monk affiliated with (or "belonged to") the cell of the little ones.[21] Another graffito and a ninth-century contract write of "the father of the little ones" and the "father of the cell of the little ones."[22] Additionally, a papyrus that may have come from Bawit also mentions such a cell.[23] Terminology is an issue in these references, as it is unclear whether the terms refer to monks of junior status or rank instead of children. But the language used is identical to vocabulary used in quotations from the Gospel of Matthew 18:2–5 in the Pachomian and Shenoutean corpora that clearly refer to children ("little ones") and has been interpreted as evidence for a small community of children at Bawit.[24]

Also in the north, in the region of Egypt known as the Fayyum, boys lived at the monastery at Naqlun (now known as the Monastery of the Archangel Gabriel).[25] The ascetics at Naqlun included monks living in a monastic residence as well as in hermitages built into the hills of the surrounding area. Of the remaining archaeological deposits, the oldest date to the fifth century, with many additional structures from the sixth century.[26] They indicate that the community consisted of a coenobium and a *lavra*, which were the cells in the hills. A monastic rule survives in Arabic, with a manuscript tradition suggesting connections to the ascetic community at Scetis.[27] Two rules explicitly prohibit monks from conversing with or associating with boys (both young boys and adolescents); one

[20] Quibell and Thompson, *Excavations at Saqqara*, 73.

[21] No. 4 in Clédat, *Le monastère de la nécropole de Baouît*, 107; see also the reference in Quibell and Thompson, *Excavations at Saqqara*, 43n1. Other inscriptions in close proximity to this one mention specific "young" or "little" monks (e.g., Nos. 6, 8, 12 in Clédat, *Le monastère de la nécropole de Baouît*, 107–08).

[22] No. 249 in Maspero, *Fouilles exécutées à Baouît*, 95; B.L. Ms. Or. 6204 line 70 in MacCoull, "Bawit Contracts," 146; see discussion in Delattre, *Papyrus coptes et grecs*, 69.

[23] *P.Lond.Copt.* 1130; see discussion in Delattre, *Papyrus coptes et grecs*, 48; Delattre, "La traduction des institutions administratives," 219–20, 223, 226.

[24] See notes 35 in Chapter 2 and 5 in Chapter 6; Delattre, *Papyrus coptes et grecs*, 48.

[25] On Naqlun generally, see Wipszycka, "Les rapports entre les monastères et les laures"; Derda, "Polish Excavations at Deir El-Naqlun"; Godlewski, "Excavating the Ancient Monastery at Naqlun." Also see the *P.Naqlun I* and *P.Naqlun II*.

[26] Godlewski, "Excavating the Ancient Monastery at Naqlun," 157–61.

[27] Wipszycka, "Apports de l'archéologie"; Derda, "Polish Excavations at Deir El-Naqlun." The rule itself is published (with a Latin translation) in *PG* 40:1065–74; a French translation appears in Breydy, "Appendice. La version des *Règles et préceptes de St. Antoine*."

instructs monks not to take on a boy as a spiritual son (i.e., as a disciple or student). Such prohibitions might lead us to conclude that children did not live at the monastery.[28] The Naqlun monastery did engage in commerce, and it may have hosted pilgrims; one could imagine children visiting the community in either of those contexts and thus the potential for monastic interactions with those children.[29] Yet one regulation charges the community to expel from the monastery any youth who had not yet taken the monastic habit or who had caused a "scandal." And the rule warning monks against mentoring boys instructs the monks not to take them on before they have donned the monastic habit. These instructions indicate that the regulations were not designed to draw boundaries only between the Naqlun monks and lay children from outside the community. Rather, they also attest to minor children, specifically boys or adolescent males, living at Naqlun in preparation for becoming monks. The rules drew boundaries between people who were living in the community, but who were of different status: adult male monks and boys who had not yet become monks. Thus, the rule suggests that, indeed, minors lived at Naqlun, but they were not considered a part of the general monastic population. Their activities must have been strictly regulated; possibly the rules restricting individual monks from associating with and instructing novice boys were directed toward the men in the hermitages in the cliffs, and the children lived in the main monastic settlement.

Unfortunately, modern excavations that have uncovered child skeletons and tunics in the cemeteries at the site cannot confirm the presence of children, since lay Christians from the nearby villages or visitors likely used those burial grounds.[30] Nonetheless, the rule from Naqlun implies that children likely lived at the main monastic residence and indicates more certainly that monks either took on children as disciples or were approached by children or their families often enough that the monastery regulated their interactions.[31] The rules indicate an assumption of children's presence in the monastery and around monks.

---

[28] Rules 4, 16, in *PG* 40:1065–74; Fr. trans. in Breydy, "Appendice. La version des *Règles et préceptes de St. Antoine*," 399–400.

[29] Wipszycka, "Apports de l'archéologie," 72–77.

[30] Godlewski, "Excavating the Ancient Monastery at Naqlun"; Czaja-Szewczak, "Tunics from Naqlun," esp. 135; Piasecki, "Skulls from Naqlun."

[31] These particular rules about young boys and adolescents do not appear to be copies of surviving Pachomian and Shenoutean rules, although more research is necessary to be definitive. Tradition erroneously attributed the rule to Antony.

Children and Manichaean Elect

Fourth-century letters from the Manichaean community in Kellis (at the Great Oasis in the western desert) indicate that some families were perhaps quite willing to devote their children to an ascetic life.[32] The *Kephalaia*, Manichaean teachings attributed to the founder Mani, urges followers to dedicate a child to the religious hierarchy.[33] The Kellis letters provide an example of at least two such families (and possibly more) who put this teaching into practice. As the editors of the Kellis documentary texts have argued, at this time the line between Manichaeism and Christianity was practically nonexistent. The authors of the letters identify themselves in ways that mark them as "Manicheans," but they use "Christian terminology" and probably "regarded themselves as Christians," specifically "the true (and perhaps more effective or spiritual) church."[34] Most of the families represented in the letters were probably catechumens and not members of the Manichaean elect, although they had close social and possibly familial networks with the elect.[35] Moreover, the Kellis papyri confirm the presence of a monastery nearby – possibly where the elect lived, although details about the monastery remain scarce.[36] Two surviving texts mention the same family in Kellis whose son has "gone to the monastery" to live with a "father Pebok," possibly to learn textile trades.[37] Unfortunately, we do not know the age of the son.

We also learn of at least one male child sent to live and journey with a member of the Manichaean elect who traveled up and down the Nile Valley, possibly with other children. The Manichaean elect were ascetics and holy people. They took vows of poverty, limited food intake by practicing vegetarianism and abstaining from wine, practiced celibacy, and prayed for the other members of their community. Therefore, a discussion of children traveling with the Manichaean elect (even if not living in a fixed monastery or monastic house per se) warrants mention here as yet another example of children living with, educated by, and raised by ascetics and monastics in Egypt.

A collection of letters written by members of one Kellis family, known as the "Makarios family documents," provides an unparalleled window into

---

[32] Gardner, Alcock, and Funk, *Coptic Documentary Texts from Kellis 1*; on the dating of the letters, see 8–10.

[33] *Keph.* 193 4–6, as cited in Gardner, Alcock, and Funk, *Coptic Documentary Texts from Kellis 1*, 39.

[34] Gardner, Alcock, and Funk, *Coptic Documentary Texts from Kellis 1*, 73.

[35] Gardner, Alcock, and Funk, *Coptic Documentary Texts from Kellis 1*, 74.

[36] Gardner, Alcock, and Funk, *Coptic Documentary Texts from Kellis 1*, 76–77.

[37] *P.Kell.G.* I 12. *P.Kell.Copt.* V 12. See discussion in Choat, "Monastic Letters," 56.

daily life and the relationships among lay religious folk, as well as between the laity and religious authorities. Their correspondence frequently references "the Teacher." Although the surviving letters never name the individual, this title was reserved for the highest office in the Manichean church.[38] One of the sons in the Makarios family, Piene, was sent from home to travel with the Teacher throughout the Nile Valley.[39] The Teacher instructed him in Latin, eventually assigning him to read in church.[40] When the Teacher traveled to Alexandria, he took Piene with him. Piene maintained contact with his family at least until he headed north to the metropolis. Makarios writes in one epistle that he has seen and spoken with Piene, suggesting that the two were in the same town or area, at least for a while.[41] Moreover, in other letters Makarios implies that other children were accompanying the Teacher.[42] Piene's older brother, Mattaios, traveled with Piene and the Teacher's group for a time and then separated from them in Antinoou; at that point the Teacher, Piene, and perhaps others journeyed to Alexandria. Mattaios writes to their mother, Maria, reporting that the Teacher "loves him [Piene] very much" and that his brother's role is a "glory" to him.[43] Piene himself writes to Maria, probably before departing for Alexandria. The editors of the Kellis letter describe the writing on the papyrus as "above normal production" – in other words, the Teacher had taught Piene well.[44]

Although the letters never state Piene's age, we have reason to believe he was a boy, or at the most an adolescent. One epistle from Piene's older brother (who was also in the Nile Valley) to their mother, Maria, refers to the boy as a "child."[45] The editors of the documents reasonably conclude that Piene was sent off with the Teacher "at a young age" for religious instruction, perhaps with the objective that he too would become one of the elect.[46] For the family of Piene, having a child who traveled with "the Teacher" as a valued student was an honor. Likewise, other families, whether Manichaean or not, may have found honor and status in dedicating a child to an esteemed religious community or revered and ascetic individual such as a monk or a Manichaean Teacher.

---

[38] Gardner, Alcock, and Funk, *Coptic Documentary Texts from Kellis 1*, 75; see also discussion of the Teacher and writing style in the Makarios collection in Gardner, "Letter from the Teacher."

[39] *P.Kell.Copt.* V 20, 24, 25, 29.   [40] *P.Kell.Copt.* V 20, 25.   [41] *P.Kell.Copt.* V 20.

[42] See *P.Kell.Copt.* V 20, in which Makarios mentions seeing Piene as well as other "little ones" (*koui*), and *P.Kell.Copt.* V 24, by which point Piene is in Alexandria and Makarios states that no more children (again *koui*) remain with him.

[43] *P.Kell.Copt.* V 25; trans. pp. 190–91.   [44] *P.Kell.Copt.* V 29; trans. pp. 203–04.

[45] *P.Kell.Copt.* V 25; trans. p. 191.

[46] Gardner, Alcock, and Funk, *Coptic Documentary Texts from Kellis 1*, 76.

Children under Monks' Legal or Economic Protection

Evidence survives from at least two fourth-century sources of monks and monasteries bringing or being urged to bring children under their legal or economic protection. These sources come from Greek papyri that document correspondence and a contract, all involving monks.

First, several letters from the monastery of Hathor testify to the close relationship the monks had with families in their community or in the community's close orbit. As we see in what follows, it is difficult to discern whether the children referenced in these documents lived with the monks or were regularly visited by the monks. Regardless, the documents provide evidence for the expectation that monks interact with children and their families and could even be called upon to provide for the children's welfare. Papyri from this collection include the earliest securely datable letters witnessing monasticism; some date back to the 330s.[47] The monastery itself was probably located in the Heracleopolitan nome, possibly near Oxyrhynchus.[48] Traditionally scholars have labeled the community "Melitian," primarily due to the account in one letter of partisans of Bishop Athanasius of Alexandria and soldiers with them attacking another group of Christians.[49]

At the end of that same letter, the author (Callistus) requests that his recipients – Apa Paiēous (the leader of the monastery) and Patabeis – pass on his greetings to "Joseph and his children (*ta paidia autou*)" and "Titouēs and his children (*ta paidia autou*)."[50] We learn nothing else of Joseph, Titouēs, and their families. Given the fluidity of honorific titles for monks and priests in fourth-century Egypt, it is difficult to ascertain whether men such as Joseph and Titouēs (who are referenced purely by their first names) are monastics in the community or lay Christians living in the area near the monastery. While the former would constitute a delightful find for a scholar researching children in Egyptian monasteries, I suspect the latter to be more likely. Epistolary conventions in late antique Egypt frequently include this type of request to pass along salutations to mutual acquaintances. Typically, the letter writer mentions colleagues, friends, or relatives whom s/he knows to be in the regional and social orbit of the addressee.[51] Callistus thus understood Joseph, Titouēs, and their children to be with

[47] Choat, "Monastic Letters," 21.
[48] Choat, "Monastic Letters," 27–28; Lundhaug and Jenott, *Monastic Origins of the Nag Hammadi Codices*, 45n112.
[49] *P.Lond.* VI 1914; Bagnall, *Egypt in Late Antiquity*, 307–08; Choat, "Monastic Letters," 25–33.
[50] *P.Lond.* VI 1914; trans. in Bell, *Jews and Christians in Egypt*, 63.
[51] E.g., many examples in Luijendijk, *Greetings in the Lord*.

the monks, nearby, or at least within the expected range of Apa Paiēous' and Patabeis' regular interactions.

Two related papyri from the Hathor community document the debt enslavement of a family (with quite young children) that the letter writer considers part of the social network of the monastery. The author ("brother Heriēous") writes to Apa Paiēous asking for money to help pay down the debts of a certain Pamonthius (also called a "brother"). According to Heriēous, Pamonthius was a wine dealer who took on significant debt and then sold all that he had in an attempt to pay off that debt. Creditors nonetheless came and took his young children (*tekna* and "quite in their infancy [*nēpia*]").[52] By the time of the second letter, Pamonthius had been arrested for failure to pay what he owed. Heriēous had secured some funds for bail but required more. He has pleaded for help from the monastic community on the basis of a shared understanding of a community obligation to each other as brethren:

> By all means then succor him without hesitation, because his creditors have carried off his children (*ta tekna autou*) into slavery; and if you hold me this man as brother (*adelphon*), join in giving help, beloved, because these straits have afflicted us exceedingly, and we ourselves will not shrink [from helping him]. Whatever we could find we have given him; yea, we have done even beyond our means.[53]

Heriēous draws on their common identity as "brother(s)" to appeal to Paiēous and the monastic community for aid.

The author's repeated reference to the children and to their young age also implies (at least from Heriēous' perspective) a particular obligation to them, to rescue them from what may be a life of enslavement. "Brother" in this context could designate several different identity formations. If we understand this letter collection to represent a Melitian monastery corresponding with Melitian lay Christians in the area, "brother" references their shared experiences as Melitians. In the fourth century, however, with a significant population still practicing devotion to traditional Egyptian and Greco-Roman gods, "brother" could refer to a shared Christian identity (whether Melitian or not). Finally, "brother" could designate an honorific title for members of the Hathor monastic community, since "brother" and "sister" are common terms monastics use to refer to each other. The latter situation strikes me as unlikely, because then we would have a wine dealer with children under the age of three who was a current

---

52. *P.Lond.* VI 1915; trans. Bell, *Jews and Christians in Egypt*, 74–75.
53. *P.Lond.* VI 1916; trans. Bell, *Jews and Christians in Egypt*, 78.

or former member of a monastery; this constellation of circumstances seems implausible. More likely, these "brothers" all identified as Christians and as members of a common religious and social network, a network built on a history of encounters and obligations. In the center of this network of monastic relationships and commitments lie children.

We do have evidence for at least one male monk in the fourth century taking on more than an informal role in a child's welfare by accepting official legal responsibility for the child. A separate Greek papyrus (*P.Lips.* 28) records a monk assuming legal guardianship for the upbringing of his nephew. Dated 381 CE, the papyrus is a contract recording the adoption of a ten-year-old boy, Paesis, by his uncle, Aurelius Silvanus, the latter identified as a *monachos* from the Hermopolite nome, though his specific monastic community remains unmentioned.[54] In later documentary papyri, the name of the coenobitic monastery would have been specified as information registering the monk's identity; either the monk was an anchorite or his community was simply not named. The child's grandmother, Aurelia Teeus, presented the child for adoption after the death of his father, who was Silvanus' brother. Much of the scholarly treatment of the text has revolved around its legal implications; technically, women could not offer a child for adoption under Roman law.[55] The document, however, is also a piece of evidence, albeit a limited one, for the relationship between children and adult ascetics. Its purpose was to record a legal and financial contract whereby the monk Silvanus agreed to become the guardian of both the boy and his inheritance; the latter was delineated in some detail: "lands and buildings and movable goods belonging to the house inventories."[56] Moreover, Silvanus promised to make Paesis the "heir of my property." As Sabine Huebner's research has demonstrated, adoption in Roman Egypt was common, and likely more frequent than a cursory review of census and other demographic sources might suggest. A higher proportion of older men report having living sons than demographic tables would predict. Likewise, orphans in census data number too few.[57] Thus, adoptions are underreported in the census tables. While contracts such as *P.Lips.* 28 express concern for the welfare of the child, adoption typically functioned to serve the needs of the adoptive parent(s) as much as the child's. Adults adopted children to secure heirs for their

---

[54] *P.Lips.* 28; trans. Rowlandson, *Women and Society*, 297–98.
[55] Kuryłowicz, "Adoption on the Evidence of Papyri," 67–69.
[56] *P.Lips.* 28; trans. Rowlandson, *Women and Society*, 297–98.
[57] Huebner, *Family in Roman Egypt*, 176–77; Huebner, "Adoption and Fosterage," 521–25; on the limits of demographic tables, see Pudsey, "Nuptiality," 73–75.

property, as the legal language of the surviving adoption contracts attests. The adoption of a son by a childless person or a person with only daughters would also guarantee a younger generation to care for them in old age. The latter motivation was common for Egyptians who were not among the elites; indeed, aging people across the Mediterranean faced such a future.[58] Some viewed the prospect of a childless old age as "the worst of all fates."[59] Various factors, then, may have motivated Silvanus' adoption of Paesis – a need to provide a legal male guardian for the child, a desire to secure an heir for Silvanus' property, an emotional attachment to the child, a wish to establish a reciprocal social and economic relationship between the two in order to support Silvanus as he aged, or some combination of these factors.[60]

Since the purpose of *P.Lips.* 28 was to record a legal relationship, it does not provide detail about the child's living arrangements. Presumably Paesis was living with Aurelia Teeus, since despite the letter of the law, it was she who was giving him up for adoption. Silvanus pledged to watch over Paesis' property and to "feed and clothe [him] in decent and appropriate fashion" as well as to "raise him in decent and appropriate fashion." The monk may have funded the boy's care while the child lived elsewhere (perhaps even staying with his grandmother); the contract's language, however, leaves open the possibility that Paesis went to live with Silvanus after the adoption.

In the eighth century in Jême, another monk designated an heir to his property. A papyrus containing the testament of the monk Paham names his son as the heir to his house and property.[61] The text dates to 725 and reports that the house was built by Paham's grandfather, willed to Paham's father, and then to him. Paham had initially designated one son named Papnoute and Papnoute's children the heirs, but they died. Paham then designated another son, Jacob, as heir. There appears to have been some dispute, with Papnoute's widow making a claim to the property. Paham lived in a monastic community on the mountain of Jême, but he maintained ownership of his property. Although his sons are likely adults, this testament demonstrates

---

[58] For a rich and thorough review of research on adoption in the Roman Empire, see Vuolanto, *Children and Asceticism,* 33–36.

[59] Huebner, *Family in Roman Egypt,* esp. 186–87; "Childless Old Age: The Worst of All Fates?" is the title of Huebner's seventh chapter.

[60] On emotional attachment and adoption, see the literature review in Vuolanto, *Children and Asceticism,* 35–36.

[61] *P.KRU* 67.

Paham's ongoing concern that his descendants, who probably include children (the grandchildren), inherit.[62]

Such social and economic connections between monks and children do not originate in this later period, but rather they date to the earliest century of Egyptian monasticism. *P.Lips.* 28 and the Greek papyri from the Hathor monastery depict a Christian landscape as early as the fourth century in which monks lived not only "in the world" but also, more specifically, in a world in which they interacted with children and were even called upon to care or provide for them. Although we do not have sufficient evidence to determine whether the children mentioned in the fourth-century papyri lived in households or communities with the monks, we can find such evidence in other sources.

Children Joining Monasteries with One or More Parents

Early monastic literature – including historical sources (such as contemporaneous letters, rules, and sermons), hagiography (saints' lives), and gnomic literature (such as the Greek, Latin, and Coptic *Apophthegmata Patrum*, or *Sayings of the Desert Fathers* [hereafter, *Sayings*]) – speaks of children joining and/or living in monastic communities with their parents, who were also monks. At times, the language of our sources makes it difficult to determine whether these sons and daughters are adult or minor children. For example, two documentary papyri from the turn of the eighth century mention a father-son pair (Moses and Theodore) at the Monastery of St. Paul in Jême. In the second papyrus, the monastic superior even allows Theodore to care for his father in his old age. Theodore's age when he joined the monastery remains uncertain.[63] Either through language or context, however, other sources tell of minor children entering the ascetic life with a parent.

Sayings mentions children surprisingly often, given its otherwise antifamilial bent. They contain stories of at least five male monks who brought children to their semi-anchoritic monastic communities. Four of these apothegms refer to fathers and their legal sons, and these pairs all lived in the desert community of Scetis, in the Wadi Natrun southeast of Alexandria. Although *Sayings* does recount traditions about monastic women in Egypt, I have not yet found any references to ascetic girls,

---

[62] See discussion in Hedstrom, *Monastic Landscape*, 193.

[63] *P.CLT* 1 and 2; trans. MacCoull, *Coptic Legal Documents*, 42–47, 51–53; see also Hengstenberg, review of *Ten Coptic Legal Texts*, by Arthur A. Schiller. An essential survey of Theban monastic wills appears in O'Connell, "Transforming Monumental Landscapes," 263–72.

much less girls joining monastic communities with a parent. In at least four cases, the boy was being raised to become a monk himself.[64] I do not take the narratives in *Sayings* as direct historical evidence for specific individual boys in fourth-century Egypt becoming monks with their fathers. An ongoing scholarly debate about the use of *Sayings* for historical research has questioned whether it provides evidence for specific "fathers" and "mothers" in the sources, for a general early monastic "wisdom" and practice, or for something even more removed in time and space, such as the educational practices of the later monks who compiled *Sayings* (some of whom may not have lived in Egypt).[65] Following Lillian Larsen, I read *Sayings* as a set of multivalent micronarratives that form part of a larger genre of gnomic sayings endemic to ancient philosophical and educational traditions. As multivalent literary provocations recorded after the events it purports to describe, *Sayings* about monks and their children testify to a monastic past, part real and part imagined, in which ascetic fathers and sons were both expected and provocative to later monastic audiences.[66]

The most extensive material pertains to the father and son duo of Carion and Zacharias. A number of sayings featuring one, the other, or both survive in multiple languages; most of my analysis pertains to the apothegms in the Greek Alphabetical Collection.[67] According to the second saying concerning Carion, the man "withdrew from the world" to become a monk, leaving a wife and two children. This apothegm goes on to evoke the intense burden and distress shouldered by family members left behind when breadwinners abandoned them to join monasteries. When a famine ensued, Carion's wife traveled to Scetis to confront him, demanding, "Who is going to feed your children?" Carion asked her to send the children to him. The son, Zacharias, stayed, while the daughter returned to her mother. The anecdotes of the Greek *Sayings* narrate that Carion then raised Zacharias among monks; his daughter merits no further mention.[68]

The other three stories that describe monks living with boys appear in the anonymous Greek collection, and two of them include father-son pairs. In one, an "old man" (*gerontos*) brings a nursing (*thēlazonta*) son to

---

[64] *AP* Carion 2, in *PG* 65:249–52. *AP Anon.* 171, 173, 187, 341, in Nau, "Histoires" (1908), 55, 56–57, 272–73; (1912), 296.

[65] On the compilation of *Sayings*, see Harmless, *Desert Christians*, 19, 169–71.

[66] On *Sayings* as gnomic and educational literature, see Larsen, "On Learning a New Alphabet"; Larsen, "Apophthegmata Patrum." For readings of *Sayings* as a historical document, see Gould, *Desert Fathers on Monastic Community*; Burton-Christie, *Word in the Desert*.

[67] *AP* Carion 2, in *PG* 65:249–52.   [68] On Carion and Zacharias, see Chapter 3.

Scetis.[69] In the other, a man brings his recently weaned son (*apogalak-tisthenta*) to Scetis and raises him there. When the latter child hits adolescence, he wishes to leave, asserting that he does not "have the strength to endure the battle" of asceticism; instead, his father sends him into the "desert" for forty days as a test and to build his strength in asceticism. The child eventually chooses to remain with the monks.[70] Finally, another saying tells of an adult monk (*gerontos*) and a boy (*paidion*) living together. The youth disobeys the older monk, receives a reprimand, and then leaves his elder without access to the room storing their bread for thirteen days.[71]

We cannot take these apothegms as concrete evidence for boys living with adult male monks in fourth-century Egyptian monastic communities, but we can discern two things. First, later monks either writing or compiling these sayings assumed early communities included fathers and sons. Second, the texts speak to and about a social world for which we have other evidence confirming monks and children living together. The writings from the White Monastery Federation, for example, contain many references to minor children, some of whom were likely the offspring of adult monastics.

The federation's most famous leader, Shenoute, mentions several family groupings specifically. In one letter, he writes of a male monk with a son, wife, and daughter all in the monastery. Shenoute has expelled the man and simultaneously forced the whole family to leave:

> This one also whom we stripped of his monastic cloak, and his son, and his wife, and his daughter, whom we cast out immediately from the congregations of our fathers – you know all his hypocrisy and his pride and his lies and his false words and all his other evil deeds.[72]

Shenoute has banished the entire family, parents and children. We know they did not leave of their own volition, because Shenoute has cast them all out and stripped the man of his monastic cloak. The one entry ritual common to most monasteries was the donning of the monastic habit.[73] To strip a monk of one's habit was to expel the monk. Although we do not

[69] *AP Anon.* 171, in Nau, "Histoires" (1908), 55, and Wortley, *Anonymous Sayings*, 114.

[70] *AP Anon.* 173, in Nau, "Histoires" (1908), 56–57, and Wortley, *Anonymous Sayings*, 114–16; trans. Ward, *Wisdom of the Desert Fathers*, 10, and Wortley, *Anonymous Sayings*, 115–17.

[71] *AP Anon.* 341, in Nau, "Histoires" (1912), 296, and Wortley, *Anonymous Sayings*, 222. See also *AP Anon.* 340 regarding novices (*neōteroi*), in Wortley, *Anonymous Sayings*, 222.

[72] Shenoute, *Why O Lord, Canons*, vol. 4, MONB.BZ 59, in Leipoldt, *Vita et Opera Omnia*, vol. 3, 141.

[73] Cassian, *Institutes* 1, in Petschenig, *De institutis*; trans. Ramsey, *Institutes*, 21–27; Harmless, *Desert Christians*, 120, 126–27, 314, 411. On oaths and the habit, see Krawiec, "Garments of Salvation"; Wipszycka, *Moines et communautés monastiques*, 365–81.

learn the ages of the son and daughter, the way Shenoute narrates the event suggests that the children were minors, still under the legal umbrella of their parents. All were forced to leave, even though Shenoute accused the children of no crime. Shenoute frequently disparages the maintenance of family ties between monks in the federation.[74] He also typically shows little restraint when criticizing people who have collaborated with transgressing monks, or who helped cover up the transgressions after the fact.[75] One would expect that at least the son would be allowed to choose his residence if he were of legal age. Thus it seems likely that this monk's son and daughter were minors rather than innocent adult children thrown out due to their close familial relation. And it would be surprising (given Shenoute's rhetorical history and leadership style) if they were adult coconspirators of some sort, and Shenoute failed to identify their transgressions.[76] We can reasonably conclude that this monastic family unit included minor children.

In another letter, this one specifically to the women's community, Shenoute names a number of women he has identified for punishment. Some of them may have had relatives in the men's communities. He provides each female monk's name, her transgression, and the punishment (generally a beating). Often, he provides familial information about the women (likely as identifiers). I excerpt here only the women's names and identifying relatives:

> Apa Hermef's daughter, Thesnoe . . .
> The sister of Apa Psyros . . .
> Hllo's younger sister Tsophia . . .
> John's younger sister, Tshenvictor . . .
> Pshai's younger sister, Taese . . .
> Takous, who is called Rebecca . . .
> Zachariah's sister, Tsophia . . .
> And her sister Tapolle . . .
> Joseph's sister, Tsophia . . .
> The sister of Apa Hllo, Tsansno . . .[77]

Thesnoe daughter of Apa Hermef, the unnamed sister of Apa Psyros, and Tsansno the sister of Apa Hllo may all be relatives of monks in one of the

---

[74] Krawiec, *Shenoute and the Women*, 161–74. See also Chapters 3 and 7 of this book.
[75] Schroeder, "Prophecy and Porneia"; Schroeder, *Monastic Bodies*, ch. 1.
[76] See, for example, Shenoute's rhetoric on the polluting nature of sin and the need to identify and punish disobedient monks, treated extensively in Schroeder, *Monastic Bodies*.
[77] Shenoute, *Why O Lord, Canons*, vol. 4, MONB.BZ 345–47, in Young, *Coptic Manuscripts*, vol. 1, 103–05; trans. 112. See also Krawiec, *Shenoute and the Women*, 42.

men's communities of Shenoute's monastery. Women in Egypt were often identified as the daughter or sister of their guardian male relative. In documentary papyri (contracts, receipts, nonliterary letters, etc.), the title "Apa" frequently designates monastics; the title also precedes the names of non-monastic clerics (e.g., presbyters) and, more rarely, men of status in their local communities who were neither monks nor church officials. Although early Greek literary texts, such as the Pachomian *vitae* and the *History of the Monks of Egypt*, use "Apa" inconsistently when naming monks, Shenoute seems to use it primarily when talking about monks, not non-monastic clerics. Besides the citations in this list of women, in the known surviving fragments of his *Canons* for monks, Shenoute uses "Apa" exclusively when writing about a particular male monk: Pshoi (*Apa Pshoi*), the founder of the Red Monastery, which was the smaller men's community in the federation. (Even in later colophons and scribal notes, where "Apa" appears more frequently, it refers to monastics.)[78] Given this usage of "Apa" in Shenoute's work and by the later scribes in his federation's library, the title "Apa" in the list of punishments for women monks likely denotes male monks, probably men also in the federation.

Only one woman on this list did Shenoute not identify by a male relative – Takous. Takous' identification raises questions about everyone else: Why was her nearest living male relative not mentioned? Because she had none, or just none whom Shenoute knew, or none in the monastery? It is possible that all but Takous had family in the men's monastery, or that we only have three – the Apa's relatives – and Shenoute identified most of the other women in the letter by male relatives outside the community. Nonetheless, we have at least one father-daughter pair (Thesnoe and Hermef).[79]

---

[78] Twice in reference to an Apa Antonios, a donor of a copy of Volume 6 of Shenoute's *Canons* to a "House of the Stewards" in the monastery; Apa Philox and Apa Zēth in the same *Canons* vol. 6 colophon, identified as housemaster and archimandrite, respectively; once in reference to a monk who is also a cleric (presbyter); and in reference to Shenoute himself as well as later archimandrites named Shenoute. Pshoi: Shenoute, *Canons*, vol. 2, MONB.XC 222, in Kuhn, *Letters and Sermons of Besa*, vol. 1, 118; *Canons*, vol. 3, MONB.YA 309, in Leipoldt, *Vita et Opera Omnia*, vol. 4, 120; see also Layton, *Canons of Our Fathers*, 118. Antony, Philox, Zēth: *Canons*, vol. 6, MONB.XF 552, in Munier, *Manuscrits coptes*, 75. We find the titles *apa* and *abba* before the name Shenoute frequently in colophons or scribal notes; see, for example, *Canons*, vol. 3, MONB.YA 554, in Young, "Five Leaves," 280. Shenoute, *Canons* vol. 8, MONB.XO 309, in Boud'hors, *Le canon 8 de Chénouté*, vol. 1, 369. Apa Psote, the presbyter monk, appears in the colophon in *Canons*, vol. 1, MONB.YW 212, in Munier, *Manuscrits coptes*, 118. For some of these citations, I am indebted to Wolf-Peter Funk for his "Work Concordance to Shenoute's Canons" and Paul C. Dilley's thorough prosopographical survey of text-bearing objects in Shenoute's monastic federation, "Inscribed Identities."

[79] See also Krawiec, *Shenoute and the Women*, 164.

Shenoute's writings also provide more general evidence for entire families joining the monastery as a commonplace practice. Rules in his *Canons* strictly regulated everyone's interactions with their blood (or legal) relatives. In an exhortation to subordinate relationships "of the flesh" to relationships and obligations to fellow monastics who are "strangers," Shenoute mentions a number of family relationships, explicitly mentioning children: "sons, daughters, brothers, sisters, parents, whether father or mother, or any other relatives of theirs according to the flesh."[80] Both male and female monks who gave some of their own food to their children, parents, or siblings faced expulsion.[81] Male monks could seek permission to travel to the women's community to visit their daughters. Men serving at the gatehouse of the women's community could not speak to any of the women; in case of emergency, a man at the gatehouse could not speak to a woman monk alone, even if that woman was his mother, sister, or daughter.[82] A man could not pray with his mother, sister, or daughter if the woman requested it, nor kiss his mother, sister, or daughter if she ran to greet him.[83] All of these rules indicate the extensive presence of biological or adoptive children and their parents together in the federation. While many of them may pertain to adult children as well as minor children, the likelihood is high that some of these families joined the community when their children were minors; we would expect most adult daughters to have left their natal family to live with their husbands and most adult sons to have married and begun their own families.

Thus, the cumulative weight of this evidence points to entire families or individual parents (e.g., widows or widowers) with minor children joining the White Monastery Federation and perhaps other monasteries. The pervasive references to children in Shenoute's rules, the circumstances of the errant monk's expulsion, and the widespread practice of families joining the federation all point to the near certainty that minor children entered this coenobitic community (and perhaps others) along with their parents or guardians. Perhaps this practice was a primary vehicle by which children came to live in the White Monastery Federation in the late fourth and early fifth centuries. At other monastic communities, the evidence is

---

[80] Shenoute, *A22*, *Canons*, vol. 3, MONB.YB 74–75, unpublished FR-BN 130² ff. 61v–62r; excerpt in Layton, *Canons of Our Fathers*, 104; trans. 105.

[81] Shenoute, *Canons*, vol. 9, MONB.DF 187–88, in Leipoldt, *Vita et Opera Omnia*, vol. 4, 106; excerpt in Layton, *Canons of Our Fathers*, 270; trans. 271.

[82] Shenoute, *Canons*, vol. 9, MONB.DF 189–90, in Leipoldt, *Vita et Opera Omnia*, vol. 4, 107–08; excerpt in Layton, *Canons of Our Fathers*, 272; trans. 273.

[83] Shenoute, *Canons*, vol. 5, MONB.XL 136–37, in Munier, *Manuscrits coptes*, 80; excerpt in Layton, *Canons of Our Fathers*, 196; trans. 197.

less firm but suggestive enough that we should consider the possibility that parents and children joined monastic communities together.

Orphaned and Abandoned Children

Many references to children in non-hagiographical sources make no note of how they came to live in monasteries or with anchorites. We have occasional references to orphans, albeit fewer than we might expect given the research on poverty, orphans, and fatherless children in Egypt. Although Egyptian census returns record only 16 percent of freeborn children under sixteen years old living without their fathers, Huebner's research into model life tables estimates that children held a one-in-three chance of losing their father before turning sixteen and a one-in-four chance of losing their mother. We would expect 11 percent of freeborn children to lose both parents. Yet fewer than 7 percent of children in the census returns lived with no parent. In fact, the percentage of children living without their parents in the census should be *higher* than the model life tables predict, since divorce and parental travel also led to children living without one or both parents. Thus, the number of orphans in the population was probably significantly higher than the 7 percent of parentless children and 16 percent of fatherless children recorded in the census tables.[84] Of course, many of these children were adopted, often by paternal relatives (such as an uncle, as in *P.Lips.* 28) to ensure inheritance and the paternal line; Huebner attributes the significant discrepancy between the census and the life tables to the frequency of adoption in late antique Egypt.[85] Nonetheless, fatherless and parentless freeborn children existed in significant numbers. Some likely lived out their childhood in their paternal family's household – perhaps even the same house as before, considering the prevalence of multigenerational households in which adult sons lived with their parents and even some siblings in late antique Egypt.[86] Yet, due to poverty and other economic factors, some surely faced more dire circumstances, including enslavement (or, for infants, exposure followed by enslavement).[87]

In the late fourth century and beyond, we know monasteries also filled in this breach in care for parentless children. Outside of Egypt, monasteries for men and women in Cappadocia reared orphaned children. At the

[84] Huebner, *Family in Roman Egypt*, 177.
[85] Huebner, *Family in Roman Egypt*, 177–78, 181–82, 184, 190–91.
[86] Huebner, *Family in Roman Egypt*, 35–53.
[87] Huebner, *Family in Roman Egypt*, 66, 197–98; Grubbs, "Infant Exposure and Infanticide," 95.

monastery founded and led by Macrina, sister to Basil of Caesarea and Gregory of Nyssa, the female monks gathered exposed infant girls and raised them in the community. The men's monastery founded by Basil also provided orphans with a home during their childhood.[88] Basil's *Asketikon* reads: "Children bereft of parents we take in of our own accord, thus becoming fathers of orphans after the example of Job's zeal."[89] Augustine also writes of monasteries caring for orphans and foundlings.[90]

The evidence from late antique Egypt is scant but suggestive. We have two documentary sources testifying to monks taking responsibility for orphaned children. In addition, Shenoute's writings mention orphans in the White Monastery Federation. And we have at least one account in *Sayings* of an abba taking in an exposed infant. Hagiography, however, proves an unreliable witness. As Vuolanto correctly notes, orphanhood constitutes a *topos* in hagiography about Egyptian ascetics (both male and female). In these accounts, saints become orphaned as children or adolescents. The death of their parents affords the narratives ideal circumstances in which to portray the young saints' moral choice to relinquish the wealth or status from their inherited property and patrimony.[91] Following a pattern established in the *Life of Antony*, the young saints embark on the ascetic life at this pivotal moment, deciding to give their property away as charity and become monks rather than live "in the world." While this phenomenon may surely have occurred, we cannot cite its abundance in hagiography as evidence for a widespread practice.[92] We find more secure footing in our contemporaneous and historical evidence, even if it is scarce. Given the demographic data about parentless children in Egypt and the evidence for early Christian monasteries outside of Egypt raising orphans, we should consider our meager surviving evidence as the visible tip of a much larger iceberg.

Orphans appear in multiple contexts – with a man, with a woman, with a likely house anchorite, and in monastic communities. The first document about an orphan we have already discussed: the ten-year-old Paesis adopted by his uncle, the *monachos* Aurelius Silvanus, in 381 CE. An ostracon from the Theban region, perhaps three centuries later, records an orphan living with a female monk (*monachē*) named Maria. Maria has written to an

---

[88] Gregory of Nyssa, *Vita Sanctae Macrinae* 26, in *PG* 46:988. See also Vuolanto, *Children and Asceticism*, 72–73, 103.

[89] Basil, *Longer Rules* 15.1, in *PG* 31:952; trans. Silvas, *Asketikon of St Basil the Great*, 200.

[90] Vuolanto, *Children and Asceticism*, 73, 103.   [91] Vuolanto, *Children and Asceticism*, 119.

[92] For a foundling (*threptariō mikrō*) living among male monks, see *AP* Gelasios 3, in *PG* 65:148–49. See also Miller, *Orphans of Byzantium*, 158.

anchorite named Kyriakos requesting his blessing.[93] At the end of the letter, she asks for prayers "on behalf of the little orphan (*orphanos šēm*)" in her care, indicating that the boy's father has died. She requests blessings and prayers specifically for her "house" (mentioning "my house" [*paēi*] twice in the short letter); the child must have lived with her in her home.

In the surviving fragments of Shenoute's *Canons* for monks, orphans are mentioned numerous times, though unfortunately not when documenting any individual whose circumstances we could discern. More disappointing, Shenoute usually uses the term *orphanos* when citing Deuteronomy in order to chastise monks who show favoritism toward their blood relatives (especially in serving food), as here: "Therefore, Oh, let us not be deceived in anything of this kind, namely to show preference by favoritism to relatives of ours according to the flesh over strangers and orphans in anything."[94] In such passages, it is difficult to determine whether Shenoute was writing literally about orphans in the community or meta-phorically. In other passages, however, his references prove more concrete. In one of these passages (which, like the passage citing Deuteronomy, shames monks for favoritism), he argues that while monks might have thought themselves virtuous for giving food to a less fortunate colleague (someone sicker or weaker), in fact they were wrong – monks were not to give extra food to anyone, not "relatives of theirs or strangers or poor or orphans or sick or lame or blind or any other person."[95] This passage contains a fairly typical list of people who would receive charity, and on those grounds we might wonder whether Shenoute mentioned orphans because they resided in the monastery or because they fit a stock charity list. We know from his *Canons*, however, that everyone else on this list indeed lived in the monastery – sick, lame, blind, poor, relatives, strangers. Additionally, in an earlier letter, Shenoute mentions the humanitarian work of the monastery, such as care for orphans, widows, and the poor.[96] Such labor surely occurred within the walls of the monastic

---

[93] *O.Brit.Mus.Copt. I* add. 23.

[94] Shenoute, *A22, Canons*, vol. 3, MONB.YB 76–77, in Layton, *Canons of Our Fathers*, 106; trans. 107. For the full (unpublished) context of this fragment, see FR-BN 130², ff. 62v–63r, online, https://gallica.bnf.fr/ark:/12148/btv1b10089625k/f125.image.r=130%20Copte, accessed December 4, 2019. Compare Deut. 10:18–19 (i.e., in the Coptic Old Testament) at *sahidic.ot Corpus*, urn:cts:copticLit:ot.deut. Coptic SCRIPTORIUM.

[95] Shenoute, *Canons*, vol. 9, MONB.DF 103, in Leipoldt, *Vita et Opera Omnia*, vol. 4, 87; trans. Layton, *Canons of Our Fathers*, 243.

[96] Shenoute, *Canons*, vol. 1, MONB.YW 89 (unpublished), in FR-BN 130², f. 7r, online, https://gallica.bnf.fr/ark:/12148/btv1b10089625k/f14.image.r=130%20Copte, accessed December 4, 2019. For

settlement, due to the fairly stringent rules and conditions the federation set on monks traveling outside of the monastery.

Finally, some indirect evidence alludes to the possibility of orphaned or exposed children within the community. The library at Shenoute's monastery contained formulas for medical treatments designed to induce lactation in women. These recipes could have formed part of a larger medical collection acquired by the monastery, of which the lactagogical elements would have remained unused. And the monastery may have acquired the medical texts well after the period under examination here. Nonetheless, they could well have been employed to induce lactation in order to nurture abandoned or orphaned babies then living at the community.[97]

Children with Living Parents: Familial and Self-Donations

We have quite varied evidence for children with living parents entering monasteries, usually at their parents' behest. Both poor and wealthy parents sent their children to monasteries in various locations along the Nile Valley.

At the White Monastery Federation, we know of at least one such named individual with living parents outside the community. Aphthonia was the daughter of a local official (a *comes*) named Alexander. After an argument with her spiritual mother (the head of the women's community at the White Monastery Federation), Aphthonia wrote home to her parents of origin to complain of abuse.[98] The surviving account of this event comes from the federation's leader at the time, Besa (successor to Shenoute). Besa's letter to Aphthonia provides a remarkable case study in familial relations – both natal and monastic familial relations.[99] Unfortunately, we do not know Aphthonia's age during this dispute, or her age when she became a monk. From what we know about women's asceticism elsewhere, and because her primary family tie is to her parents (not her children, brother, or in-laws), she probably joined the community as a girl, younger than or just on the cusp of the age of marriage, and not as a widow. Her

---

further discussion of this passage, see also Schroeder, "Prophecy and Porneia"; Schroeder, *Monastic Bodies*, ch. 1; Emmel, "Shenoute the Monk." Crislip takes these references as prima facie evidence for orphans; Crislip, *From Monastery to Hospital*, 135.

[97] Crislip, "Care for the Sick," 26.

[98] Besa, *Aphthonia* 1.5, in Miyagawa et al. urn:cts:copticLit:besa.aphthonia.monbba, Coptic SCRIPTORIUM; Engl. trans. Miyagawa and Zeldes, urn:cts:copticLit:besa.aphthonia.monbba. Coptic SCRIPTORIUM.

[99] See Chapter 8.

father's title means she came from a wealthy and influential family in the region.

An ostracon from further south, in Western Thebes (late antique Jême), records a letter from a man who had given his daughter to a nearby, unnamed monastery.[100] In contrast to Aphthonia's household, this family likely was not well off. The father, Psalom, had requested that a certain "Victor" (possibly a priest) write to "Apa Dios" of the monastery where his daughter was ensconced. The text refers to Psalom as "this poor man" (*peiheēke*). In it, the father begs the monastery not to return the girl to his household, even offering to provide a monetary deposit to the monastery to ensure that the monks would not send her back. Although Psalom does not describe his circumstances in detail, the language suggests economic distress. Coptic epistolary frequently includes tropes of humility, especially when a person of lower status writes to request something from a correspondent of higher status. Yet the Coptic term *hēke* typically refers to economic poverty, suggesting that adverse material conditions, not just traditional humility, motivate Psalom.[101] Plausibly, he could afford to bestow some money on the monastery in return for its care of his daughter, but he could not support the child's entire upbringing and/or dowry.[102]

Papyri from the eighth-century Monastery of Phoibammon near Jême (Thebes) record several families donating children to the monastery or to the healing shrine run by the monastery, especially after sickness.[103] This collection is unique, so it is difficult to derive generalizations about practices throughout Egypt based on practices at one particular monastery.[104] Moreover, they date to the eighth century, later than the main period of study in this book; we cannot retroject onto earlier eras (particularly the fourth and fifth centuries) based on a period with significant legal and economic differences, one in which monasticism also was more widespread, legally sophisticated, and hierarchically complex. Finally, Gesa Schenke has recently argued that the children mentioned in the documents were dedicated not to the monastery per se but to the healing shrine of St. Phoibammon, which was run by the monastery.[105] Despite these cautionary considerations, as a major institution in southern

---

[100] *O.Brit.Mus.Copt.* I LXVI/1; see also Wilfong, *Women of Jeme*, 107.
[101] Crum, *Coptic Dictionary*, 664a; also see editors' comments in Hall, *Coptic and Greek Texts*, 93.
[102] On dowries, see Huebner, *Family in Roman Egypt*, 64, 84, 87.
[103] *P.KRU* 78–114; German trans. in Till, *Die koptischen Rechtsurkunden aus Theben*, 149–88; English trans. of some documents in MacCoull, "Child Donations and Child Saints," MacCoull, *Coptic Legal Documents*, and Schenke, "Healing Shrines."
[104] On one other possible donation record, see Schenke, "Kinderschenkungen."
[105] Schenke, "Healing Shrines."

Egypt at the tail end of the historical period examined in this book, the monastery provides an important case study for the history of children and Christian monasticism.

Several papyri record the oaths of parents (single mothers, fathers, and couples) who promised their children to the monastery after a visit to the community had cured them. The documents are both contractual and literary; legal language delineates the rights of various parties, and emotional, narrative language draws on hagiography and literature.[106] For example, one text narrates the travails of a premature baby and his mother, Tachel. Tachel vowed to give the boy to the monastery if God saved him. He was cured, and then she reneged on her agreement. He became seriously ill again, which she interpreted as a reminder of her broken promise. She swore to abide by the original agreement if the monastery healed her son a second time.[107] Another papyrus tells a similar story, this time of a couple who promised their son Peter to Phoibammon's monastery at the time of his birth. As Peter grew up, the parents reconsidered their vow, and then the boy received the "scourge of sickness." A visit to the monastery healed him, and the papyrus reaffirms their commitment to donating the child.[108] It was not always a broken contract that propelled the recording of the donation. A certain Pesynte and Tasia promised their boy, Panias, to the monastery after the monks healed him from a near fatal illness.[109]

Parents could sometimes choose between sending their children to live at the monastery and keeping them home, while sending the earnings from their labor to the monastery. In one contract, the *oikonomos* asks the family, "Do you wish that he come to the holy place and serve in it? God and you shall command it. Or do you wish that he hand over his labor to the holy place?" The parents defer to the monastery's preference: "We will give him in the way that you impose upon all the boys of the holy place."[110] In the documents, the boys are often promised as enslaved persons or servants (Coptic *hmhal* and *cauon*), and the monastery is named as their owner or lord (*joeis*).[111] Such language is legal as well as biblical; Paul's letters in the New Testament enjoin believers to remember they are all enslaved to their lord, Jesus Christ.[112] Sometimes families also promise a small annual

---

[106] Richter, "What's in a Story?"   [107] *P.KRU* 86.17–32.   [108] *P.KRU* 100.14–43.

[109] *P.KRU* 91.5–13.

[110] *P.KRU* 91.23–26; trans. MacCoull, "Child Donations and Child Saints," 410–11, mod.

[111] E.g., *P.KRU* 88.7, 12. See discussion and literature reviews in Papaconstantinou, "Notes sur les actes de donation d'enfants"; Richter, "What's in a Story?"

[112] Rom. 6:16–22; 1 Cor. 6:20; 7:22–23; 2 Cor. 4:5; Martin, *Slavery As Salvation*; Martin, *Corinthian Body*.

donation to the monastery, which in one case may be for the basic expenses of the child's food and care.[113] Additionally, at least one adult donates himself to the monastery under similar circumstances (illness), using the same language of servitude.[114]

All of the children mentioned in the Phoibammon papyri are boys, and the contractual language indicates a routine practice of assimilating boys into the monastery (e.g., "the way that you see to all the boys of the holy place"). These children thus comprised an identifiable, integrated population at the monastery. The focus on production and labor in many of the documents has inspired a scholarly debate about the role and status of these children: were they enslaved, wards, or novice monks?[115] Earlier sources from the Pachomian and Shenoutean monasteries do not mention enslaved children (or enslaved adults), and rarely address the amount of labor required for the monasteries to function fully (particularly to complete large-scale building projects, such as a church). The monasteries may have enslaved individuals or contracted them for hire from regional families. Even if the donated children were not enslaved in a traditional sense, the Phoibammon papyri require us to ask: Were any of the laborers at early Egyptian monasteries children? Were any of the children enslaved? Unfortunately, such questions are nearly impossible to answer due to the near absence of slavery from the earliest monastic sources.[116]

Hagiography, of course, frequently depicts "holy children" who become ascetics, often with their parents' encouragement or support. Although the most famous names associated with the earliest ascetic movement are those of men who converted to the ascetic life as adults (e.g., Antony, Pachomius, and Macarius the Great), child saints appear early in monastic hagiography and panegyric. These sources tend to attribute early ascetic prowess (not poverty or parental tragedy) to the phenomenon of child monks. They follow the traditions of Greco-Roman biography and panegyric for people considered favored by the gods, as well as biblical models (Samuel, Jesus in the Gospel of Luke, etc.).[117]

The *Life of Shenoute*, for example, recounts a childhood in which the monk was already marked by God in his youth. On his own initiative, the

---

[113] *P.KRU* 78.25–26.

[114] *P.KRU* 104; trans. Schenke, "Healing Shrines," 516–17, and MacCoull, *Coptic Legal Documents*, 163–65.

[115] See also Chapters 6 and 7.

[116] For more, we await an article in progress by Jennifer Cromwell on Coptic evidence for slavery.

[117] Wiedemann, *Adults and Children in the Roman Empire*, 51–52, 54–55; Caseau, "Childhood in Byzantine Saints' Lives," 128–29, 137–39.

boy prayed every night with such fervor that the fingers of his outstretched hands burned "like ten flaming lamps." So strong was the child's ascetic aura that the local monastic leader Pcol greeted Shenoute by calling the *youth* "my father and archimandrite." The young Shenoute exorcised a demon and was protected in his sleep by a guardian angel. He then entered ascetic life, guided by the man who founded the monastery Shenoute would eventually lead. According to this tradition, while Shenoute was still a child, God pronounced him "archimandrite of the entire world!"[118]

The Tenth Sahidic *Vita* of Pachomius similarly traces the ascetic expertise of one of Pachomius' successors back to an extraordinary childhood. Theodore would eventually lead the Pachomian federation after the founder's death and an intervening period.[119] According to the Bohairic *Life*, Theodore joined the community at the age of twenty, but the Greek *Life* puts the age at fourteen, the Tenth Sahidic *Life* describes him as a "boy" when he joined, and the *Letter of Ammon* states that he was thirteen years old.[120] In the Greek *Life of Pachomius*, Theodore "stood out above the others" early in life, bewailing "the things of this world" that came between him and God. Purportedly, he often fasted during the day and generally avoided "expensive meats and foods like a monk" until he left the family household in order to live in a monastery.[121] These accounts of Theodore's childhood, like those of Shenoute's, portray a child destined for ascetic greatness as an adult. In contrast, no such trope surfaces in documentary or contemporary historical sources. Neither young Piene's family, who sent him to travel with the Teacher, nor Psalom, who requested a monastery not return his daughter, cite the moral virtue of their children as motivation for sending them to live among ascetics. I have yet to find such a commentary in the authentic writings of Shenoute or Besa.

This motif continues in later Egyptian hagiography. The *Life of Moses of Abydos*, for example, presents Moses' monastic destiny as prophesied from a time before he was born by none other than Shenoute. Moses' parents,

---

[118] *Life of Shenoute*, 4–9, in Leipoldt, *Vita et Opera Omnia*, vol. 1, 9–13; trans. Bell, *Besa: Life of Shenoute*, 42–45. See the work on the "vita" of Shenoute as panegyric by Lubomierski, "*Vita Sinuthii*: Panegyric or Biography?"; Lubomierski, *Die Vita Sinuthii: Form- und Überlieferungsgeschichte*; Lubomierski, "Coptic Life of Shenoute."

[119] On the succession of leaders in the Pachomian federation, see Harmless, *Desert Christians*, 132–39; Rousseau, *Pachomius*, 183–91.

[120] V. Pach. Bo 31, V. Pach. G¹ 33, V. Pach. S¹ Fragment 4; ed. and trans. Veilleux, *Pachomian Koinonia, Volume One*, 57, 321, 453; Ep. Ammon 9, in Goehring, *Letter of Ammon*, 130; trans. 164.

[121] V. Pach. G¹ 33, in Halkin, *Sancti Pachomii Vitae Graecae*, 20–21; ed. and trans. Veilleux, *Pachomian Koinonia, Volume One*, 320–21.

recognizing that the Holy Spirit had blessed their child, dedicated him to God when he was just five.[122] In the Synaxarion, a number of saints are recognized as holy while still children.[123]

Given the hagiographical genre of these texts, it is difficult to use them as evidence for specific families donating sons or daughters to monasteries because of perceived virtue in the children at young ages. These accounts promote an ascetic theory about monastic children expressed elsewhere in the Pachomian saints' lives and in *Sayings*. As later chapters explore, monastic literature characterizes the ascetic potential of children as greater than the potential of those who converted to monasticism as adults. Nonetheless, although the pervasiveness of this trope means that we cannot take these accounts of individual monks as historically accurate biographies, we do see an important trend in the literature, signaling how late antique monastic writers valued children. These literary accounts portray a late antique monasticism where children dwelled among monks and monasteries raised children. This social milieu is not wholly in conflict with our firmer historical evidence for children living in monasteries.

Similarly, another trope appears in the Pachomian literature, that of young males who commit to the ascetic life immediately on the cusp of adulthood. Ammon, in his *Letter* describing the three years he lived in the Pachomian federation, claims he decided to join a monastery upon turning seventeen, the age of young adulthood. At that milestone, he became a Christian and attended a sermon of Bishop Athanasius of Alexandria. The bishop's preaching inspired him to become a monk.[124] Similarly, one section of the Bohairic *Life of Pachomius* narrates the origin story of one of the communities in the federation, Thbew. According to this account, a young man named Petronios from a wealthy, high-status family left his household to become a monk. He established a monastery on his parents' property, at some distance from the main residence, and eventually merged his community with the Pachomian federation. Judging from the Bohairic *Vita*, monasticism was a "family affair" for Petronios; he converted relatives, including his father, and they lived together in the monastery until death.[125] While these narratives served to laud their central characters (regardless of whether the saints *did* these things), they also present virtuous models for managing social phenomena we know existed in late

---

[122] *Life of Moses of Abydos*, in Moussa, "Abba Moses of Abydos," 15–18; trans. 28–29.
[123] Basset, "Arabic Synaxarion," *PO* 3:283–84, 431, 443; *PO* 11:517–18, 682–85.
[124] *Ep. Ammon* 2, in Goehring, *Letter of Ammon*, 124.
[125] *V. Pach. Bo* 56; ed. and trans. Veilleux, *Pachomian Koinonia, Volume One*, 77. See discussion in Rousseau, *Pachomius*, 153–55.

antique Egypt: families with individuals who joined the monastic life, at times in conflict with other relatives in their household.[126]

Children Passing Through

The monastery in late antique Egypt also served as an institution that sheltered children during moments of personal or social crisis. During military incursions from the south by people Shenoute calls the Blemmyes, the White Monastery Federation temporarily housed thousands of lay people, financed ransom for kidnap victims, and paid doctors to care for the sick and for the fifty-two babies born there.[127] At the sixth-century Palestinian Monastery of St. Stephen, children's bones were secured along with adult bones in a large ossuary. A study of the skeletons revealed that many showed signs of disease, suggesting that these children sojourned at the monastery while receiving healthcare.[128] If the children died on site, the monks interred their remains on the property. Perhaps monasteries also housed adolescent runaways. When Ammon, mentioned earlier in this chapter, left home to join the Pachomian federation, his parents went searching for him, knocking on the doors of all the monasteries.[129] Does this detail hint that monasteries were a known refuge for runaways?

Additionally, we do not know whether children, especially those donated by parents, were oblates dedicated to God and the monastery for their entire lives, or whether they were living in the communities merely for a time in order to be educated.[130] An anecdote in the chapter about John of Lycopolis in the *History of the Monks of Egypt* is sometimes cited as an example of the latter scenario. John, who himself became a monk as an adult, visited the home of an officer and his pregnant wife. After the woman survived a difficult birth that nearly killed her, John instructed the man to raise the child in their household until he turned

---

[126] For an account of such conflicts in the wider Mediterranean and the role of ascetic literature in managing them, see Vuolanto, *Children and Asceticism*, 95–129.

[127] Schroeder, *Monastic Bodies*, 117; Lopez, *Shenoute of Atripe and the Uses of Poverty*, 56–63.

[128] Leyerle, "Children and Disease." [129] *Ep. Ammon* 30, in Goehring, *Letter of Ammon*, 152.

[130] The term "oblate" can be confusing, since today it can designate people committed to a religious order who are not officially monks and nuns. Also, in the early medieval Latin West, debate raged over whether child oblation was irrevocable. Specifically, could parents remove oblates or could the children themselves decide to leave a monastery or nunnery upon reaching puberty? The tenth Council of Toledo in 656 decreed oblation irrevocable, except in the case of boys and girls donated after reaching the age of ten; those children had the right to decide for themselves whether to stay. The Toledo decision, however, cannot be taken as a universal statement on the practice of oblation across Europe in the early Middle Ages. See de Jong, *In Samuel's Image*, ch. 1, esp. 40–46.

seven and then to send the boy "to the monastics in the desert."[131] The story, however, ends there, with the child's fate in adulthood uncertain. John's instruction could also be interpreted as a command to donate their child to God permanently. Only in the later medieval and Byzantine periods do we find extensive sources for a debate over revoking a child oblation.[132]

Monasticism and the Family: Social Preservation

Some of the most famous literature about Egyptian monks emphasizes the early ascetic movement as one of familial renunciation. Such discursive positioning occurs in both hagiographical and historical sources. In this chapter alone, we have seen the leaders of the White Monastery Federation – in their letters, rules, and sermons – seek to break bonds between family members, whether those relatives live inside the federation or without, challenging the very framework of "family" in late antique society.

Yet, when we peer more closely at the sources, especially those pertaining to children, we see an equally prominent thread: one in which Egyptian monasticism acts as a social institution to preserve the welfare of children and even families. This dissonance is productive, allowing monasteries as institutions to carve out their own position in the social infrastructure of the late antique Mediterranean.[133]

The family persisted as an institution monastics could never fully renounce. Even in sources hostile to marriage, family, and childbearing – early hagiography and *Sayings of the Desert Fathers*, for example – the family requires reckoning as much as renouncing. In the Greek *Life of Pachomius*, we find the founder testing new monks *and their parents* before novices join the community.[134] Within their own communities, monks created practices and networks that replicated the functions of the family; Pachomius reportedly raised

---

[131] *Historia Monachorum*, John of Lycopolis 10, in Festugière, *Historia Monachorum in Aegypto*, 12; trans. Russell, *Lives of the Desert Fathers*, 53. See discussion in Crislip, *From Monastery to Hospital*, 134–35.

[132] De Jong, *In Samuel's Image*, 40–46; Vuolanto, *Children and Asceticism*, 102–03; Greenfield, "Children in Byzantine Monasteries," 253–56.

[133] Jacobs and Krawiec, "Fathers Know Best?"; Jacobs, "Let Him Guard Pietas"; Krawiec, "From the Womb of the Church." On asceticism outside of Egypt constructed as beneficial to the traditional family, see Vuolanto, *Children and Asceticism*, 131–45.

[134] *V. Pach. G¹* 24, in Halkin, *Sancti Pachomii Vitae Graecae*, 14–15; ed. and trans. Veilleux, *Pachomian Koinonia, Volume One*, 312.

Theodore as if he were his own son.[135] The Hathor monastery regularly interacted with families and children, to the extent that another Christian turned to them for help in releasing a man and his children from imprisonment and enslavement. The female monk Maria took in an orphan. Ascetics in Egypt maintained extensive networks with families and children outside the monastery. From the Manichaean Teacher to the Monastery of Phoibammon, care for children provided essential social and educational services to wider communities. In late antique Egypt, children were part of the fabric of ascetic life.

---

[135] *Ep. Ammon* 9, in Goehring, *Letter of Ammon*, 130; trans. 164.

CHAPTER 2

The Language of Childhood

At the Monastery of Saint Phoibammon, the settlement founded amidst the ruins of the ancient pharaoh Hatshepsut's temple, Deir el-Bahri, near ancient Jême (Western Thebes), the following inscription was found: "Do not approach a child; you yourself are a child."[1] This maxim plays with the slippery semantics of the language of childhood, at once bringing to mind a child of a tender age and an adult with the ascetic status of a child.

Children lived in varied early Egyptian monasteries, whether alone or as part of an entire family who joined, as discussed in the previous chapter. As we discovered in Shenoute's federation, our evidence often fails to reveal important information about the children: their age. Were they minor children or adult children (the mature descendants of either monks or other individuals mentioned in the sources)? We know men and women came into the monastery with their sons and daughters but not whether these children were young children, adolescents, or mature adults.

Complicating our study, Egyptian monks used the terminology for childhood to denote monastic status and rank. The Shenoutean corpus in particular contains a vast number of references to children, and yet it is very often difficult to determine whether these "boys," "girls," and "little ones" are minor children or monks of junior or low status. Whereas the previous chapter sought to document the presence of children in the monasteries of late antique Egypt, this chapter provides a philological analysis of the vocabulary of childhood in monastic sources. This study has two objectives: to discern how to craft a social history of underage children in early monasteries when the language of our sources is contextually clear in some places and multivalent or ambiguous in others, and to examine how the language of childhood operates ideologically and

---

[1] Deir el-Bahri inscription no. 26 in Godlewski, *Le monastère de St. Phoibammon*, 149. Modified by Jürgen Horn, personal correspondence. Orig.: *mpo hōr ehōnšēre šēm ntkoušere šēm hōk*. Horn: *mpr hōn ehoun ešēre šēm ntkoušere šēm hōk*.

symbolically to construct ascetic ideals and hierarchies of power within early monasteries.

The analysis mines the corpus of Shenoute's writings primarily and utilizes the Pachomian corpus, other hagiography, and documentary sources secondarily. The centrality of Shenoute's corpus is simply practical: his writings present us with more references to "children" than sources from or about any other early monastery in Egypt, and quite possibly any other Christian monastery in the late antique Mediterranean world. Since many of Shenoute's texts are unpublished, untranslated, or both, this philological survey is thorough but not exhaustive. I have examined all relevant vocabulary in the published editions of Shenoute's *Canons* for monks and in many of the unpublished manuscripts. I have not consulted all unpublished manuscripts. When I have found a relevant term in a published section of one of Shenoute's writings, I have then consulted as many of the unpublished folios of that text as possible. (Some manuscript fragments, such as those at the Coptic Museum in Egypt, can be difficult to access.) I also reviewed some additional unpublished manuscripts I had collected in the course of prior research.

The Coptic vocabulary for childhood in monastic sources, including Shenoute's corpus, is diverse, albeit not as varied as Greek. The most frequent terms are "boys" (*šēre šēm*), "girls" (*šeere šēm*), and "little ones" (*koui*). We also find occasional references to "youths" (*hršire* and *lelou*) and "orphans" (*orphanos*). Unlike in Greek, common and distinct terms for infants, newborns, and babies do not in exist in Coptic. "Boy," "girl," and "little one" encompass children of all ages, including babies.[2] Coptic has a compound word for someone who breastfeeds (i.e., an unweaned infant), but I have not found this noun (*ouamerōte*) attested in monastic literature suitable for social history.[3] As this chapter demonstrates, however, almost none of this vocabulary can be understood to refer straightforwardly and exclusively to minor children living in the monastery. Notably, much of the time the most common Sahidic Coptic vocabulary for children – *šēre šēm* (boy), *šeere šēm* (girl), and *koui* (child, little one) – clearly designates not age or physical maturity but monastic status. At other times, the contexts of these terms in specific instances indicate that these groupings of boys, girls, and little ones included minor children. Chapter 1 documented *where*

---

[2] Crum, *Coptic Dictionary*, 94a, 584b. See also Luke 10:21 and 18:15 in Horner, *Coptic Version of the New Testament*, vol. 2.

[3] Crum, *Coptic Dictionary*, 58b. Crum notes a reference in the Coptic *Life of Daniel of Scetis*; this text, however, is on the later end of the period studied in this book and may be more removed from its monastic social context than even most hagiography. See Dahlman, *Saint Daniel of Sketis*.

children lived in monasteries and how they may have come to be there. Chapters 7 and 8 delve more deeply into the daily lives of these young children and adolescents. This chapter surveys the vocabulary of childhood, arguing that the most common terms used to identify minor children also denote monastic rank or spiritual status of some adult monks; contextual analysis is required to discern when passages concern minor children, spiritually "junior" adult monks, or both. The ambiguity and multivalence of the Coptic language of childhood also underscores the influence of the family model on monastic institutions, particularly on the structure of hierarchical relationships within their networks. We begin with the least common terms (for orphans and youths) and conclude with the most common (for boys and girls).

Orphans

The word for orphan (*orphanos*, a loanword from Greek) appears infrequently in Egyptian monastic literature. Although the term appears occasionally in the Pachomian sources, it does not explicitly signify a population living in the monasteries. The Pachomian and Shenoutean monasteries leave no direct evidence for the practice (especially among female monastics) of claiming abandoned infants, a practice attested in Cappadocia and North Africa.[4] This despite the inclusion of women's communities in both federations. In the Pachomian dossier, mentions of *orphanos* typically are metaphorical, describing people who become *like* orphans when someone dies, such as monks when their monastic superior passes away.[5] The term signifies vulnerability and loss, pointing to a need for a new monastic "father" to lead the community.

Similarly, in Shenoute's *Canons* for monks, while *orphanos* appears in eight passages, few references can be taken to mean that Shenoute was talking about orphaned children living somewhere in his monastery. Most of the usages are rhetorical or abstract, occurring most commonly in lists of people deserving charity, as discussed in Chapter 1. The orphans receiving aid may live in the monastery or the nearby village. In Shenoute's rhetoric, *orphanos* signifies a minor child, since adults without fathers would not necessarily appear on a list of charity recipients; women should be married (and thus in a new household) and men should be working, establishing

---

[4] See Chapter 1.
[5] *S⁷*, *S⁹*, and *S⁵*, in Lefort, *S. Pachomii Vitae Sahidice Scriptae*, 96, 102, 183, 184. Pachomius, *Instruction Concerning a Spiteful Monk*, 49, in Lefort, *Oeuvres de S. Pachôme*, vol. 1, 20.

their own households. Shenoute also accuses people of becoming like orphans by turning their backs on their monastic companions.[6]

For Shenoute, as in the Pachomian material, orphans signify vulnerability. In particular, they represent a population defined by *need* – need for resources or familial relationships. In Shenoute's discourse of monastic power, both of these needs the monastery can fulfill, either through charity or through monastic networks and hierarchies of relationships.

Other evidence for orphans and exposed children is inconclusive. Elsewhere in the White Monastery Federation documents, a later manuscript with medical formulas to induce lactation survives. As discussed in Chapter 1, however, we have no independent confirmation that women (whether monks, enslaved women, or hired wet nurses) received this medical treatment in order to nurture infants in the monastery. An ostracon from Thebes dated to the seventh or eighth century contains a letter addressed to a monk at an unnamed community. It mentions orphans and other children, but unfortunately the text is too damaged and fragmentary to discern much further.[7]

Youths and Adolescents

Early Egyptian monastic sources contain only a handful of occurrences of the Coptic terms for youths or adolescents (*lelou* and *hršire*). The Sahidic term *lelou* typically means "youth" in either masculine or feminine forms and often appears with the adjective for "small" (*šēm*), which may emphasize the young age of the person.[8]

I have found only two instances of the term in Shenoute's writings (not including parallel manuscript witnesses to the same text). Both appear in Volume 9 of his *Canons* for monks. Although pages apart, the passages are word-for-word copies of each other and forbid youths (*lelou šēm*) from gathering dates. Shenoute reasons that such a task is not work for "children" (*šēre šēm*).[9] *Canons* thus equates the category of "youths" (*lelou šēm*) with "children" (*šēre šēm*).

---

[6] Shenoute, *A22*, *Canons*, vol. 3, MONB.YA 202, in Leipoldt, *Vita et Opera Omnia*, vol. 4, 119; parallel manuscript witness in MONB.ZE 203–4 in Lucchesi, "Deux feuillets coptes," 176–77.

[7] *O.Brit.Mus.Copt.* I XLV/1. [8] Crum, *Coptic Dictionary*, 141b, on *lelou*.

[9] Shenoute, *Canons*, vol. 9, MONB.DF 48 (GB-BL 3581A f. 69v), in Crum, *Catalogue of Coptic Manuscripts*, 84; *Canons*, vol. 9, MONB.DF 177–78, in Leipoldt, *Vita et Opera Omnia*, vol. 4, 98 (parallel manuscript witness to the same passage appears in MONB.XK 199, in Amélineau, *Oeuvres de Schenoudi*, vol. 2, 516); see also excerpt of MONB.DF 177–78 in Layton, *Canons of Our Fathers*, 258.

A variant of this term for "youth" (*lelou šēm*) also occurs in a letter on an ostracon found at Karnak (Thebes), dating to around the eighth century.[10] The text reads *nelaue šēm*, which is probably meant to be *nelelaue šēm*, and the editors take the reference to mean children.[11] The letter contains a request for prayers from a certain person named Pekosh to two named monks (Apa Ananias and Pisrael) and "youths" (*nelaue šēm*). Since a variant of "youth" is paired here with the adjective *šēm*, the letter is likely addressed to a mixed group of adult men and children.

Bringing together the examples from Shenoute's writings with the ostracon from Thebes, we have evidence for adolescents residing in monasteries as early as the 300s or 400s and as late as the eighth century. Moreover, Shenoute's contextual use of the term indicates that at times, the monastery differentiated the responsibilities and labor of adolescents and children from the responsibilities and labor of adults. Although Shenoute's corpus does not survive in its entirety, the word thus far surfaces only in the reference to date-harvesting. This rare usage, however, is not evidence that adolescents themselves were rare in Shenoute's federation. Since Shenoute here pairs *lelou* with the more common term for child (*šēre šēm*), it is likely that in the *Canons* the latter phrase is used to refer to minors of all ages (infants to adolescents) and encompasses people who might also be called *lelou*.

The other Sahidic Coptic word for adolescent or youth, *hršire*, also occurs infrequently in our early coenobitic sources, albeit slightly more frequently than *lelou*. A variant of *šēre*, it can mean youth, young person, or young servant, and, in Coptic literature, turns up often in biblical passages, including in place of the Greek *neōteros* in Jer. 14:3, *paidarion* in 1 Kgs. 1:6, *anēr* in Isa. 5:15, and *brotos* in Job 14:10.[12] Shenoute too uses it in biblical citations, most notably of Jeremiah. For example, riffing on Jer. 6:11 in his first letter in *Canons*, Volume 1, Shenoute writes: "I will pour out my anger upon the children (*šēre šēm*) outside and upon the congregation of these youths (*hršire*) together."[13] Shenoute also uses it in another section of the same letter, where he criticizes the monastery for misdirecting the energy of its youth, elders, and children toward misguided deeds and away from

---

[10] *P.Mon.Epiph.* 359. On the history of the monastery, see Dekker, "Chronology of the *Topos* of Epiphanius," 755–67.

[11] Winlock and Crum, *Monastery of Epiphanius I*, 139; referring to *O.Brit.Mus.Copt.* I XX/4.

[12] See Crum, *Coptic Dictionary*, 585–86, for a fuller listing.

[13] Shenoute, *Letter 1*, *Canons*, vol. 1, MONB.XC 14, in Leipoldt, *Vita et Opera Omnia*, vol. 3, 196; three total references in MONB.XC 14–17, all quoting or paraphrasing Jeremiah.

fasting, prayer, ascetic discipline, and night vigils.[14] Given the intertextual references to Jeremiah earlier in the letter, and the term's
relative scarcity in Shenoute's corpus, Shenoute may have been evok-
ing Jeremiah's vocabulary in order to emphasize the biblical and
prophetic foundation of his critique rather than referring to
a specific population of young people, perhaps adolescents, in the
monastery. (Of course, both a concrete social context of adolescents
and a prophetic emphasis through exegesis are possible; Shenoute
deploys such rhetorical moves elsewhere in Volume 1.)[15] I have found
only three other usages in Shenoute's corpus, one of which is also
a biblical paraphrase.[16]

The two more promising citations for the social historian lie in Volume
9 of the *Canons*. In one passage, Shenoute explains why he requires the
monks to report suspicious activities to him: "Therefore, I shall tell the
innocent people and especially the youths (*hršire*) and children (*šēre
šēm*) ... "[17] He then goes on to justify the rule. Elsewhere in Volume 9,
Shenoute prohibits children and young people from medically treating
others: "No child (*šēre šēm*) or youth (*hršire*) shall give medication to
a person in these congregations, without having asked the ones who
supervise them."[18] The general Coptic etymology and usage of *hršire*
suggests Shenoute is talking about children or young people – identifying
a specific population of younger people in the monastery who, in the first
instance, are more innocent or naïve than the older monks and need
Shenoute's culture of surveillance explained to them. In the second
instance, *hršire* have their activities restricted; they have not yet matured
and earned the rights and privileges of full monks.

For reasons that will become clear shortly, however, *hršire* may signal
that Shenoute is talking about a specific monastic population that included
adults, not one exclusively comprised of underage children and adolescents. Each of these references to *hršire* make sense when translated as

---

[14] Shenoute, *Letter 1, Canons*, vol. 1, MONB.XC 89–90 (unpublished), in FR-BN 130² f. 7, online
https://gallica.bnf.fr/ark:/12148/btv1b10089625k/f14.image.r=130%20Copte, accessed December 4,
2019. See also Emmel, "Shenoute the Monk," 164–69; Schroeder, *Monastic Bodies*, 28–39, on the
background of the text.
[15] Schroeder, "Prophecy and Porneia."
[16] Shenoute, *A22, Canons*, vol. 3, MONB.YB 100 (unpublished), in FR-BN 130² f. 38v, online, https://
gallica.bnf.fr/ark:/12148/btv1b10089625k/f77.image.r=130%20Copte, accessed December 4, 2019.
Prv 19, possible Prv 23. Thanks to Frederic Krueger for his transcription.
[17] Shenoute, *Canons*, vol. 9, MONB.YZ 222, in Young, "Two Leaves," 295; trans., 296.
[18] Shenoute, *Canons*, vol. 9, MONB.FM 185, in Leipoldt, *Vita et Opera Omnia*, vol. 4, 160; see also
excerpt in Layton, *Canons of Our Fathers*, 288.

"adolescent" – adolescents need to be taught the ways of the monasteries, and they require supervision, especially around sensitive material such as medical supplies. Yet, as the chapter demonstrates (and as the passage from the Monastery of Phoibammon alludes), the term for "child" or "children" may also signify adults of lower status or rank in the monastery; the same may also be true for *hršire*. Given the traditional meaning of *hršire* in Coptic and its relative infrequence in monastic literature, I think it more likely that *hršire* refers to adolescents, but the usage of other terms for age and family relationships to mark monastic status requires us to consider the possibility that *hršire* are a class of monks that include adults.

Sons and Daughters

The Sahidic words *šēre* and *šeere* typically mean "son" and "daughter," which is how Shenoute, the Pachomian materials, and other monastic sources typically use them. In monastic literature, however, "sons" and "daughters" may indicate one of several possibilities: biological or legal children of various men and women, metaphorical or theological children, monastic "children" (monks subordinate to Shenoute or another monastic leader in the community), or finally (as we see in Chapter 8) generations of descendants in a genealogy.

We have already examined several examples of the first case – parents and their legal or biological children – in Chapter 1. In some of these instances, the sources are in Coptic and the terminology involves a straightforward use of *šēre* and *šeere* (without *šēm*). Recall the female monk Thesnoe, the daughter (*šeere*) of Apa Hermef, as well as the male monk whom Shenoute expelled along with the man's wife, son (*pefšēre*), and daughter (*pefšeere*).[19]

In other cases, "sons" and "daughters" are metaphors or theological references. They designate Jesus the son of God, or the biblical daughter Zion. They appear in citations or paraphrases of the apostle Paul's discussions of children of light and darkness (1 Thess. 5:5 and the possibly pseudonymous Eph. 5:8).

Monks also use the language of kinship as a form of address between teacher and student, superior and inferior. "Sons" and "daughters" can be spiritual disciples or adult men and women over whom the author or speaker has an authoritative relationship. This is a consistent feature of

---

[19] Shenoute, *Why O Lord, Canons*, vol. 4, MONB.BZ 59 and 345, in Leipoldt, *Vita et Opera Omnia*, vol. 3, 141; Young, *Coptic Manuscripts*, vol. 1, 103.

monastic literature with roots in Egypt. For example, in *Canons*, Volume 1, Shenoute records the first leader of the monastery crying out, "My children." In the same volume, Shenoute identifies himself as a "son" in relation to his monastic father, the monastery's second leader.[20] All the monastic leaders in this federation were called "father."[21] In *Sayings of the Desert Fathers*, monks call the more experienced ascetics "father" (Apa), while senior monks call male disciples "son."[22] A major turning point in the *Life of Pachomius* occurs when Pachomius' older brother, who has accompanied his younger sibling into the ascetic life, turns to Pachomius and calls him "Father."[23]

The Pachomian tradition expresses some ambivalent feelings about the use of the titles "father" and "son" among monks. As Philip Rousseau has noted, the *vitae* use the title "father" for Pachomius, and they record Pachomius himself ascribing the title of "father" to the monk Theodore, who would later become one of his successors. On the other hand, the sources also claim that Pachomius resisted this appellation and insisted that the title belongs to God alone: "Just as a corpse does not say to other corpses, 'I am your head,' so too I never considered that I am the father of the brothers. God himself alone is their father."[24] This vignette exposes an underlying anxiety about the hierarchical system of monastic rank emerging in Egypt. At the same time, it overtly impresses upon its readers Pachomius' dedication to the virtue of humility. Despite the hagiographical Pachomius' protestations, however, the usage of "father" prevailed, enduring throughout the coenobitic tradition in Egypt. Slightly later sources from the Monastery of Apa Apollo in Bawit document "father" as the title and form of address for the community's leader.[25] Texts and inscriptions at the Monastery of Epiphanius in Thebes and the Monastery of Jeremias in Saqqara also document this commonplace.[26]

---

[20] Shenoute, *Letter 1, Canons*, vol. 1, MONB.XB 43 (unpublished), in FR-BN 130² f. 89r, online, https://gallica.bnf.fr/ark:/12148/btv1b10089625k/f178.image.r=130%20Copte, accessed December 4, 2019; a possible paraphrase of or allusion to Hos. 7:13.

[21] Layton, "Some Observations on Shenoute's Sources."

[22] For examples, see *AP Syst.* Humility 16–18, in the *Verba Seniorum* (*PL* 73:957). See also the many examples in the Coptic *Sayings: apophthegmata.patrum Corpus*, urn:cts:copticLit:ap. Coptic SCRIPTORIUM, available at this query https://corpling.uis.georgetown.edu/annis/?id=a334f1e5-e79f-4a6b-acba-1616c290b378, accessed June 18, 2019.

[23] *V. Pach. Bo* 20, in Lefort, *S. Pachomii Vita Bohairice Scripta*, 19–20; ed. and trans Veilleux, *Pachomian Koinonia, Volume One*, 43.

[24] *V. Pach. G¹* 108; ed. and trans. Veilleux, *Pachomian Koinonia, Volume One*, 373–74. See also Rousseau, *Pachomius*, 109.

[25] Clackson, *Orders from the Monastery of Apollo*.

[26] Crum and Evelyn-White, *Monastery of Epiphanius II*; Quibell and Thompson, *Excavations at Saqqara*.

Boys and Girls, Children and Little Ones

The Coptic vocabulary for "boy" and "girl" – *šēre šēm* and *šeere šēm*, respectively – comprises modifications of the words *šēre* and *šeere*. Literally meaning "little son" and "little daughter," they are the most common Sahidic terms for boy and girl. Likewise, *koui* (lit. "little") as a noun can mean "little one" or child. With these terms, we begin to see more textual evidence for minors living in monastic communities, though even these words are not as straightforward as they seem. The Pachomian corpus uses both *šēre šēm* and *koui* specifically for minor children, as in this passage from the Tenth Sahidic *Life of Pachomius*:

> [Pachomius] set a little one (*koui*) in the midst of his disciples saying, "'Anyone who shall receive a young child (*šēre šēm*) such as this in my name receives me (cf. Matt 10:42).' But as for other little ones (*koui*) who have acquired an evil bent in their [youth] ... [the manuscript breaks for a few words] ... [as Solomon] says, 'Anyone who lives wantonly from his youth (*tefmntkoui*) shall become a slave [cf. Prov. 29/31:21].' And so my brothers, every young child (*šēre šēm*) as well as those who are older (*noc*) whom the Lord has brought to us for the rebirth, let us be zealous ... many times, let us teach them."[27]

The biblical references, in which Jesus clearly talks about children and Solomon uses "youth" to signify an early life stage, indicate the monastic usage of both *šēre šēm* and *koui* as terms of age; these are minor children of whom the *vita* speaks.

Shenoute also mentions "children" in contexts that make quite clear that these people are young. In a list of rules near the beginning of Shenoute's very first letter in Volume 1 of *Canons*, this regulation appears: "Cursed is anyone who will defile and touch a child (*šēre šēm*), saying, 'I would know whether he has come of age.'"[28] This rule seems designed to address a specific situation, namely an adult monk caught in the act of touching a child monk and trying to come up with a plausible excuse for doing so. The vocabulary leaves no room for doubt; the final verb, "to come of age" (*r-hēlikia*), derives from a Greek loanword and means to mature physically and temporally.[29] This rule thus concerns adult interactions with underage children.

---

[27] *V. Pach. S^{10}* Fragment 2, in Lefort, *S. Pachomii Vitae Sahidice Scriptae*, 33–34; ed. and trans. Veilleux, *Pachomian Koinonia, Volume One*, 451–52.
[28] Shenoute, *Letter 1*, *Canons*, vol. 1, MONB.XC 7–8, in Schroeder, "Early Monastic Rule"; see also excerpts in Layton, *Canons of Our Fathers*, 92–96.
[29] Lampe, *Patristic Greek Lexicon*, 605; Liddell and Scott, *Greek-English Lexicon*, online, Perseus Digital Library.

Minor children, therefore, resided in the monasteries of the Pachomian and Shenoutean federations. We cannot, however – at least at Shenoute's monastery, and perhaps in others – interpret every mention of *šēre šēm*, *šeere šēm*, and *koui* as indicating underage persons. For the language of age and familial relationship also designates rank or status in the monastery. We can see this usage very clearly in a rhetorical move Shenoute makes throughout his writings, as seen in the following examples taken from various volumes of the *Canons* for monks. In each case, "great" (*noc*) and "small" (*koui*) can also mean "old" and "young," respectively, as we have already seen with the word *koui* on its own:

1. Each year during Lent, no one among us shall be able to store bread at all, whether male or female, or great (*noc*) or small (*koui*), until all of Lent is completed[30]

2. . . . and the Lord shall bless everyone who hopes in God and who is of a single heart and the ones who teach them among us, whether male or female, whether great (*noc*) or small (*koui*),[31]

3. . . . then why also did you commit these great evil things in his presence, from your great (*noc*) men to your boys (lit. small sons [*šēre šēm*]), from your great (*noc*) women to your girls (lit. small daughters [*šeere šēm*]),[32]

4. Cursed is everyone who will kiss or who will embrace each other passionately with desire, whether small (*koui*) or great (*noc*), whether parent or child (*šēre*), whether male or female.[33]

5. We know who all of them are, from their small (*koui*) to their great (*noc*).[34]

6. But we are afflicted and we grieve day and night because of those who are disobedient to the gospel of the Lord Jesus, this one that says, "Unless you change yourselves so that you are like these children (*šēre šēm*), you shall not go into the kingdom of heaven" (Matt 18:3). Now see how much is revealed, namely the ignorance of them . . . among us, whether male or female, whether great (*noc*) or small (*koui*).[35]

---

[30] Shenoute, *Canons*, vol. 5, MONB.XL 185, in Leipoldt, *Vita et Opera Omnia*, vol. 4, 58; see also excerpt in Layton, *Canons of Our Fathers*, 168.

[31] Shenoute, *Canons*, vol. 4, MONB.GI 138–39, in Leipoldt, *Vita et Opera Omnia*, vol. 3, 172.

[32] Shenoute, *Letter 1, Canons*, vol. 1, MONB.XC 18, in Leipoldt, *Vita et Opera Omnia*, vol. 3, 199.

[33] Shenoute, *Letter 1, Canons*, vol. 1, MONB.XC 7, in Schroeder, "Early Monastic Rule"; see also excerpt in Layton, *Canons of Our Fathers*, 92.

[34] Shenoute, *A22, Canons*, vol. 3, MONB.YA 296, in Leipoldt, *Vita et Opera Omnia*, vol. 4, 116.

[35] Shenoute, *A22, Canons*, vol. 3, MONB.YA 297–98, in Leipoldt, *Vita et Opera Omnia*, vol. 4, 116–17.

7. Why does this one for his part weep, or do you yourself weep, from your old men (*hllo*) to your small boys (*šēre šēm*)?[36]

Shenoute, as these examples demonstrate, employs a distinct rhetorical maneuver throughout his writings in order to emphasize the scope of authority embedded in his instructions. Each of these seven examples contains a turn of phrase that brings together opposites of status and rank in late antiquity. Shenoute names people occupying each end of at least one of the common hierarchies of gender (male and female), age (old men and boys), and social status and/or age (great and small/old and young). As Rebecca Krawiec persuasively argues in her book *Shenoute and the Women of the White Monastery*, the phrase "whether male or female" is a rhetorical device Shenoute uses to emphasize that all of the monastic federation must follow a "universal" monasticism.[37] Shenoute's instructions pertain to all monks, whether they live in the men's communities or the women's. None may profess ignorance of a regulation applying to them. As these examples show, Shenoute uses this same rhetorical device with the vocabularies of age and status. Old or young, great or small – Shenoute's words apply to all. The language of youth and age signifies inclusivity, completeness, universality.

Other terms of youth, age, and familial relationship also function as codes for monastic status or rank in Shenoute's federation. Table 1, adapted from Bentley Layton's scholarship, lists the terms for monks of different ranks or status in Shenoute's federation.[38] Most of them are somehow derived from words for age or familial relationship. For each rank, the chart provides a useful English title based on the Coptic and the context, a fairly transparent translation of the Coptic term(s) used by Shenoute, and the original Coptic term(s). I have organized the chart by gender, but we should remain mindful of the fact that in almost all cases, masculine plurals (when the plurals have different masculine and feminine forms) collectively refer to groups containing male and female members.

Thus seniority in the monastery is often indicated by the language of age and/or kinship. While Shenoute is "father," his male deputy is the Elder; likewise, the leader of the women's community is the female Elder or

---

[36] Shenoute, *He Who Sits upon His Throne, Canons*, vol. 6, MONB.XF 16, in Amélineau, *Oeuvres de Schenoudi*, vol. 2, 198–99.

[37] Krawiec, *Shenoute and the Women*, 92–119.

[38] Layton, "Social Structure and Food Consumption," 29. I have provided documentation only for titles and ranks not included by Layton (who based his chart primarily on *Canons*, vol. 4) and for material that differs from Layton's presentation of the monastic social structure.

Table 1 *Terms of rank and status in the monastic hierarchy of Shenoute's federation (Layton, mod.)*

Father (*eiōt*) of the Congregations	
Men's Community(ies)	*Women's Community*
the Elder: "the old man" (*phllo*)*	the Elder or Mother: "the old woman" (*thllō*), "the mother" (*tmaau*)[39]*
elders: "old men" (*hlloi*)	elders: "old women" (*hlloi*)[40]
senior monks: "great men" (*noc nrōme*)[41]	senior monks: "great women" (*noc nshime*)
parents and house leaders: "parents" (*eiote*), "house leaders" (*rmnēi*)	
subordinates: those "who come after them"	
brethren (female monks, male monks, or male+female monks[42]): "brothers" (*snēu*)	
brother, monk: "brother" (*son*)	sister, monk: "sister" (*sōne*)[43]

* *Note:* The female Elder's absolute authority over the women was contested, with Shenoute frequently imposing the male Elder's authority over her.[44]

mother.[45] "Old men" are the senior monks; "old women" are the senior female monks. "Great" men and "great" women (where "great" renders *noc*, the opposite of the word *koui*, "little") are also senior monks. Shenoute refers to monastic "parents," who are generally respected monks, house leaders, or division leaders in the community. A "brother" or "sister" is a fellow monk.

The prevalence of vocabulary for age and familial relationship requires us to ask whether the terms for children – like the terms for "father," "mother," "brother," and "sister" – can also designate rank or status. Shenoute does not use a separate word for "novice," new monk, or monk of low status in the monastic hierarchy. As the seven passages cited earlier in this chapter demonstrate, "son" stands in contrast to "father," the "little" in contrast to the "great," and "children" in contrast to the "old" and

[39] On the female Elder as "mother," see Shenoute, *Canons*, vol. 2, MONB.XC 232–33, in Kuhn, *Letters and Sermons of Besa*, vol. 1, 124–25; trans. vol. 2, 119.

[40] On *hlloi* specifically for women, see Shenoute, *Canons*, vol. 2, MONB.XC 232–33, in Kuhn, *Letters and Sermons of Besa*, vol. 1, 124–25; trans. vol. 2, 119.

[41] E.g., in Shenoute, *You God the Eternal, Canons*, vol. 5, MONB.XS 353, in Leipoldt, *Vita et Opera Omnia*, vol. 4, 60; see also excerpts in Layton, *Canons of Our Fathers*, 174.

[42] Krawiec, *Shenoute and the Women*, 92–119.

[43] For "brother" and "sister," see Shenoute, *God Is Holy, Canons*, vol. 7, MONB.GO 52, in Amélineau, *Oeuvres de Schenoudi*, vol. 2, 1.

[44] Krawiec, "Role of the Female Elder."

[45] Layton translates Shenoute's deputy's title as "Eldest." On the female Elder, see Krawiec, "Role of the Female Elder."

"great." Yet, as Layton's work on monastic hierarchy has demonstrated, "old" and "great" are not always markers of *age* but rather are markers of *monastic status*. Thus, "boys," "girls," and the "little ones" might consist of those men and women who have not yet matured *as monks*, whose status or rank remains junior to full monks. We are reminded of the inscription at the Monastery of Phoibammon, where "child" (*šēre šēm*) means both an underage minor and a spiritually immature monk. The term for "little" (*koui*), we have already seen, both (1) refers to minor children in unambiguous passages in monastic literature (such as quotations of Matthew 18) and (2) is used rhetorically in opposition to "the great," who, as Layton has shown, are moderately high *status* (senior monks). Might "little ones," "boys," and "girls" thus have dual meaning, in the way that "old man," "great woman," "father," and "mother" do? The "children" and "little ones" are probably "junior" monks, as Krawiec translates the term.[46] Thus a revised monastic hierarchy would include another section for junior monks, provided in Table 2.

These multiple usages of the vocabulary for children raise several questions, most notably how to interpret the terms (especially with respect to age). If the language of age and relationship is the language of monastic rank, and minor children indeed live in the communities, then when does

Table 2 *Full monastic hierarchy in the monastery of Shenoute*

Father (*eiōt*) of the Congregations	
Men's Community(ies)	*Women's Community*
the Elder: "the old man" (*phllo*)	the Elder or Mother: "the old woman" (*thllō*), "the mother" (*tmaau*)
elders: "old men" (*hlloi*)	elders: "old women" (*hlloi*)
senior monks: "great men" (*noc nrōme*)	senior monks: "great women" (*noc nshime*)
parents and houseleaders: "parents" (*eiote*), "houseleaders" (*rmnēi*)	
subordinates: those "who come after them"	
brethren (female monks, male monks, or male+female monks): "brothers" (*snēu*)	
brother, monk: "brother" (*son*)	sister, monk: "sister" (*sōne*)
junior monks: "children"/"little ones" (*šēre šēm, koui*)	
junior male monks: "boys" (*šēre šēm*)	junior female monks: "girls" (*šeere šēm*)

[46] Krawiec, *Shenoute and the Women*, 142, 149, 164, 166, 170; see also Schroeder, *Monastic Bodies*. Young translates "children" (*šēre šēm*) as "novices" at times in *Coptic Manuscripts*. In contrast, see Layton, *Canons of Our Fathers*, 55n7.

"boy" or "girl" or "little one" indicate a minor child? When does "boy" or "girl" or "little one" indicate a junior monk? Or are "boys," "girls," and "little ones" inclusive terms for *both* minor children and adult junior monks?

The terms for "boys" and "little ones" at other monasteries, even in inscriptions, prove equally flexible. Some of the documentary sources discussed in Chapter 1 are understood to refer to minor children.[47] It is possible, however, that at these locations (Thebes, Saqqara, Bawit) our sources similarly refer to monks of junior status. The term "small" (*šēm*) in the phrases meaning "boy" (lit. "small son") and girl (lit. "small daughter") has in a monastic context been translated by Sarah Clackson as "humble" – in other words, small of ego.[48] Shenoute also calls the person who writes down his dictation "our little brother" (*penson šēm*).[49]

Finally, two instances of the universalizing language seen in Shenoute's rhetoric ("whether great or small" and "from small to great") occur in other Egyptian monastic sources. The *Regulations* attributed to Horsiesius, one of Pachomius' successors, specify that no monks, "whether great or small," may eat outside the appointed mealtimes, except for "little" ones: "Let no one, whether great (*noc*) or small (*koui*), eat before the signal is given to eat. If the little one (*koui*) wishes to eat, he may not eat at all in the oven-room or among the brothers who are not eating; rather let him be given bread and let him go elsewhere to eat by himself."[50] In this context, "little" or "small" may have double meaning, referring either to a child or to a monk of junior rank. We have already, however, seen *koui* used for minor children in the Tenth Sahidic *Vita*. With this in mind, as well as the context of this rule (concerning physical needs, which would be particularly relevant for children, who are physically more vulnerable), we may assume that this occurrence of *koui* in the *Regulations* indicates minor children. In a later text, the *Life of Samuel of Kalamun*, the phrase "from the smallest to the greatest" clearly refers to monastic status. Chapter 7 of this text contains an account of Chalcedonian sympathizers attempting to force all the elders of the monastery "from

---

[47] Chapter 1 of this book. For an example of other Coptologists understanding these to be children, see Winlock and Crum, *Monastery of Epiphanius I*, 139n7; Crum and Evelyn-White in *P.Mon.Epiph.* 359 (text and trans.).

[48] Clackson, *Orders from the Monastery of Apollo*.

[49] Shenoute, *Canons*, vol. 2, MONB.XC 226–27, in Young, *Coptic Manuscripts*, vol. 1, 116; trans. 120.

[50] Horsiesius, *Reg.* 41, in Lefort, *Oeuvres de S. Pachôme*, vol. 1, 93; ed. and trans. Veilleux, *Pachomian Koinonia, Volume Two*, 210–11, mod.

their small (*koui*) to their great (*noc*)" to commit to the Tome of Leo.[51] Here all monks regardless of *status* were pressured to abide by the theological doctrine of the Tome.

Thus, the vocabulary of "children" in Coptic monasticism contains fluid terms, words that are often ambiguous without further context. Not only in Shenoute's corpus but also elsewhere, the words stymie modern translators because of their multivalence. Moreover, the usage of *koui* and *šēre/šeere šēm* does not appear to differentiate between categories of people in the community, with one term denoting physical age and the other monastic status. (See examples 3 and 5 in the list of sample rules from Shenoute cited earlier.) Additionally, "boy" and "girl" *cannot* refer exclusively to adult junior monks; *šēre/šeere šēm* clearly designates age in many of our examples. Although minor children were present in late antique Egyptian monasteries, then, the fluidity of the vocabulary for children complicates research. At Shenoute's monastery, and perhaps at others, the phrases for "boys" and "girls" (and possibly "little ones") functioned inclusively, as a category of "junior" monks, which might include novice adults as well as minor children living at the monastery.

In contrast, the sources from the Pachomian communities do not utilize the language of childhood to systematically designate junior monks. (The one possible exception is the rule of Horsiesius about food.) The Pachomian corpus has its own methodological and linguistic complications: the texts survive in a range of genres (hagiography, epistolary, rules) – some of them only in Jerome's Latin translations – and in three different languages (with more than one dialect of Coptic represented). Additionally, the paucity of references to children in the Pachomian corpus prohibits a more detailed language study. As we have already seen, the Tenth Sahidic *Life* uses both *koui* and *šēre šēm* for minor children.[52] New monks, who would later be called "novices" in the Benedictine Rule, appear rarely in the sources as an identifiable group of monks with a particular status, and they are not called "children." Chapter 6 presents a more detailed study of children and the emerging category of the novice in Egypt, but a brief glance at the vocabulary in the Pachomian sources demonstrates that no one term for "novice" emerges in that corpus;

---

[51] Isaac the Presbyter, *Life of Samuel of Kalamun*, 7, in Alcock, ed. and trans., *Life of Samuel*, 6; trans. 80.

[52] *V. Pach. S^to* Fragment 2, in Lefort, *S. Pachomii Vitae Sahidice Scriptae*, 33–34; ed. and trans. Veilleux, *Pachomian Koinonia, Volume One*, 451–52.

perhaps the Pachomian Federation did not have a rank of "novice" as we understand it from later monasticism.

Thus, constructing a history of children and childhood in early monasticism faces a significant hurdle: the very vocabulary in our textual sources. The problem is most pronounced in the vast and potentially rich corpus of Shenoute, but we can see it in the inscriptions and documents from other communities as well. In some cases, we can begin to overcome our linguistic obstacle by examining the contexts of the rules. Contextually, we can discern that some regulations indeed pertain specifically to minor children, though others may address a broader group of youth and adult *šēre/šeere šēm*.

PART II
Representations

CHAPTER 3

Homoeroticism, Children, and the Making of Monks

As we have seen in Part I, children lived in early monasteries or, in a place like the Hathor Monastery, were part of a social network of monastic care. In literary texts about the monastic life – texts that may tell us more about ideals and ideology than social history – we also see children appear in key roles. In this representation of asceticism, children embody the tension between, on one hand, the ascetic expectation on monks to renounce sex, reproduction, and family, and, on the other, the social expectation on monks to reproduce themselves as a community and to serve the lay Christian families around them in Egypt.

Despite children's presence in early Egyptian monasteries, ideological threads about the dangers children pose remained tightly woven into the fabric of monastic literature. A famous admonition ascribed to the monk Macarius the Great apocalyptically attributes the downfall of one of Egypt's most famous early monastic communities to children: "When you see a cell built close to the marsh, know that the devastation of Scetis is near; when you see trees, know that it is at the doors; and when you see young children, take up your sheep-skins and go away."[1] This saying resembles the apothegm discussed in this book's Introduction, a famous prohibition against children attributed to Isaac of Kellia: "Do not bring young boys here. Four churches in Scetis are deserted because of boys (ta paidia)."[2] These two ominous warnings appear in a Greek version of Sayings of the Desert Fathers. They seem somewhat cryptic – what danger, one might ask, do boys pose? Yet, read in the context of other stories about children in Sayings, these pithy warnings evoke, among other things, anxieties about sex and the social construction of boys as sexually desirable.

Children posed several challenges – requiring food, education, and constant care. They also symbolized both the homoeroticism present in

---

[1] AP Macarius the Great 5, in PG 65:264; trans. Ward, Sayings of the Desert Fathers, 128.
[2] AP Isaac of Kellia 5, in PG 65:225; trans. Ward, Sayings of the Desert Fathers, 100.

early Christian communities of celibate males and emerging taboos about homoeroticism.[3] In the saying attributed to Isaac, the Greek term *paidia* means children, including adolescents but not young adults, and leaves no doubt that the monk is talking about minors.[4] Christian ascetic literature from the fourth through sixth centuries frequently construes children as obstacles to the spiritual progress of the adult monastic. A ban on playing with boys in the rules of one of the earliest coenobitic monasteries (founded by Pachomius) constitutes one of the few references to children in that community's corpus.[5] Such admonitions seem a reminder that Christian monasticism should not be confused with classical Greek culture, in which sexual relations between men and boys were accepted, even idealized.[6] And yet these admonitions also remind us modern readers that in these monasteries and among these monks, the classical standards of beauty, in which the adolescent male form represented the erotic ideal, lingered.

Given the legacy of Greek culture in late antique Egypt, an admonition against bringing a young male into a celibate, homosocial community should seem obvious and unsurprising. Yet, although the presence of young males within the monastery is eschewed, early Egyptian monastic texts embrace boys and adolescent males within their pages. Despite the sources' overt disavowal of sexual contact between men and boys, the circulation, retelling, and rereading of these texts – with their stories and rules about sex with children – kept homoeroticism and the representation of boys as sexually desirable objects alive in the ascetic imagination.

This chapter examines the role of children in the construction of monastic male sexuality. It focuses on adult men and boys due to our surviving source material. A few monastic sources (predominantly from the White Monastery Federation led by Shenoute) mention women having sexual relationships with other women, and I have found only one that refers to homoeroticism between women and

---

[3] Richlin, "Not before Homosexuality."

[4] Thus including boys younger than future emperor Marcus Aurelius, who was eighteen when he met his tutor Marcus Cornelius Fronto: Aurelius and Fronto, *Marcus Aurelius in Love*.

[5] Pachomius, *Precepts and Judgements* 7, in Boon, *Pachomiana Latina*, 66; ed. and trans. Veilleux, *Pachomian Koinonia, Volume Two*, 177.

[6] Foucault, *History of Sexuality, Vol. 2*, esp. Part IV; Lear and Cantarella, *Images of Ancient Greek Pederasty*; Halperin, *One Hundred Years of Homosexuality*, esp. 30–31, 55–59. See also Amy Richlin's critique of Halperin, based on her argument that sexual mores in the Roman Empire differed from those in classical Greece: Richlin, Review of *One Hundred Years of Homosexuality*, by David Halperin; Beaumont, "Shifting Gender," 203–04.

girls.[7] We cannot conclude from this sparse evidence that such sexual practices were extraordinarily rare among female monks in late antique Egypt. Rather, this near absence of mention is probably due to our male authors' general disinterest in women (and subsequently women's sexuality) unless women intersected somehow with these men's concerns. There are, of course, numerous examples of ascetic and monastic men with sexual interests in girls, particularly teens of marriageable age or demons taking the form of young virgins. What I am particularly interested in is the role of children in adult formulations of monastic sexuality, as well as what these constructions of sexual ideals and taboos may tell us about the social circumstances of children in the monasteries. Due to the nature of our surviving sources, this dynamic can be analyzed primarily in men's monasticism, not in women's.

This chapter focuses on children and male sexuality in two examples from late antique Egypt: stories from the Greek *Sayings of the Desert Fathers* and the writings of the monastic leader Shenoute. *Sayings* contains anecdotes, teachings, and sayings attributed to monks in the fourth and fifth centuries, but they were collected and written down in later years.[8] Shenoute was a fourth- and fifth-century monk and eventually leader of a monastery comprised of thousands of male and female monks who resided in separate, sex-segregated residences. In some ways, these sets of texts differ extraordinarily. The Greek *Sayings* comprises gnomic apothegms that may be wholly untethered from the historical moments they purport to describe. Shenoute's writings, on the other hand, are contemporaneous Coptic letters, rules, sermons, and treatises by a known, historical monastic author. Despite these divergent contexts and genres, however, both sets of sources build idealized visions of ascetic masculinity based upon certain classical ideals of masculinity, while simultaneously seeking to resist classical models of eroticism in which the adolescent male represents the ideal sexual partner. Both sources are designed to be recited or retold as edifying ascetic literature. Both circulated in monastic communities where boys also resided. Thus, despite their overt disavowal of sexual contact between men and boys, the retelling and rereading of these texts eroticize the monastery, authorizing and normalizing a voyeuristic gaze on the part of adult male monks.

---

[7] Shenoute, *Canons*, vol. unknown, MONB.XR 399, in Leipoldt, *Vita et Opera Omnia*, vol. 4, 169–70; see excerpt in Layton, *Canons of Our Fathers*, 308. See also Brooten, *Love between Women*, 349–50; Krawiec, *Shenoute and the Women*, 37–38; Wilfong, "Friendship and Physical Desire."

[8] Harmless, *Desert Christians*, 169–71.

Voyeurism and Sin

Sayings depicts communities of monks where children resided alongside adult monastics, even if in low numbers. It records anecdotes about at least five male monks living with "boys," usually their biological sons.[9] A few other snippets address other monks and unrelated minor children. Two anecdotes underscore the literature's biting ambivalence about the sexual passion of adults for youth, particularly the homoerotic pleasure in gazing upon young male bodies. The first, the story of Abba Carion and his son Zacharias, exemplifies the sexual tension that young males and stories about them produced.

Zacharias joined his father at the monastic community of Scetis when he was still a boy (after his mother shamed Carion into caring for him, as described in Chapter 1).[10] Gossip about their living arrangements commenced among the other ascetics as Zacharias "grew older" – presumably when he entered puberty. Although the scandal is mitigated by the fact that Zacharias is Carion's biological son, the father nonetheless suggests that they leave, due to the "murmuring" of the other ascetics. Gossip was a common strategy for regulating power relations between ascetics, something the child monk seems to understand.[11] For Zacharias objects, pointing out that at least at Scetis, everyone knows that they are father and child, "but if we go somewhere else, we can no longer say that I am your son." Zacharias is, of course, correct, for when they go south, the murmuring follows them. So they return to Scetis, where again the gossip continues, until finally Zacharias soaks himself in a lake of natron – the substance used to mummify corpses – until his body resembles that of a leper.

Although the narrative's explicit concern is the unseemly nature of an adult male living with a boy or adolescent, it implicitly exposes the voyeuristic tendencies of the male monks who do not live with children and who profess to object to such cohabitation. Zacharias represents a sexual temptation to the other monks; their murmured accusations are effective only insofar as the boy's status as object of desire is mutually understood. Seeing a threat to their own battles to extinguish sexual desire, the monks use gossip about him and his father to coerce the comely youth to leave. In the end, Zacharias mutilates his body, so that his appearance is no longer pleasurable when he is in the sight of other monks. No physical sex occurs in the story; instead, much of the narrative revolves around appearances – Zacharias' physical appearance but also what it means

---

[9] See Chapter 1.   [10] *AP* Carion 2, in *PG* 65:249–52.   [11] Gleason, "Visiting and News."

socially and culturally for a man and child to be seen together. The visible invites speculation about the invisible; a man and boy seen together in public must be having sex out of sight. Despite the absence of any visual evidence of sex, the monks' murmuring indicates the spinning of licentious tales; through their titillating accusations, the gossiping monks participate as oral and aural voyeurs in fantasies of sex acts they are forbidden to commit. As a story of sexual voyeurism, Zacharias' predicament reveals the pleasure experienced when male monastics viewed the adolescent male body, as well as the pleasure enjoyed in telling tales about that body.

Zacharias' disfigurement also serves to justify the continued erotic gaze of his fellow ascetics. Although his leprous form invites (even anticipates) revulsion, it simultaneously authorizes their gaze. Pleasure is not excised from the narrative; his self-mutilation removes the guilt from this guilty pleasure. Although exhibiting the body of an undesirable old man, he remains a youth. The horror of his figure – seen by the monks within the narrative and envisaged in the mind's eye of later monks, listeners, and readers – is a paradigm of loss, the loss of beauty and erotic physicality. As one of many stories of reverse transfiguration in early Christianity, Zacharias' corporeal disfigurement represents less a break with the past than a visual reminder of it.

The hagiographical account of a famous prostitute turned monk provides a parallel example of such a reverse transfiguration, in which a saint's holiness and spiritual virtue is made manifest in the physical body's declining aesthetic splendor. In the Christian tradition, the archetypal "transfiguration" occurs in the New Testament Gospels (Matt. 17:1–9, Mark 9:2–8, Luke 9:28–36), when Jesus becomes radiant with light, his clothes turn pure white, and Moses and Elijah appear near him. In the narratives, this moment of aesthetic splendor visually reinforces Jesus' status as "Son of God," which a voice from heaven simultaneously intones. Early Christian hagiography as well as *Sayings* narrate the lives of saints in ways that evoke the life of Jesus. Some saints experience a bodily transfiguration, in which physical beauty expresses the spiritual virtue of the ascetic; others experience a reverse transfiguration, in which their holiness can be witnessed by their *disfigured* bodies, often a result of severe physical ascetic discipline. In the *Life of Mary of Egypt*, Mary renounces her profession after encountering a vision of her namesake, the mother of Jesus, and turns to a life of ascetic repentance in the desert. There she lives for decades without clothing, shelter, or food – except what God provides. Mary's withered, emaciated form, blackened by exposure to the sun, serves as a physical witness to the pleasures of her past harlotry; her tortured figure evokes the memory of the perfumed, decorated, and hedonistic prostitute who had sex with men not just for the money but also for pleasure.[12]

Reading about and mentally visualizing the pain of Zacharias' transformation can also elicit pleasure. In writing about the pornography of pain, Susan Sontag reflects, "It seems that the appetite for pictures showing bodies in pain is as keen, almost, as the desire for the ones that show bodies naked." Religious art portraying saints experiencing pain is particularly evocative. "No moral charge attaches to the representation of these cruelties. Just the provocation: can you look at this? There is the satisfaction of being able to look at the image without flinching. There is the pleasure of flinching."[13] The account of Zacharias' dip in the natron evokes the mental image of his body both before and after. (Did you flinch when reading of Zacharias entering the natron? Did you take pleasure in the flinch?)

Zacharias' story also exemplifies the tension between the homoeroticism in early male monasteries and the masculine ascetic ideal of self-control. The tale narrates two disruptions in this masculine ideal. First, the responsibility for the preservation of male ascetic chastity rests in significant part upon the object of male desire (not on the self-control of the desiring male subject). It is the young Zacharias who must make himself less attractive in order to restabilize the erotic lives of the adults. Second, the story affirms the adolescent male body's eroticism. It does not challenge the notion that the adolescent male body represents an erotic ideal. The adult monks are not required to repress or reorient their erotic imagination, but rather Zacharias must make his body less attractive.

Sayings also records the tale of a senior monk (an "old man") stumbling upon another monk who is "sinning with" a boy (*paidiou*) who had originally come to the monks to be healed. The senior monk watches the encounter, saying nothing to the other monk and doing nothing to stop it. He then reflects, "If God who has made them sees them and does not burn them, who am I to blame them?"[14] The conclusion is surprising, because it seems to exculpate the monk abusing the boy and to condone the sexual encounter. The account also makes no further mention of the ill child; he came to the monastic community seeking help, and presumably he was never healed from his original ailment. The saying refuses to pass judgment on the monk.

The tale could be read as one among many admonitions against the sin of judgmental pride. A rather self-satisfied monk should not be too smug if

[12] *PG* 87(3):3697–726; *PL* 73:671–90.   [13] Sontag, *Regarding the Pain of Others*, 41.
[14] *AP* John the Persian 1, in *PG* 65:256; trans. Ward, *Sayings of the Desert Fathers*, 107.

his own ascetic efforts appear superior to those of a neighbor (the "judge not lest ye be judged" lesson of Matt. 7:1). But the story condones voyeurism as well, even attributing the guiltless act of voyeurism to God himself. God watches and does not judge. So too might another monk watch and neither judge nor be judged.

In the telling and retelling of the story, the eye of God becomes the eye of subsequent generations of monks, who as readers gaze upon this "sin" with neither verbal censure nor threat of punishment. This eye of God is no panopticon, no Big Brother from whom one cannot escape. Hagiography often renders the ascetic gaze as an instrument of shaming and assimilation. For example, Symeon Stylites, the famed solitary pillar-saint from Syria, previously lived in a communal monastery where he engaged in acts of self-mortification. Most notably, he wound a rough cord made of palm around his waist until it cut deeply into the skin. He hid the cord and wounds under his cloak, for fear that his difference, his extremism, would render him an "other" even among his closest peers. Simeon's worries proved justified, for his colleagues' reactions upon the discovery of his bleeding sores forced him to abandon the monastery.[15] By contrast, in the saying about the monk, the boy, and the peeping ascetic, the gaze provides no instrument of discipline or forced conformity but rather asserts a method of justified voyeurism. While uncomfortable, it is nonetheless acquiescent.

Seeing and Doing

In hagiography and other late antique literature, the boundaries between seeing and doing are porous. As Georgia Frank has taught us, visiting and viewing in the flesh the living saints of late antiquity allowed Christian pilgrims to imbibe and partake of their holiness. Travel literature that describes famous ascetics – the very monks enshrined in *Sayings* – expresses "the belief that seeing the holy provides an active, tactile encounter with it."[16] This entry in *Sayings* furnishes a textual recording of one man's sexual encounter with a boy, preserved for all to see in the mind's eye. Do the observant monk and his successors, who learn and reflect upon the story, see and thus absorb the holy or the demonic? In her essay "Visceral Seeing," Patricia Cox Miller has argued for the physical and affective elements of

---

[15] Theodoret, *Religious History*, 26.4–5, in Theodoret, *Histoire des moines de Syrie*, vol. 2, 164–70; trans. Price, *History of the Monks of Syria*, 161–62.

[16] Frank, *Memory of the Eyes*, 14.

reading about seeing. She analyzes an account of Saint Artemius curing a man's diseased testicles, and the supplicant's subsequent exposure of his healed body parts for all to witness the miracle:

> This is visceral seeing at its most intense, not only because of the image's sensate effect on the reader but also because the saint's gaze invites the reader's eye to look at body parts that would normally be taboo. The affective quality of this image, especially when it is repeated over and over again, not only brings materiality and meaning very close together, it also demonstrates the close alignment of insistent physicality and equally insistent looking that characterized late ancient constructions of the holy body.[17]

To see was as if to touch, to experience viscerally within oneself the bodily transformation of another.

Is this true of monastic seeing as well? The art of discernment in Egyptian asceticism held as its goal the elimination of sin and temptation; to recognize evil, including evil in the form of a demon, for its true self – not to mistake it for the thing which it hoped to appear to be – was the first step in rendering it powerless. In the case of the older monk who observes his colleague's sexual indiscretions, discernment does not extinguish the erotic power of the moment. Although forbidden to touch a young boy with desire, the monk's erotic voyeurism is now authorized, even ritualized, in the form of an edifying text. As Miller writes, "[V]oyeuristic scenes of manifest realism bridge the divide between reader and text. Further, the ocular and affective quality of these images is an appeal to the sensory imagination of the reader. . . . They are figuratively real – that is, they are narrative pictorial strategies that seduce the reader into forgetting that these are images in texts."[18] Indeed, even the monks who "watch" by reading also see and thus themselves participate in the sexual taboo. The texts invite the reader to identify neither with the youth, nor with the sinning monk, nor with young Zacharias but with the ascetics who look upon these youthful bodies, and whose voyeurism is justified either by the nonjudgmental gaze of the almighty or by the sacrifice of their object of desire.

Both Zacharias' immersion in the natron and the encounter between monk and demoniac boy are short but intensely visual moments. They function as verbal snapshots, economic hagiographical ekphrases of iconic scenes suspended in time. As textual photographs, they invite the viewer to identify with the monks who gaze upon the bodies of the boys. As Sontag

---

[17] Miller, "Visceral Seeing," 400.   [18] Miller, "Visceral Seeing," 402–03.

writes, "Memory freeze-frames; its basic unit is the single image."[19] These pithy, vivid, and thus memorable sayings fix in the ascetic imagination the image of the monk with the boy, or Zacharias' naked form before and after the natron.

Abuse and Agency

Perhaps Zacharias' dip into the natron could be seen as an act of agency, even seduction. Let us return to Mary of Egypt, the penitent harlot. In *Sex Lives of the Saints*, Virginia Burrus rereads this hagiography as a love story in which Mary's sacrifice of her body has led to a new series of sacred seductions.[20] Mary seduces the male monk Zosimus, the purported narrator of the story, who discovers her in the desert and is so taken by her that he cannot stop thinking of her and must return to experience her presence again. She seduces even God himself when she challenges him to return to her a love as intense as the love she has given her Lord. And even after her death, she seduces Zosimus' ascetic colleagues, whom he regales with tales of the fantastical Mary. Finally, she seduces all subsequent readers of her saint's life.

Perhaps the figure of Zacharias does not extinguish the erotic when he steps into the natron; perhaps instead he allows it to flourish. His reverse transfiguration allows the presence of the adolescent male in an environment in which the homosocial easily morphs into the homo-erotic. It also presents a material and textual reminder of the hyper-sexual body he once inhabited. In this reading, Zacharias' character is doubly disturbing to the modern reader, as an eroticized child who then takes on the physical trauma of the natron. This reading also raises concerns about the repercussions of this apothegm for children in monastic communities, their potential position as hypersexualized yet nonetheless responsible for protecting their own purity, even taking on acts of self-harm to do so.

Alternatively, Zacharias' actions could be read as an act of resistance, a refusal on this figure's part to be reduced to a sexual object. He acts in an effort to realign the erotic tensions in the community. Similarly, Paula and Blaesilla, friends of the church father Jerome, undertook severe fasting and radical dress in their ascetic pursuit. Burrus characterizes the resulting disfigurement as "an effective act of resistance. In performing a denaturalized 'body,' risking a hyperembodiment of 'culture,' Blaesilla

[19] Sontag, *Regarding the Pain of Others*, 22.   [20] Burrus, *Sex Lives of Saints*, 158.

and Paula walk a dangerous edge."[21] Perhaps Zacharias was staking his claim to the ascetic territory, a territory denied to him by a culture that viewed his body as inherently sexual. By stepping into the natron, does he interrupt the gaze that reduces him to object and produces sexually desiring yet ascetic adult subjects? In manipulating the viewing subjects' senses and imagination, perhaps Zacharias turns himself into a mirror, exposing the monastic viewer's (or reader's or hearer's) status as an "object" of his own "voyeuristic pleasure."[22]

These two snapshots about likely fictional children underscore the ambivalence about children and sex in monastic culture. These stories circulated in communities where boys and men lived together and where, we see in what follows, men engaged in sexual activity with underage boys – what we would deem abuse and what even the monks of that time would classify as sin. Yet concern for the well-being of these children is absent. Symbolically, the boys represent beauty or temptation and also the sidestepping of adult culpability.

Children and Adult Self-Control

The letters of Shenoute too exhibit anxieties about the stability of masculine ascetic identity. Like *Sayings*, Shenoute purports to eschew classical models of eroticism in which the adolescent male represents the ideal sexual partner. However, his masculine ideal builds upon other classical ideals of masculinity, especially the Stoic control of the passions, and Shenoute identifies *youth* as a specific challenge to self-control. His monastic rules forbid a number of undesirable behaviors, including sexual contact (or potentially erotic situations involving children). The rules on sex also explicitly prohibit certain forms of contact with young monks. As addressed in Chapter 2, the language in some of these rules raises questions. In Shenoute's monastery and possibly elsewhere, the Coptic phrase typically translated as "child" or "boy" (*šēre šēm*) denotes minor children (as determined by age), adolescents, and "junior monks" or novices of any age. That the term includes minor boys is obvious from one rule pertinent to our study here – a rule that condemns anyone who justifies touching a boy by claiming he is only trying to determine whether the child has come of age.[23]

---

[21] Burrus, *Sex Lives of Saints*, 89.   [22] Žižek, *Looking Awry*, 109–10, 180n6.
[23] Shenoute, *Letter One, Canons*, vol. 1, MONB.XL 7, in Schroeder, "Early Monastic Rule," 35, trans. 37; see also excerpt in Layton, *Canons of Our Fathers*, 94.

The prohibitions on sex with minors in Shenoute's federation are not limited to basic admonitions toward chastity. Moreover, although they contain some parallels with rules from the more famous communal monasteries founded by Pachomius, Shenoute's regulations are far more detailed and at times reflect different ascetic ideologies than the Pachomian material.[24] Shenoute's rules contain very specific prohibitions against kissing children, touching children, and unsupervised activity with children (such as anointing or bathing them). They also forbid children from engaging in potentially erotic activities with each other (such as shaving or pulling a thorn from another boy's foot).[25]

These and other admonitions against both heteroerotic and homoerotic behavior often invoke a discourse of the passions taken from the Greek philosophical tradition of Stoicism; a proper monk, like the proper Greek man, maintains control of his desires. In a variety of Egyptian monastic literature, the combat with the passions is a primary means by which ascetic subjectivity is formed. As David Brakke has argued, "this Stoic approach to virtue" is a particularly useful "paradigm by which to understand monastic accounts of conflicts with demons."[26] In Brakke's reading of the *Life of Antony*, the famous early anchorite seeks to "preserve his natural state" – "one not dominated by the passions" – in the face of external forces, such as demons, which target the soul.[27] The Stoic understanding of the natural state of humanity is a useful paradigm for interpreting some of Shenoute's monastic rules as well. Shenoute specifically invokes the passions as an acute source of distress. One rule condemns kissing a boy with desire (the Greek *epithumia*). (Although Shenoute wrote in Coptic, he used common Greek loanwords, including *epithumia*, *pathos*, and *hēdonē*.) Other regulations prohibit a man embracing another man with a polluted desire (*epithumia*) or kissing a boy with desire (*epithumia*). Burning with polluted desire (*epithumia*) for either an adult colleague or a child also receives censure.[28] A more blanket prohibition condemns anyone – male or female, old or young – who kisses or embraces another with passionate desire (*epithumia* + *pathos*).[29]

---

[24] Schroeder, *Monastic Bodies*, 68–81.
[25] Shenoute, *Letter One*, Canons, vol. 1, MONB.XC 7–8, in Schroeder, "Early Monastic Rule," 34–35; see also excerpt in Layton, *Canons of Our Fathers*, 94.
[26] Brakke, *Demons*, 39.   [27] Brakke, *Demons*, 38–39.
[28] Shenoute, *Letter One*, Canons, vol. 1, MONB.XC 15–16, in Leipoldt, *Vita et Opera Omnia*, vol. 3, 197–98. These rules begin with the formula declaring "cursed is" or "cursed be" the person who commits the sins; on this formulation, see Timbie, "Writing Rules."
[29] Shenoute, *Letter One*, Canons, vol. 1, MONB.XC 7, in Schroeder, "Early Monastic Rule," 34, trans. 36; see also partial text in Layton, *Canons of Our Fathers*, 92, 94.

The opportunities for sexual contact presented by everyday situations in a monastery also represented a threat to celibacy, and these opportunities included situations involving children. Some of Shenoute's rules specifically target adults or senior monks interacting with children and junior monks. These rules resemble in content and style rules prohibiting sexual interactions among adults, and not all the rules invoke the passions. Shenoute specifically forbids bathing or anointing youth without reference to the passions. But other rules, as we have shown, do identify the problematics of passion and desire. It is not merely a homosocial environment or the presence of minors that troubles Shenoute. It is not simply embracing another monk that poses the threat but embracing with passion; not simply kissing a child but kissing with passion. We can imagine liturgical and ritual settings in which monks should embrace or kiss – a kiss of greeting or the kiss of peace during a eucharist celebration, for example.[30] And certainly in a monastery comprised of thousands of ascetics, the close quarters afforded ample opportunity for physical contact. In one rule, monks are censured for allowing "defiled thoughts" to take root in their hearts, or for enabling "polluted *epithumia*" to become established in their spirits after shaving another, being shaved, taking the thorn out of another's foot, or having a thorn taken out of one's own foot. Monks who touch each other while lying on the same mat receive censure when the touching occurs "with a passionate desire" (*epithumia + pathos*).[31] Again, it is not solely the physical intimacy of these activities that threatens the monk but the passions that the monk might allow to take hold. Monks must even bathe their own faces and feet with care, to avoid bathing themselves with desire (*epithumia*), passion (*pathos*), and pleasure (*hēdonē*).[32]

In his earliest letters, Shenoute uses the rhetoric of femininity to shame his fellow monks. Comparing sinful monks who break the monastic rules to the harlots of the Hebrew Scriptures, he likens insufficient ascetic discipline in the monastery to the uncontrolled sexuality of these biblical "loose women."[33] The monks have become scriptural whores. In his rules about sexuality, we also see the converse – the construction of an ideal masculinity, of the man in control of his passions.

[30] Penn, *Kissing Christians*, 43–56.
[31] Shenoute, *Canons*, vol. 3, MONB.YA 314–16, in Leipoldt, *Vita et Opera Omnia*, vol. 4, 124; see also partial text in Layton, *Canons of Our Fathers*, 124, 126.
[32] Shenoute, *Canons*, vol. 3, MONB.YA 303, in Leipoldt, *Vita et Opera Omnia*, vol. 4, 118–19; see also excerpts in Layton, *Canons of Our Fathers*, 116.
[33] Schroeder, "Prophecy and Porneia."

Gazing upon the bodies of one's fellow monks exacerbates the monk's vulnerability to the passions. Both men and women should avoid peering lustfully upon the nakedness of monks in their cells, or in public, when their garments accidentally reveal their genitals:

> Cursed are men or women who will gaze or who will look desirously (*epithumia*) upon the nakedness of their neighbors in their bedrooms, or stare at them at any other place, either when they are on a wall or up a tree, or when they urinate or walk in mud or bathe, or while they are sitting down and they expose (themselves) inadvertently, or when they were drawing a log to a place that is up high, or when they are working with one another or even when they are washing their clothing in the flow at the canal or by the cistern, or when the brethren who make the bread reach into the ovens or (are busy) at any other task which some would be doing in our domain or in your domain too and unwittingly bare (themselves). And those who will gaze at them desirously (*epithumia*) with a shameless eye shall be cursed. And also those who will gaze with a desirous passion (*epithumia* + *pathos*) upon their own nakedness shall be cursed.[34]

One should expect to encounter nudity during the daily operations of a monastery. Nakedness, even seeing nakedness, is unavoidable, but to look with intentionality and passion invites the devil. To return to Miller's work, passion and intentionality produce *visceral* seeing. Implicit in these rules lies the belief that monks can control their vision and passions and thus prevent sin.

Myth and Memory

Shenoute's instructions and admonitions, while of a strikingly different literary genre from *Sayings*, thus are also intensely visual. They too produce textual photographs of monks kissing, embracing, or accidentally revealing themselves. And despite their different literary forms, both *Sayings* and Shenoute's writings were read and reread, recited and re-recited by generations of monks. The traditional view of *Sayings of the Desert Fathers* is that it consists of compilations of sayings and anecdotes that likely circulated orally in ascetic circles for decades before being recorded on parchment or papyrus in the late fifth and early sixth centuries in Palestine, not Egypt.[35] The Greek text claims that its authors have "committed to writing a few

---

[34] Young, *Coptic Manuscripts*, vol. I, 271–73, trans. mod.
[35] Harmless, *Desert Christians*, 170–71.

fragments of [these monks'] best words and actions," in order to preserve their heritage in the Christian memory.[36] So although the stories themselves are often mythic and fantastical, the recounting and preserving of these "memories" served an important didactic purpose; as William Harmless has written, "this community [of later ascetics] remembered [the early monks] because it was convinced that remembering provided access to the holy, to salvation." Later generations of monks desired these words because they "desired holiness and sought pathways to find holiness ... past wisdom that might serve the present quest."[37] Likewise, Shenoute's letters and rules were compiled (in part by Shenoute himself) into a library of authoritative documents for the community, to be read at the monastery several times a year.[38] What was the effect of this repetition of visually evocative stories and rules? Cannot the passions attack the monk through the mind's eye as well as the body's? By keeping the images of partially nude or sexually intimate monks alive in the ascetic imagination, Shenoute's own writings destabilize the very self-control he seeks to cultivate, presenting an eroticized monastery as normative.

The relationship between body and society transformed during the process of the Christianization of the ancient Mediterranean.[39] *Sayings* and the writings of Shenoute expose both the fragility of this transformation and the ambivalence in the ascetic community about its claims to success. Monastic attitudes toward young males and the control of the passions express an uncertainty about ideals of masculinity that ascetics have inherited from the classical past. The monastery itself is envisioned as a space pulsing with erotic potential. Just as the male citizen in the Greco-Roman city had to discipline his passions to succeed in the complex negotiations of urban relationships, so too was the monk required to maintain self-control in daily interpersonal encounters.

Ironically, eroticism flourished in the writing and reading of ascetic literature. In *Sayings*, the adolescent or preadolescent male remains an ideal sexual partner for male monks. Furthermore, beneath the narratives of self-control and de-eroticization in Shenoute's writings and

---

[36] *AP* Greek Alphabetical Collection, in *PG* 65:72; trans. Ward, *Sayings of the Desert Fathers*, xxxvi.
[37] Harmless, *Desert Christians*, 211.
[38] Emmel, *Shenoute's Literary Corpus*, vol. 2, 562–63; Emmel, "Shenoute the Monk," 154–55; Schroeder, *Monastic Bodies*, 28.
[39] Brown, *Body and Society*.

the story of Zacharias lies a textual voyeurism authorized in no small part by the genre of the text. Like the monk who observes his colleague "sinning" with the boy, the monks who read, hear, and rewrite these texts participate in a voyeuristic erotic experience about which the texts themselves express decided ambivalence.

CHAPTER 4

Child Sacrifice
From Familial Renunciation to Jephthah's Lost Daughter

Violence loomed large in the lives, imaginations, and imagined lives of late antique persons on the path to adulthood. Augustine's beatings for failing to learn in school, John Chrysostom's advice against using corporal punishment, and Gregory of Nyssa's nocturnal beating by the forty martyrs all testify to the pervasiveness of such violence.[1] The same is true of the lives and imagined lives of children in monastic culture in late antique Egypt.

Despite an impulse in some monastic literature to paint an idealized portrait of a celibate, prayerful life, in which children and all other reminders of a prior life are pushed aside, children make themselves known. As we have already seen in Chapter 3, they materialize in a number of scenes in the Greek *Sayings of the Desert Fathers*. In addition, in *Sayings* and other monastic literature, children appear as possessed by demons, and demons appear in the guise of children. The literature also recounts lay Christians bringing their ill, paralytic, and deformed children to monks for healing, as we see in Chapter 5. Male monks struggle to renounce and forget their biological children. Yet others bring their children into the ascetic life with them. Despite a variety of representations of children, many of these young people share a common experience: trauma. They undergo trauma from acts of violence, violence narrowly averted, self-inflicted deformities, disease, and demonic possession.

The Greek *Sayings* even contains accounts of child killings and attempted killings. In one saying in the Alphabetical Collection, a man who seeks to join a monastery in Upper Egypt is commanded to throw his son in the river as a requirement of admission:

> One of the inhabitants of the Thebaid came to see Abba Sisoes one day because he wanted to become a monk. The old man asked him if he had any

---

[1] Augustine, *Confessions* (1992), vol. 1, 8, 11–12; trans. Chadwick in Augustine, *Confessions* (1991), 11, 17. Chrysostom: Leyerle, "Appealing to Children," 265–66. Gregory of Nyssa: Limberis, *Architects of Piety*, 65.

relations in the world. He replied, "I have a son." The old man said, "Go and throw him into the river and then you will become a monk." As he went to throw him in, the old man sent a brother in haste to prevent him. The brother said, "Stop, what are you doing?" But the other said to him, "The abba told me to throw him in." So the brother said, "But afterwards he said do not throw him in." So he left his son and went to find the old man and he became a monk, tested by obedience.[2]

Although Abraham and Isaac are never mentioned by name, this morality tale is clearly modeled on the biblical account of the sacrifice of Isaac in Genesis 22. This scene seems to have resonated with monastic writers and audiences. Similar retellings of the sacrifice of Isaac within a monastic milieu also appear in the Greek Anonymous Collection of *Sayings* and the Latin version known as the *Verba Seniorum*.[3] John Cassian, who practiced asceticism in Egypt and wrote two books for monks in Gaul, also included in his works two accounts of monks and their sons modeled on the Abraham and Isaac story.[4] Even within late antique and medieval Egyptian monastic culture, depictions of child killings and attempted killings extend beyond *Sayings*, and they are not all ascetic retellings of Genesis 22. This chapter examines accounts of child killings (but not those of child martyrs) in Egyptian monastic textual and visual culture through an analysis of the Greek *Sayings*, paintings of the sacrifice of Jephthah's daughter and the averted sacrifice of Isaac at the monasteries of Saint Antony on the Red Sea and Saint Catherine at Sinai, and the exegesis of the same biblical narratives in the writings of the Egyptian monk Shenoute as well as more broadly among late antique ascetic authors.[5] The art and diverse ascetic texts point to a monastic culture in which violence or attempted violence conveys meaning beyond the ascetic injunction to abandon family.

These child killings or attempted killings are expressed in conjunction with powerful moments or rituals of transition and transformation, such as the initiation into a monastery, the performance of sacramental duties, or a conversion from heterodoxy to orthodoxy. Additionally, they also typically contain sacrificial elements. As such,

---

[2] *AP* Sisoes 10, in *PG* 65:391–407; trans. Ward, *Sayings of the Desert Fathers*, 214.

[3] See discussion of *AP Anon.* 295 later in this chapter. *Vit. Patr.* 14.8 (in the chapter on obedience) is nearly identical to *AP* Sisoes 10 (in *PL* 73:949).

[4] Cassian, *Institutes* 4.27–4.28, in Petschenig, *De institutis*, 65–67. Cassian, *Conferences* 2.7, in Petschenig, *Collationes*, 46; trans. Ramsey, *Conferences*, 89. See Chapters 8 and 9 of this book.

[5] My analysis does not include child martyrs. In the child killings or attempted killings considered here, the *perpetrators* – not the victims – are figures ultimately reckoned as pious or faithful in Christian tradition.

these visual and textual streams combine to create a monastic culture in which child sacrifice is an undercurrent. Yet the motif of child killing and child sacrifice is not simply renunciatory, repressive, or destructive – something that brackets off aspects of life and culture (family, children) that are no longer accessible to monks. Child killings ironically prove to be a rather fruitful literary theme. In mimetic readings of the texts and art, monks are invited to identify with a parent willing to kill their child for God, a girl whose sexual purity is offered to God, a biblical patriarch whose life was saved by God, and an orthodox theology equating liturgical bread and wine with Jesus' actual body and blood – all in the process of forging a multigenerational community of holy men. For although some monasteries had women's residences, most of these sources have imagined audiences that are male. The narration of child killings and attempted killings is theologically, politically, and even socially generative.

Biblical Sacrifice in Art and Apothegms

Two significant artistic representations of child sacrifice exist in monasteries in Egypt, one at the Greek Orthodox Saint Catherine's Monastery in Sinai and the other at the Coptic Monastery of Saint Antony at the Red Sea. Their sanctuaries display paintings of the two most iconic moments of child sacrifice in biblical literature: the averted sacrifice of Isaac in the book of Genesis and the completed sacrifice of Jephthah's daughter from the book of Judges. At Saint Catherine's, two seventh–eighth century encaustic paintings (one of each sacrifice) stand near the bema of the great church. The portraits frame the altar, hanging on twin marble pilasters, with Abraham on the left and Jephthah on the right (Figures 1 and 2).

The Abraham painting has sustained some damage from rubbing. The Jephthah painting is very damaged, since an icon of St. Catherine had covered it until 1960. St. Catherine's tomb blocks the marble pilaster, making it difficult to see or photograph the image today. Originally, it would have been visible from the nave.[6] The renovations honoring St. Catherine date to 1715. At Saint Antony's, a thirteenth-century wall painting depicting both events is likewise placed in a prominent location over the altar (Figure 3). These images have traditionally been interpreted

---

[6] Weitzmann, "Jephthah Panel," 342–44; van Loon, *Gate of Heaven*, 155–56.

Figure 1 The sacrifice of Isaac, circa 700 CE. Saint Catherine's Monastery. Encaustic icon on marble revetment. Reproduced through the courtesy of the Michigan-Princeton-Alexandria Expedition to Mount Sinai.

primarily as visual representations of biblical, typological prefigurements of Jesus' sacrifice. Positioned at the altar, where the priest would perform the ritual reenactment of Christ's sacrifice through the administration of the

Figure 2 Jephthah and his daughter, circa 700 CE. Saint Catherine's Monastery. Encaustic icon on marble revetment. Reproduced through the courtesy of the Michigan-Princeton-Alexandria Expedition to Mount Sinai.

Figure 3 The sacrifices of Isaac and Jephthah's daughter, thirteenth century. Monastery of Saint Antony on the Red Sea. Photograph by Patrick Godeau. Reproduced through the courtesy of the American Research Center in Egypt.

eucharist, the parental figures express the biblical roots of the priest's function and the divine origins and sanctification of the sacrament.[7]

At Saint Antony's in particular, the paintings hang in a circumscribed space; the sanctuary is bounded by wooden screens to protect the holiness of the altar. In this period, the sanctuary screen was typically understood to symbolize the veil of the tabernacle. It protected the priest from the nave and from seeing potentially "dangerous" sights (such as women or sinners), which could damage his own sanctity while performing the prayers and sacraments.[8] At this church, the painting's first audience would indeed be a priestly one. The art, however, is positioned high enough on the wall so that a person standing in the sanctuary can partially see it over the current wooden screens dividing the sanctuary from the nave. At least some of the painting would likely have been visible in the thirteenth century as well.[9] Assuredly monks who lived in the monastery would have known of its presence, even if they stood in parts of the nave that did not afford a view. The images carried a particular resonance for the monastic audience in this church: as Elizabeth S. Bolman has noted in her study of St. Antony's sanctuary, the paintings evoke the ascetic's vow to offer his or her life as a sacrifice to God.[10]

The paintings at Saint Antony's and Saint Catherine's express a multiplicity of meanings and should be revisited in light of Egyptian monastic literature, particularly *Sayings*, which contains striking vignettes of child killings and attempted killings, at times modeled on the biblical story of a father and his child. Art in monastic settings functioned as objects of mimetic veneration. While participating in the church liturgies, or even while praying before an image in his own cell, the ascetic experienced a ritual transformation in which he or she identified with the figure represented in the art. As Bolman has argued in her study of the interplay between monastic literature (especially *Sayings*) and monastic art, the monk "achieves the imitation of these exemplars through acting like them, through hearing or reading about them, and through learning to see them." In viewing the images of spiritual beings within their sacred space, the monks "learned to become like them, and indeed to become

---

[7] Weitzmann, "Jephthah Panel"; van Moorsel, "Jephthah?" 273–78; Bolman, "Theodore, 'The Writer of Life,'" 66; see also the description of the paintings at Saint Antony's in van Loon, *Gate of Heaven*, 91–98, 154–58.

[8] Bolman, "Veiling Sanctity," especially 95–97, 104; Frank, *Memory of the Eyes*, 122–26.

[9] The original screens no longer exist. On screening and protective elements in the art before the altar at Saint Antony's, see Bolman, "Veiling Sanctity," 101.

[10] Bolman, "Theodore, 'The Writer of Life,'" 66.

them."[11] The paintings of Isaac and Jephthah's daughter, in conjunction with monastic literature, raise provocative questions about the person(s) with whom the viewer and reader are to identify: Abraham, Isaac, Jephthah, or his daughter? In order to answer this question, we must first examine the broader monastic context in which these paintings were created and understood.

The religious communities at Saint Antony's and Saint Catherine's would have been well versed in *Sayings*. The text was copied and translated widely in the late antique and medieval eras. Saint Catherine's library currently houses Greek, Syriac, Georgian, Old Church Slavonic, and Arabic manuscripts of *Sayings* dating from the eighth to seventeenth centuries.[12] Although St. Antony's monastery was looted in the fifteenth century, making the library's precise contents unknown, it housed a thriving and influential monastic population and a significant manuscript collection in the medieval era.[13] The monks certainly would have studied *Sayings*, since *Sayings* circulated widely throughout the late antique and Byzantine Mediterranean, appearing variously in Greek versions as well as in Latin, Armenian, Syriac, Ethiopic, and Sahidic.[14] The copy of the Sahidic Coptic version most scholars use originates from a monastic library – namely, the monastery of Shenoute, or White Monastery.[15] Today the library in the Monastery of Saint Antony contains manuscripts of Arabic versions of *Sayings*. These manuscripts date from the fourteenth through eighteenth centuries, and some of them are likely twelfth- and thirteenth-century translations from Coptic and Greek versions. The size and characteristics of this collection indicate that the monks of Saint Antony's read *Sayings* collectively and individually during the history of the monastery.[16] Also at Saint Antony's, paintings of the monks profiled in *Sayings* and in other monastic literature line the nave of the church.[17] Although the master artist, Theodore, did not originate from Egypt, but rather from Syria or Palestine, other painters on his team were Egyptians, and he was familiar with the literary traditions about Egyptian monasticism. The monastic saints on the walls of the old church at Saint Antony's do not all draw from a later liturgical text, the *Synaxarion*; one figure

[11] Bolman, "Joining the Community of Saints," 46, 44.

[12] See Clark, *Checklist*, 7, 15, 18, 19, 36; Kāmil, *Catalogue*, 28–36 passim, 59, 76–90 passim, 148.

[13] Gabra, "Perspectives," 173–74; Gabra, *Coptic Monasteries*, 73.

[14] Regnault, *Les sentences des Pères*, 208–11, 238–39, 262–63.

[15] Chaîne, *Le manuscrit de la version copte*.

[16] Samuel Rubenson, personal correspondence, May 18–19, 2011. Rubenson is currently conducting research on the Arabic versions of *Sayings*.

[17] Bolman, "Theodore, 'The Writer of Life,'" 48–54.

(Sisoes) is featured in *Sayings* but not the *Synaxarion*.[18] As Bolman has shown, the iconography in the old church of Saint Antony's is steeped with references to events, characters, and ascetic teachings from *Sayings*.[19] A later painter at the nearby monastery of St. Paul seems to have similarly consulted with *Sayings* as he created his art.[20]

In addition, the image of Jephthah's daughter cannot be dismissed as a mere import of a foreign artist but must be understood within the context of Egyptian monasticism as well as Eastern Mediterranean culture more broadly. Religious politics and cultural innovation crossed geographical boundaries during this period, such that Egyptian and Syrio-Palestinian artistic trends influenced each other. We know that an influential Coptic family during the thirteenth century had houses in both Damascus and Cairo.[21] Images and motifs in the wall paintings at Saint Antony's and the neighboring Saint Paul's Monastery share elements with Byzantine art from elsewhere in the Mediterranean.[22]

At both Saint Antony's and Saint Catherine's, the theological matrix in which these paintings were created was infused with a rich literary tradition in which the stories of Isaac and Jephthah's daughter were told, explained, exegeted, justified, asceticized, and even reconfigured for a monastic community. Moreover, this literary culture included accounts of child sacrifice or killings that extended beyond retellings of Genesis and Judges.

Monastic Sacrifice

In four accounts in the Greek *Sayings* in which monks engage in violence against children, these acts are presented as occurring during sacrificial events: three explicit stories of child sacrifice or sacrifice averted and one story of the murder of a pregnant woman in which the death of the fetus is counted as a separate crime. In three of the stories, the monks hearing and reading *Sayings* are implicitly invited to identify with the person conducting the killing, since that person becomes a monk like themselves.

All four of these tales are sacrificial in nature, containing a constellation of elements Kathryn McClymond has identified as cross-culturally endemic to ritual sacrifice.[23] McClymond theorizes sacrifice as a matrix of ritual elements rather than a statically defined phenomenon. Various

---

[18] Pearson, "Coptic Inscriptions," 222, 268n36.
[19] Bolman, "Theodore, 'The Writer of Life,'" esp. 37.   [20] Lyster, "Reviving a Lost Tradition," 231.
[21] Davis, *Coptic Christology in Practice*, 253.
[22] Bolman, "Theodore's Program," 99–102; Bolman, "Medieval Paintings," 168, 171–72.
[23] McClymond, *Beyond Sacred Violence*.

combinations of the seven criteria appear in sacrificial activities: (1) the "selection" of "the appropriate sacrificial substance," (2) "association" of the event with a deity or deities, (3) "identification" of the offering or ritual with a "patron who benefits from the sacrifice," (4) "killing," or the "intentional execution of the offering," (5) "heating" the offering with fire, (6) "apportionment" of the offering to "specific ritual participants," and (7) "consumption" of the offering.[24] As McClymond argues, these seven elements – not all of which need appear – are "basic activities that generate sacrificial events when combined," and thus she moves scholars of religion beyond the question of whether an event is or is not sacrifice and urges us to ask instead whether it is more or less sacrificial in nature.[25] These examples from *Sayings* each contain at least four of McClymond's seven sacrificial elements.

The art and apothegms exemplify another theoretical conceptualization of the role of sacrificial events: the gift exchange, especially between the devotee and the divinity, in which blood sacrifice is particularly transformative.[26] *Sayings* and paintings depict sacrificial events in which bloodshed occurs or is anticipated during a gift exchange between a person and his deity or sanctified community. Through these exchanges, sacred relationships and communities are forged or reinforced.

Earliest asceticism was commonly understood as a sacrificial act – namely, a sacrifice of family and offspring (among other things). For example, Shenoute praises those who left behind their sons and daughters "because of their love for God and his blessed son."[27] Interpretations of Luke 14:25–27 were especially foundational in wider ascetic arguments for the abandonment of family.[28] As we have seen already in this book, however, representations of the ascetic life as a complete rejection of traditional family are somewhat exaggerated; at Shenoute's monastery and elsewhere, siblings or parents and children joined monasteries together. Frequently monks *maintained* kinship networks in the face of

---

[24] McClymond, *Beyond Sacred Violence*, 29–33. [25] McClymond, *Beyond Sacred Violence*, 25, 27.

[26] Mauss, *The Gift*; Burkert, *Homo Necans*; Burkert, "Sacrifice, Offerings, and Votives," 325–26. The literature on sacrifice as a religious category is too vast to summarize here. The theories of Burkert and Mauss (among others) have come under increasing scrutiny. McClymond critiques the centrality of blood and violence (*Beyond Sacred Violence*, 44–64, esp. 44–46). She raises legitimate concerns; nevertheless, blood and violence (real or anticipated) are central to the art and text in this study.

[27] Shenoute, *Canons*, vol. 7, MONB.XU 100–101, in Amélineau, *Oeuvres de Schenoudi*, vol. 2, 153. For an extensive treatment of ascetic interpretations of the Bible in Greek and Latin writers, see Clark, *Reading Renunciation*, 177–203.

[28] Clark, *Reading Renunciation*, 198.

Shenoute's admonitions otherwise.[29] Nonetheless, the ascetic ideal of familial renunciation remained, and narratives of child sacrifice in *Sayings* reinforce this ideal.

The story of Abraham's averted sacrifice of Isaac in Genesis serves as the dramatic and obvious model for the ascetic sacrifice of family. In the tale from *Sayings* quoted at the beginning of this chapter, the aspiring monk's actions mirror the biblical patriarch's.[30] Like Abraham, the father's commitment to God is tested by a command to kill his son, and like Isaac, the son is saved by a last-minute intervention on his behalf. Despite his physical survival, the child nonetheless serves as a sacrificial object; though he lives, the father leaves him behind without even an afterthought as a sign of his devotion only to God in pursuit of his ascetic vocation. The story provides opportunity for a doubled mimesis; the reader (or hearer) imitates both the esteemed monk of *Sayings* and the patriarch Abraham (whom the monk of the story in turn has imitated) in adopting the ascetic life.

In a parallel story of ascetic child sacrifice in the Anonymous Collection, one monk does follow through with an attempted murder of his biological son. This man is a more established ascetic, who had left his three children behind to join a monastery three years earlier. He becomes depressed over his separation from his offspring and speaks about it to his abbot, who orders the monk to find the children and bring them to the monastery. He discovers that two have died and returns with the third, a son. He seeks out his abbot, whom he finds in the monastery's bakery. The abbot covers the child with kisses and asks the monk, "Do you love him?" and then, "Do you love him very much?" When the monk replies affirmatively, the abbot commands him to throw the son in the bakery's furnace "so that it burns him." The monk casts his child into the furnace, which "immediately became like dew, full of freshness."[31] The transformation of the oven to dew may mean that the child survives. It may also imply that the child has been conveyed to heaven, and thus that his earthly life, at least, has been extinguished. Dew has a biblical association with heaven and divine benevolence. The "dew of heaven" is a treasured gift of God in Genesis. According to Numbers, manna would fall from heaven "when the dew fell on the camp" of the Israelites. Dew signifies God's blessing in Psalm 133. In the book of Daniel, heavenly dew "bathes" Nebuchadnezzar during his seven years of exile, indicating that despite suffering and tribulations, the

---

[29] Krawiec, *Shenoute and the Women*, 161–74. See also Chapter 8 in this book.
[30] *AP* Sisoes 10, in *PG* 65:391–407; trans. Ward, *Sayings of the Desert Fathers*, 214.
[31] *AP Anon.* 295, in Nau, "Histoires" (1909), 378; trans. Ward, *Wisdom of the Desert Fathers*, 47 (saying numbered 162).

king is saved, sanctified, and eventually right with God; his exile from "human society" is simultaneously a punishment and a divine embrace.[32] Whether the child is to be understood as living or miraculously conveyed to heaven, this oblique reference effectively ends his life, for *Sayings* makes no further mention of the boy or his prospects. Instead, the account ends with a commentary on the actions of the biological father: "Through this act, he received glory like the patriarch Abraham."

These two ascetic retellings of the sacrifice of Isaac illustrate a motif in the symbolic representation of children in *Sayings*: children as sacrificial objects. Both men receive commands from their institution's leadership to sacrifice their children as part of a ritual of initiation. In the first story, the sacrifice functions as a primary ritual of initiation; he must kill the child in order to prove his faith and join the community. In the second story, the monk becomes a true and tested monk only once he has enacted the sacrifice. That the abbot *commanded* the monk to seek out his children indicates that this is an institutionally authorized act designed to test the man's obedience to monastic authority, with the abba as patron. (This saying also appears in the section of Latin *Sayings* on the theme of obedience.) The monk fully affirms and embraces his monastic identity once he reenacts Abraham's sacrifice of Isaac. Though he has lived at the monastery for three years, his initiation is complete only upon the enactment of the sacrifice.

Remarkably, in both of these accounts, the fate of the *child* remains unstated. This shared narrative element signifies two important themes in the stories: the primacy of the parent as the ritual agent in the sacrifice and the extinguishing of the child as the sacrificial object. In Genesis, Abraham continued to parent Isaac, and Isaac himself went on to become no minor figure in biblical tradition. Isaac's very survival leads to the establishment of the covenant between God and Abraham, Isaac, and Isaac's descendants. The story of the sacrifice of Isaac is rather the story of the survival of Isaac and the engendering of an entire people. But *Sayings*'s storyline follows the father and his dedication to God. It too narrates a story about community but about the father's community and his acceptance into it through the excision of his children from his life. The ascetic life is an act of mimesis, modeling oneself on the dedication of the biblical parent willing to kill his child for God. The parent's future depends upon the narratological (if not literal) death of the child. As the parents' storylines flourish, the children's narrative threads die. Levitical notions of sacrifice depend upon the

---

[32] Gen. 27:28; Num. 11:9; Ps. 133:3; Dan. 4:15, 4:23–25, 4:33, 5:21.

immolation or destruction of the sacrificial offerings. As Caroline Walker Bynum has noted, Christian interpretations of this type of biblical sacrifice and theorizing about Christ's death often express anxiety about this fundamental element of sacrifice inherited from the Jewish scriptures. According to Bynum in her study of blood piety, the essential element of Christ's sacrifice is sometimes interpreted to be his death (the extinguishing of his life), but often emphasis turns to interpreting the crucifixion as an offering from which the violent act of killing has been expunged; the offering up of his blood provides an example. Christ's blood becomes an oblation to God, a gift strangely dissociated from the act that enabled its existence.[33] The children of these monks do not die; rather, they are extinguished as gift-offerings that evoke the blood of physical sacrifice but are strangely dissociated from physical death. They are extinguished from the monks' lives, communities, and identities.

The extinguishing, destruction, or "killing" of a sacrificial object need not be bloody or violent, as McClymond has persuasively argued; sacrificial substances are "manipulated" in a variety of violent and nonviolent ways. What the religious theorist should attend to is what the "killing" or manipulation of the sacrificial object enables.[34] The stories of child sacrifice in *Sayings* participate in sacrificial discourses in which offerings subject to immolation and destruction generate power or facilitate relationships. We scholars should question our tendencies to label all religiously imbued deaths or bloodlettings "sacrifices."[35] Curiously, the child sacrifices in *Sayings* are sacrifices but not bloody slaughters. They contain several of McClymond's sacrificial criteria: selection, association, identification, and killing (here, symbolic killings). They express late antique Christian ambivalence about the legacy of blood sacrifice in the theology and practice the tradition has inherited and adapted. Even though these children are not killed, they function narratologically, symbolically, and mimetically as ritual blood sacrifices. They function as offerings to God, which only carry transformative meaning when extinguished.

In this way, the accounts in *Sayings* recall the story of another biblical child sacrifice – one also depicted at Saint Antony's and Saint Catherine's, and one whose life is literally extinguished: that of Jephthah's daughter. In the book of Judges, Jephthah vows to sacrifice the first living thing that walks through his door to greet him upon his return if God will provide him with victory in battle. Tragically, the first person who welcomes him

---

[33] Bynum, *Wonderful Blood*, 234.   [34] McClymond, *Beyond Sacred Violence*, 44–46, 64.
[35] Frankfurter, "Egyptian Religion."

home is his daughter, his only child. Jephthah, with his daughter's consent, fulfills his vow and enacts the sacrifice (Judg. 11:30–40). The monks' stories mirror Jephthah's in two ways, as sacrifices of destruction and as sacrifices enacting a gift exchange. Like Jephthah, the monks in *Sayings* offer their children, and like Jephthah's daughter, the children's role in the narrative ends with their sacrifice. Though neither of the monks in *Sayings* takes a monastic vow during the course of the narrative, these sacrificial acts are part of their ritual fulfillment of their obligation to God through a monastic initiation. Some monastic communities in Egypt required a vow or established a ritual of initiation. Monks at Shenoute's monastery swore an oath upon entrance.[36] The most famous coenobitic community, the Pachomian monasteries, did not seem to have ritualized an oath of initiation, but other ascetic sources mention the taking of vows or the donning of the monastic habit as inherent to the ascetic life.[37] The ascetics' promise to dedicate their lives to God mirrors Jephthah's oath. Their offering of their children functions as a gift-offering that fulfills their obligation to God, the gift required to fully enter the community of living saints that is the monastery, just as the sacrifice Jephthah performed repays his obligation to God for his victory in battle. Human sacrifice, even child sacrifice, may have been normative (albeit rare) in parts of the ancient Near East, and passages in the Christian Old Testament (including Judges 11) may provide evidence that child sacrifice to the God of the Israelites was acceptable.[38] I do not propose that these literary rituals of initiation recollect historically enacted rituals of monastic initiation in which living children were killed or almost killed. The elimination of the child from the monk's family constitutes a death or a loss, one that is simultaneously metaphorical and anchored in the material realities and consequences of sacrificial events. Egyptian monks did not kill children as part of an initiation ritual, but ceremonies of initiation involved renouncing a former life through ritual acts, such as donning the monastic garb or taking monastic oaths. The ritual act transformed the monk, in no small part because it involved a renunciation of the man's former life, a life that

---

[36] Krawiec, *Shenoute and the Women*, 20–21; Schroeder, *Monastic Bodies*, 4.

[37] Athanasius, *Ep. virg. I* 33; trans. Brakke, *Athanasius and Asceticism*, 285; Cassian, *Institutes* I, in Petschenig, *De institutis*; trans. Ramsey, *Institutes*, 21–27. See also Harmless, *Desert Christians*, 120, 126, 127, 314, 411; Krawiec, "Garments of Salvation"; Wipszycka, *Moines et communautés monastiques*, 365–81. I thank William Harmless for references and insights.

[38] Burkert, "Sacrifice, Offerings, and Votives," 333–36; Logan, "Rehabilitating Jephthah"; Finsterbusch, "First-Born between Sacrifice and Redemption"; Lange, "They Burn Their Sons and Daughters"; Bauks, "Theological Implications of Child Sacrifice."

would have included living with and maintaining constant communication with his biological family.

McClymond argues that sacrificial elements are visible, ritual categories even in moments that are "not traditional sacrifice" – episodes or traditions that have "translated" sacrifice into "symbolic or internalized forms."[39] The renunciation of family praised by Shenoute and enacted in initiation rituals or vows certainly qualifies as such an "internalized" sacrifice, in which the gifts or sacrificial objects are the monk's family and secular life path. Looking at the early Christian context, David Biale has shown that early Christian authors re-narrate, reinterpret, and reframe biblical stories of blood sacrifice. In such rewritings, the materiality of blood is not wholly washed away by its symbolic interpretations. Blood, the shedding of blood, the sharing of blood, and the spreading of blood signified community. Christian sacrificial discourse spiritualized the practice of blood sacrifice while it continued to traffic in ancient blood symbolisms.[40] Likewise, Egyptian monastic culture did not completely detach from the bodily and bloody acts depicted in *Sayings* and the paintings at Saint Antony's and Saint Catherine's. The narratives in *Sayings* about fathers sacrificing their children mimic Abraham and Isaac (a child sacrifice averted, a young boy saved), but elements of these narratives also evoke Jephthah and his daughter. As I explain in what follows, standing near the monastic altars at the moment of her death, Jephthah's daughter signifies a more complete blood sacrifice. In a parallel sacrificial act, the gift-offering of the monks is complete, for they have given up real biological children or the potential to have biological children in order to pursue lives of holiness.

Priests, Penance, and Infanticide

Monastic literature's accounts of violence against children extend beyond ascetic rewritings of these biblical dramas. Two accounts in *The Sayings of the Desert Fathers* present the butchering of babies as turning points in "edifying" narratives about adult monks. In one, three monks debate whether the eucharist is truly the flesh and blood of Christ. One expresses skepticism, asserting the bread and wine are merely symbols. The next Sunday, the monks attend church services together. As the priest places the bread on the table, a small child also appears. As the priest prepares the

---

[39] McClymond, *Beyond Sacred Violence*, 154–55, and also the discussion of the spiritualization of Genesis 22 on 157–59.

[40] Biale, *Blood and Belief*, 45.

eucharist, an angel pours the child's blood into a chalice, chops the child into little bits, and offers the once-skeptical monk a "morsel of bloody flesh." Afraid, the man shouts aloud that he believes the eucharist indeed to be the body and blood of Christ.[41] Thus the flesh and blood of the child prove the ontological status of the bread and wine in the church's ritual sacrifice. This story seems to be directed against Origenism, Melitians, or other "heresies" that believed that the eucharist was only a "symbol" or a "type" of Christ's flesh and blood, rather than an actual ritual manifestation of his physical body.[42] In yet another anecdote, Apa Apollo, before becoming a monk, is moved by the devil to tear open a pregnant woman and rip the fetus from her body, killing them both.[43] He is struck with remorse and joins a monastery to live a life of prayer.

The moral freight both of these butchered children carry is sacrificial. The eucharistic child quite obviously represents Jesus Christ and his sacrifice for the repentance of sins. The physicality of the butchered child testifies to the physicality of both Jesus' original sacrifice and the eucharistic bread and wine.

This textual image of child sacrifice fits well with eucharistic interpretations of the art at Saint Catherine's and Saint Antony's. And it provides a reason for the specific inclusion of Jephthah's daughter in the iconographic programs, even though her death is rarely depicted in art. The paintings at both monasteries portray Jephthah's daughter as a blood sacrifice whose ritual is in the process of completion. They share some iconographic similarities, such as the positioning of the figures, but they are not identical; Jephthah's clothing, for example, differs.[44] Despite damage to the painting at Saint Catherine's, Jephthah is partially visible and can be seen in the process of cutting his daughter's throat (Figure 2). Likewise, at Saint Antony's, the dagger is in the girl's neck (Figure 4). In both, Jephthah stands behind his daughter and pulls her head back by grasping her hair and tugging downward. These paintings contrast with their twins, the sacrifice of Isaac, in which Abraham's blade is poised above the child's neck (Figures 1 and 5). Whereas Isaac is a sacrifice averted, Jephthah's daughter is a more complete prefigurement of Christ's death (which is celebrated in the eucharist). Her blood is shed, and she is killed. Just as in the graphic imagery in *Sayings*, the girl's physical death reminds the viewer of the physicality of Christ's death and the equation of the eucharist with his sacrificial body. While a lamb

---

[41] *AP* Daniel 7, in *PG* 65:156–160; trans. Ward, *Sayings of the Desert Fathers*, 53–54.
[42] Clark, *Origenist Controversy*, 64–66.
[43] *AP* Apollo 2, in *PG* 65:133–36; trans. Ward, *Sayings of the Desert Fathers*, 32.
[44] Van Loon, *Gate of Heaven*, 155.

Figure 4 The sacrifice of Jephthah's daughter, thirteenth century. Monastery of
Saint Antony on the Red Sea. Photograph by Patrick Godeau. Reproduced through
the courtesy of the American Research Center in Egypt.

hovers in the background of both Isaac panels, reminding the viewers of the
coming of Christ as the lamb of God, Jephthah's daughter prefigures God's
completed sacrifice of his own flesh and blood, his own child. Medieval
Coptic texts also viewed her typologically. She foreshadowed Christ's crucifixion, although her blood redeemed her alone and not all of humanity.[45]

The fetus in the story of Apollo also plays a role in a sacrificial drama.
Although the incident is narrated as a tremendous sin motivated by the

---

[45] Van Loon, *Gate of Heaven*, 157.

Figure 5 The sacrifice of Isaac, thirteenth century. Monastery of Saint Antony on the Red Sea. Photograph by Patrick Godeau. Reproduced through the courtesy of the American Research Center in Egypt.

devil, it is nonetheless the sin that propels Apollo to convert to the ascetic life. While couched as an act of murder, the fetus's death is a necessary event in the narrative. On a narratological level, the unborn child's future, and that of its mother, are sacrificed so that Apollo might come to live a "life of God." This tale recounts a sort of inverted sacrificial event, in which two are slaughtered in a multilayered "gift" exchange. In this case, Apollo takes something (their lives), which he then has an obligation to repay. He offers his life (a life spent in atonement), for which he then

receives something sacred in return (his monastic community and relationship with God). The monk, the woman, and the fetus are all sacrificial
substances manipulated by the narrator and Apollo in turn. As interpreters
of the text, we should attend to the dead victims but also, in the words of
McClymond, to what the killings enable: sacred relationships, expressed in
Apollo's admission to the monastic community. Homiletical parallels in
contemporaneous Christian exegesis of Judges 11 confirm that this account
can be understood as inherently sacrificial. In early Christian hermeneu-
tics, Jephthah's daughter's death often serves a moral purpose similar to
that of the fetus's death. In the words of Jerome, the girl dies so that "he
who had improvidently made a vow, should learn his error by the death of
his daughter."[46] Although wrong, her death enables Jephthah's spiritual
growth. In a similar vein, the pregnant woman's death functions as a tragic
necessity, enabling Apollo's spiritual growth.

That stories of child sacrifice and child killings are featured in texts as
popular and authoritative as *Sayings* is somewhat surprising given the
accusations of cannibalism, infanticide, and other similar horrors that
"pagans" levied against Christians in the pre-Constantinian era. Coptic
texts like the *Panegyric of Macarius of Tkow* revive charges of human
sacrifice but enlist them against the people in Egypt who continue to
worship traditional deities. In other words, other accounts of child sacrifice
appear in Egyptian Christian literature, but they represent a reversal of the
ancient Roman polemic against Christians: Christians demeaned their
opponents with the very accusations of human sacrifice they themselves
had once faced. David Frankfurter argues that in a text like the *Panegyric*,
such "details of human sacrifice . . . derive from polemical and literary *topoi*
of subhuman religion."[47] Infanticide, in particular, is a form of the "widespread myth of the Other in antiquity."[48] Building on Frankfurter's
analysis, the Isaac story in the Christian tradition can serve as a story of
Christian superiority: unlike the religions of the "Other," the Christian
God does not demand human sacrifice to venerate him. However, some
tension emerges between the accounts I have examined from *Sayings* and
the polemical tropes of infanticide and sacrifice Frankfurter discusses. In
Sayings, the children are sacrificial not in the service of "pagan" religiosity,
but rather they are sacrificial in narratives of initiation into the Christian
ascetic life or conversion to orthodox Christian eucharistic theology.

---

[46] Jerome, *Iou.* 1.5, 23, in *PL* 23:226, 252–54; trans. in *NPNF* 2, vol. 6, 349, 363. I thank Elizabeth
A. Clark for this reference.
[47] Frankfurter, "Illuminating the Cult of Kothos," 182.
[48] Frankfurter, "Illuminating the Cult of Kothos," 187.

Child Sacrifice Rejected and Redeemed in Early Ascetic Exegesis

The images at St. Catherine's and St. Antony's monasteries were created in a religious culture in which these motifs of child sacrifice existed in literature. Both the art and the texts held authoritative positions and possessed mimetic qualities for their communities. But with whom in these stories and images is the reading or listening monk to identify? Whom is the monk to imitate? How is this identification and mimesis expressed and understood? And what does it mean for a monk to identify either with the children or the parents, the dead child or the spared child? Finally, what would images and stories of child sacrifice mean for communities in which children were living among adult monks? Monastic texts suggest that sacrificial imagery was profoundly multivalent. Ascetic and monastic writings, including those of Shenoute, revisit the stories of Jephthah's daughter and Isaac in order to impart ascetic wisdom to their readers. The two figures served to reinforce church doctrine about the eucharist as well as the ascetic obligation to renounce family and procreation.[49]

In none of the texts of *Sayings*, however, is the monk asked to identify with the sacrificial child. Rather, the sacrifice is part of a ritual (either the eucharist or an explicit or implicit ritual of initiation) in which the monk functions as the ritual subject and agent. Yet elements of the paintings – especially of Jephthah's daughter's story – do indeed suggest a monastic identification with the object of sacrifice. In later Jewish and Christian interpretation, the power of Jephthah's daughter's death lay largely in her virginity. Jewish author Pseudo-Philo wrote a lament for the girl in which she does not express grief over her impending death but proclaims her own willing decision to offer herself as a sacrifice; thus she becomes the model for holiness and righteousness.[50] As a virgin, she is a pure sacrifice, dying before she can live a life that has fulfilled its potential.

In early Christian literature, most "church fathers" interpret Jephthah's act as one of foolishness; his vow serves as a lesson to future believers never to make such a ridiculous oath.[51] The earliest Christian reference to Jephthah comes, of course, in the New Testament book of Hebrews (11:32), where he is listed alongside other military leaders and "righteous"

---

[49] This section presents an abbreviated survey of early Christian ascetic exegeses on Jephthah's daughter; the fuller survey can be found in an earlier version of this chapter published as Schroeder, "Child Sacrifice in Egyptian Monastic Culture."

[50] Baker, "Pseudo-Philo and the Transformation of Jephthah's Daughter."

[51] Weitzmann, "Jephthah Panel," 350–52; Thompson, *Writing the Wrongs*, 100–38.

men (such as David); no mention is made of his daughter. Ascetic authors of the patristic age, however, did not avoid speaking of her and in fact found much to say about the vow that led to the military victories honored in Hebrews. One approach, exemplified by Ambrose of Milan, avoids openly criticizing Jephthah for fulfilling his vow but questions making such a promise in the first place and pillories him for setting a poor example for later church officials making their own vows to God.[52]

Ascetic authors nonetheless found redemption in the figure of the daughter and considered her a pious exemplar. For Ambrose, she turns "an impious accident" into a "pious sacrifice."[53] Some commentators characterize her as a martyr, a prefigurement of Christ in her bodily sacrifice *and* a model for ascetic sacrifice. Ephrem the Syrian links her blood to the blood of Christ's crucifixion and the blood of a virgin's hymen.[54] For Ephrem, the girl's own virginal status mirrors the monks' vows of virginity. In this reading, the figure of the daughter would resonate with monks gazing at the paintings. Other Latin and Greek ascetic writers in the fourth century also praise Jephthah's daughter as a model for female asceticism.[55] The paintings would thus invite the monks to identify with her not just because they, like Jephthah's daughter, offer their lives to God, but also because they, like Jephthah's daughter, offer their sexual purity to God. Although the depiction of women other than Mary in early monastic church art is rare, and exceedingly rare in Egypt, holy women do appear as objects of male monastic mimesis in the church at the Monastery of Saint Paul.[56] Thus the sacrificial images in the paintings of Genesis 22 and Judges 11 invite predominantly male monks to identify their own ascetic dedication with a female figure as well as a male.

Ascetic commentators frequently compare Jephthah and Abraham, and typically Jephthah comes up short. Nonetheless, juxtaposing the two patriarchs produces a curious effect. Jerome condemns Jephthah in *Against Jovinian*, but twenty-five years later, in his *Commentary on Jeremiah*, he reverses himself and praises Jephthah's intentions (though not his execution of them).[57] Many cite Jephthah as an example of what not to do, and as a reminder that men should *not* attempt to emulate

---

[52] Ambrose, *Off.* 1.255, in Davidson, *Ambrose*, vol. 1, 266–67, 400–03.
[53] Ambrose, *Off.* 3.12.81, in Davidson, *Ambrose*, vol. 1, 404–05.
[54] Ephrem, *Hymns on Virginity* 2:10–11, in Beck, *Des heiligen Ephraem des Syrers Hymnen de Virginitate*, 7; trans. McVey, *Ephrem the Syrian*, 268–69; Weitzmann, "Jephthah Panel," 351–52.
[55] Thompson, *Writing the Wrongs*, 114–15.
[56] Lyster, "Reviving a Lost Tradition," 223, 225, 226, 346–47n113.
[57] Jerome, *Iou.* 1.5, 23; see also Thompson, *Writing the Wrongs*, 121–24.

Abraham. Yet the combination of Abraham and Jephthah is provocative given the sacrificial imagery in the monastic texts. When linking Abraham with Jephthah, early Christian authors tacitly admit that it looks bad for a patriarch of the tradition to commit child sacrifice. Procopius of Gaza and Ambrosiaster take pains to explain that Jephthah's act *cannot* be compared to the events of Genesis 22.[58] Augustine questions whether Jephthah killed his daughter at God's command and is resolute in maintaining that he should not be admired. God provides Jephthah's story as warning to all those who might imitate Abraham.[59] (Abraham's test, apparently, was unique, not to be repeated.) Some commentators argue that Jephthah's improvident promise serves pedagogical purposes. It functions as the vow to end all such vows.[60] Jephthah's daughter sacrifices her life so that others may learn the folly of her father's ways.[61] Despite efforts to distance Abraham and later Christian tradition from Jephthah, we nonetheless find commentators seeking to resolve their differences. The tendency to refer to Abraham and Isaac when the question of Jephthah arises suggests that the commentators indeed protest too much.[62] Visually, these two prominent paintings paired the men in important monastic churches. Their continual association validates Jephthah's act by deploying it for additional pedagogical, theological, and symbolic purposes.

To return to the Egyptian context, a handful of late antique and medieval Coptic texts mention Jephthah, typically with praise. One encomium compares him to Abraham and faults him not for offering his daughter as a sacrifice but for lamenting her impending death. Another encomium follows the example of Hebrews and lists him among several saints and righteous men.[63] One Coptic author invokes Jephthah's daughter as a model for asceticism, alongside Jephthah, Abraham, and Isaac. In a sermon entitled "I Have Been Reading the Holy Gospels," Shenoute expounds upon the importance of the vow to ascetic life. Written in 431, soon after Shenoute's return from the Ecumenical Council at Ephesus, the

---

[58] Proc. G. *Gen.-Jud.* 11.30, as quoted in Thompson, *Writing the Wrongs*, 132. Ambrosiaster *Qu. test.* 43, as quoted in Thompson, *Writing the Wrongs*, 124.

[59] Aug. *Civ.* 1.21, in Dombart and Kalb, *De civitate dei*, 23; trans. Dyson, *Augustine*, 33–34. Aug. *Quaest. Hept.* 7.49, in De Bruyne and Fraipont, *Quaestionum in Heptateuchum, libri VII*, 358–73. See also Thompson, *Writing the Wrongs*, 125–30.

[60] Chrys. *stat.*14.3, in *PG* 49:147–48; trans. in *NPNF*, vol. 9, 434 [numbered Homily 14.7]. See also Thompson, *Writing the Wrongs*, 116–18.

[61] Weitzmann, "Jephthah Panel," 351.

[62] Only a few later commentators, including Peter Chrysologus in the East and Paschius Radbertus in the West, uncritically blend Jephthah's daughter's story with Isaac's (Thompson, *Writing the Wrongs*, 134, 135).

[63] Van Loon, *Gate of Heaven*, 157.

text contains an extensive treatment of the monastic vow and the clerical vow, particularly the oath of celibacy or virginity.[64] When addressing monks who break their vows after the fact, Shenoute pairs the concepts of fidelity and sacrifice. He begins by speaking of God's love for humanity and offers Jesus, including his death, as the major sign of God's love. God sacrificed his only son for the sake of humanity, insists Shenoute, and so the least monks and clergy can do is hold fast to their own vows, which constitute much smaller sacrifices. He singles out not only men who fail to maintain their celibacy but also men who strive to become monks or clergy with questionable motives. He asks God, "[D]o you discover among us that someone will say, 'I did something for you?' As for him who says, 'I have done a deed for you,' it is for himself that he is actually doing it." Christ's death models Shenoute's ideal of a selfless sacrifice. Jesus' sacrifice leads Shenoute to write of other fathers who sacrificed their children – namely, the biblical patriarchs Jephthah and Abraham. The citation is brief, yet powerful:

> If some have offered up to you their children as sacrifices, like the great Abraham the patriarch and Jephthah, while others again did not do it for you, it is you who rewarded them with what they had no power ever to obtain. You rewarded all of them here and allowed them to inherit eternal life, these among whom Christ came in the flesh, your only-begotten Son who exists before the ages. It is he whom you sent to the world at the last days, [who] gave himself for our sins and for our impiety, and [who] rose on the third day.[65]

Shenoute quickly pivots back to the topics of Christ's incarnation, sacrifice, and resurrection, but the implication is clear: monks who either renege on their promises or pledge celibacy with selfish motives compare poorly to the true, selfless sacrifices committed by Abraham and Jephthah, men who both maintained their commitments to God and, according to Shenoute, were willing to carry out a selfless sacrifice.

Shenoute reconfigures even Isaac, the iconic sacrifice-deferred, to signify an actualized ascetic sacrifice. He identifies Isaac as a model for discipline in which ascetics, in sacrificing themselves to God, are asked to imitate Abraham and his son simultaneously. Paraphrasing Romans, he refers to Isaac as a model sacrifice that all monks should imitate in their endeavors to

---

[64] Moussa, "I Have Been Reading," 1; for more on the historical context and dating of the sermon, see 1–8, 13–19.

[65] Shenoute, *I Have Been Reading the Holy Gospels* 19, *Discourses*, vol. 8, in Moussa, "I Have Been Reading," 57; trans. 151.

purify their bodies through ascetic discipline. Monks should obey God, just as Abraham obeyed without hesitation, so that they too may offer themselves as pure sacrifices to God.[66]

Reviewing the vast history of Jewish and Christian commentary on Judges 11, much less both Judges 11 and Genesis 22, is beyond the scope of this chapter. But focusing on even a selection of ascetic exegetes is illuminating. The combination of ascetic commentary with the images at Saint Catherine's and Saint Antony's suggests that not only Isaac, not only the eucharist, but also the story of Jephthah's daughter, with her bloody death, lurk behind accounts of child killings and sacrifice in monastic literature. She and Isaac are multivalent symbols in an ancient multimedia culture referencing renunciation, virginity, martyrdom, obedience, and the eucharist.

Child Sacrifice, Cultural Heritage, and Monastic Reproduction

The accounts from *Sayings* examined in this chapter are disturbing, for they present children and monks in ways that disrupt conventional mores. Righteous fathers do not throw their sons in rivers or ovens. Grown men do not drink the blood of babies. Holy men do not murder pregnant women. Their power lies in their ability to provoke. Their unsettling natures require contemplation, interpretation, and explanation. Despite their shocking qualities, these tales are not completely renunciatory in nature. As I have already shown, within their larger literary and artistic monastic context, they are theologically generative, in that they produce eucharistic theologies both visually and textually. Moreover, they are socially and politically generative, creating monastic communities through genealogies engendered by ascetic sacrifice rather than biological reproduction.

One of the more provocative aspects of Apollo's crimes is that the death of the fetus haunts him more than his murder of the pregnant woman. His continued penance over the fetus's death raises questions about the cultural value of children as represented in the text. Apollo reportedly spends his life in prayer, becoming convinced that God has forgiven him for the sin of murdering the woman, "but for the child's murder, he was in doubt." Another monk who heard his prayers one day told him, "God has forgiven you even the death of the child, but he leaves you in grief because that is

---

[66] Shenoute, *The Lord Thundered, Discourses*, vol. 4, MONB.GG, ff. 27–28, in Amélineau, *Oeuvres de Schenoudi*, vol. 2, 142; trans. Timbie and Zaborowski, "*The Lord Thundered*," 107.

good for your soul."[67] Why does the death of a fetus weigh more heavily on Apollo's soul than the death of a woman? One reading might turn to innocence for the explanation: the death of the child represents the death of an innocent, compared to the death of the adult woman. Yet, although the innocence of children has roots in early Christianity, the concept of the "innocent childhood" and the accompanying cultural semiotics of children signifying purity and innocence take their strongest hold in modernity.[68] Another contextually Roman cultural signification of children privileges the fetus's life over the woman's. For Greco-Roman families, the cultural and symbolic value of children lay in their reference to the future. Children represented the family's and the society's legacy – a legacy of culture, economics, and reputation. To kill a child was to kill the future. For example, legislation about abortion in the Roman world focused not on a moral equivalency between murder and terminating a pregnancy but on the issue of legacy; women who aborted their children deprived their husbands and their society of their legacy.[69]

Thus the story of Apollo the murderous monk can also be read as a discourse on traditional Greco-Roman family values. Despite being a fetus-killer – perhaps even *by* being one – Apollo affirms the importance of children in late antiquity, even in late antique *monastic* culture. Although Apollo embarks on the more virtuous life of celibacy and familial renunciation, his tale implicitly reifies the cultural significance of children as society's legacy. Killing the future is a greater sin than killing the past. The dead fetus has dual meanings. Apollo as a literary character exists within a monastic literary collection populated by children who typically experience severe trauma, even attempted murder or death. In this way, the monastic culture appears distinctively anti-child. But the fetus, due to Apollo's eternal penance, also speaks to a monastic culture that embraces children as symbols of a society's legacy.

The child killings are also paradoxically productive, rather than renunciatory, when examined as narratives of sacrificial rituals. Anthropologist and religious theorist Nancy Jay has argued that particularly in male-dominated cultures, ritual sacrifice is intricately connected to modes of cultural and biological reproduction. "The practice of sacrifice affects

---

[67] *AP* Apollo 2, in *PG* 65:133–36; trans. Ward, *Sayings of the Desert Fathers*, 32.

[68] Heywood, *History of Childhood*, chs. 1–3, esp. 4, 20, 33; on innocence and infants in Eastern and later Syriac traditions (in contrast to Greek and Latin patristic views), see Doerfler, "The Infant, the Monk and the Martyr."

[69] Grubbs, *Law and Family in Late Antiquity*, 96; Grubbs, *Women and the Law in the Roman Empire*, 203, 311n28.

family structures, the organized social relations of reproduction within which women bear their children."[70] Examining the practice of sacrifice in cultures as diverse as ancient Greece and Rome, Hawaii, and West Africa, Jay contends that ritual sacrifice "identif[ies], and maintain[s] through time, not only social structures whose continuity flows through fathers and sons but also other forms of male to male succession that transcend dependence on childbearing women ... [I]t identifies social and religious descent, rather than biological descent" and thus produces genealogies that are "no longer directly dependent on women's reproductive powers for continuity."[71] Ritual sacrifice thus encodes and maintains a genealogy in which women's role in reproducing that society is deemed less relevant than other modes of social and cultural reproduction.

Sacrificial rituals often promote social communion or expiation. In communion sacrifice, members of a community are initiated into the group or their membership in the group is affirmed through participation in a sacrifice. In expiation sacrifice, sin, guilt, pollution, or some other disruptive element is expelled during the ritual. The line between these two forms of sacrifice is not bright; like expiation sacrifices, communion sacrifices are rituals of differentiation – they distinguish members of the enculturated group from outsiders; similarly, expiation sacrifices promote internal cohesion by ridding a person or group of difference.[72] Although aspects of Jay's theories remain controversial, the political and social functions of sacrifice are widely acknowledged.[73] Sacrificial activities, as McClymond summarizes, construct and reinforce communities with distinctive and often politically charged identities: "sacrifice is often the arena in which certain people distinguish themselves from others, community versus community, social rank versus social rank, modern religion versus ancient religion."[74] David Biale, in his examination of blood in Judaism and Christianity, also notes that rituals and discourses of blood sacrifice had a significant political dimension, which overtook their theological dimension. In the Hebrew Bible, blood and blood discourse had an "indexing" function, pointing to one group's sacred authority over some of the wider community's social practices, and even over certain

---

[70] Jay, *Throughout Your Generations Forever*, xxiv.

[71] Jay, *Throughout Your Generations Forever*, 37.

[72] Jay, *Throughout Your Generations Forever*, 17–20.

[73] Jay has received criticism for universalizing specifically Western cultural categories and, in imposing them on non-Western cultures, misinterpreting her evidence. See Goode, "'Creating Descent' after Nancy Jay"; McClymond, *Beyond Sacred Violence*, 2, 11–13, 45–46.

[74] McClymond, *Beyond Sacred Violence*, 3.

constituencies within that community. As Biale has argued, a key constituency is women: blood discourses in the Hebrew Bible concerning sex, animal slaughter, and criminality index priestly authority over food and over women.[75]

The art at Saint Catherine's and Saint Antony's and the accounts of child killings and averted killings in *Sayings* Christianize and transform some of the discourses of blood found in the Christian Old Testament, but they retain an indexing function. Child killing is authorized in the context of prefiguring or conducting the priestly act of distributing the eucharist. Child killing is rationalized as a martyrdom, virginal offering, or precursor to monastic conversion. Child killing is also questioned through the mimetic act of identifying with Isaac or Jephthah's daughter.

Jay is especially interested in how sacrificial rituals between and performed by men establish and perpetuate explicitly patrilineal lines of descent. She writes, "Man born of woman may be destined to die, but man integrated into an 'eternal' social order to that degree transcends mortality."[76] Sacrifice, with its "twofold movement" of "integration and differentiation," or "communion and expiation," in her words,

> is beautifully suited for identifying and maintaining patrilineal descent. Sacrifice can expiate, get rid of, the consequences of having been born of woman . . . and at the same time integrate the pure and eternal patrilineage. Sacrificially constituted descent, incorporating women's mortal children into an "eternal" (enduring through generations) kin group, in which membership is recognized by participation in sacrificial ritual, not merely by birth, enables a patrilineal group to transcend mortality in the same process in which it transcends birth.[77]

In other words, male ritual experts create male-to-male, patrilineal genealogies through sacrificial rituals of initiation and assimilation.

In three of the four tales from *Sayings* examined here, sacrificial child killings and attempted killings occur during or immediately prior to rituals of initiation, in which the monks enter a patrilineal group and differentiate themselves from others. The fourth (the killing of the Christ child) occurs during a ritual of transformation (the eucharist) in which the monks join the ranks of Christian orthodoxy. Likewise, the art in St. Catherine's and St. Antony's monasteries affirms (male) priestly authority (by invoking

---

[75] See the treatment of sacrifice and priestly power in Biale, *Blood and Belief*, 13.
[76] Jay, *Throughout Your Generations Forever*, 39.
[77] Jay, *Throughout Your Generations Forever*, 40. As McClymond notes, Jay's attention to expiation is very Girardian, in that sacrifice rids a community of a perceived problem – namely, women or biological descent (*Beyond Sacred Violence*, 45).

prefigurements of Christ and the eucharist) as well as the sacred boundary of the celibate male community (by depicting the virginal sacrifice of Jephthah's daughter). These textual and visual acts of sacrificial child killings are a socially and culturally generative process that allows celibate men to regenerate their own social group, one not dependent on biological reproduction but nonetheless one in which fathers beget sons who carry on a social and cultural legacy.

Conclusions

The role of sacrifice in constructing an exclusively male, sacred, authoritative community is not unproblematized in the Egyptian monastic material. On one hand, the story in *Sayings* narrating Apollo's crimes confirms Jay's insights: his murders propel him to join the monastery, where the killing of the *woman* does not jeopardize his relationship with God and his status as a monk. On the other hand, the inclusion of Jephthah's daughter simultaneously affirms and troubles the patriarchal paradigm. The girl dies at the hand of a father who lives on as a righteous man in Christian culture. But at the same time, her presence in the monastic churches demonstrates that masculinity cannot subsume into itself all the social contributions and cultural codes women provide. While the priest may identify with the fathers, the monk may identify with them or with the girl. The texts and paintings contribute to a rich and multifaceted symbolic culture.

In the texts and art examined here, sacrificial events represent a transformation of sacrificial rituals but do not translate into a simple one-to-one replacement of sacrifice with ascetic renunciation. Just as the sacrifices in Genesis and Judges allow for and enable the genesis and survival of a sacred community as well as the production and continuation of a sacred genealogy, child killings and attempted killings in monastic art and literature result in the creation and continuation of a sacred monastic community, organized as much around ascetic mimesis, genealogical production, theological orthodoxy, and sacred authority as around familial renunciation.

In this way, the central tenet of familial renunciation stands not in contrast to but in creative tension with other monastic discourses and practices that preserve family. The following chapter examines this dynamic in accounts of monks healing children.

CHAPTER 5

Monastic Family Values
The Healing of Children

Monastic culture represents children as problems, as barriers to the ascetic endeavor, judging by the material in the previous two chapters. Whether potential sexual temptations or symbols of sacrifice, children are config-ured by many adult monks as obstacles to overcome or avoid. This under-standing of the function of children in a monastic "family" runs through monastic literature, beyond the passages examined in the previous chapter. Material on children, sex, and sacrifice are the tip of the iceberg. For example, the Greek *Sayings of the Desert Fathers* contains the following apothegm, which encapsulates this view of children:

> Abba Olympius of the Cells was tempted to fornication. His thoughts said to him, "Go, and take a wife." He got up, found some mud, made a woman and said to himself, "Here is your wife, now you must work hard in order to feed her." So he worked, giving himself a great deal of trouble. The next day, making some mud again, he formed it into a girl and said to his thoughts, "Your wife has had a child, you must work harder so as to be able to feed her and clothe your child." So, he wore himself out doing this, and said to his thoughts, "I cannot bear this weariness any longer." They answered, "If you cannot bear such weariness, stop wanting a wife." God, seeing his efforts, took away the conflict from him and he was at peace.[1]

Family and children, Olympius learns, are incompatible with monasti-cism. As Douglas Burton-Christie has observed, the desert fathers and mothers have long weathered criticisms for being, at their core, "antisocial and anticultural, thereby contributing notably to the decay of humane culture and civilization in late antiquity."[2] The disdain for traditional family and children, the building blocks of late ancient Mediterranean society, shown in this saying surely contributed to such scholarly dismissals

---

[1] *AP* Olympius 2, in *PG* 65:313–16; trans. Ward, *Sayings of the Desert Fathers*, 160–61.
[2] Burton-Christie, *Word in the Desert*, 11. Burton-Christie is summarizing earlier scholarship, with which he disagrees.

of early monasticism. The scholarship of recent decades has gone a long way toward reorienting our view of the roles of asceticism and monasticism in the mainstream economies, politics, and institutions of late antiquity.[3] Nonetheless, the strong ideological threads about children and family already examined in this book still exist; the traditional family and household as classically conceived can still seem a realm far removed from the holy men and women of Egypt. Early monasteries organized and represented themselves as alternative forms of family, but the men and women within these communities were nonetheless encouraged to withdraw from traditional family structures and kinship networks. Olympius' story is but one among many passages – whether literary or prescriptive – depicting familial renunciation at the heart of early Egyptian monasticism.

After reading about child sacrifice in the previous chapter, we would be tempted to conclude that early Egyptian monks *had* no "family values" – that they were anti-family. In fact, one of the tensions in our sources is that the literature of family renunciation and child sacrifice exists alongside numerous literary accounts of monks healing sick children. This chapter argues that such accounts constitute another thread in Egyptian monasticism, one that construed children as symbolizing the future, as representatives of familial and cultural legacies. Early Egyptian monasticism shared this understanding of children and family with the larger Roman world. Monasteries, in their care for sick or demonically possessed children, acted as agents in the support and continuation of traditional families. Lay Christians corresponded with monks to request their intercessory prayers for sick children and even brought children to monks for healing. In this way, monasteries – communities of celibate ascetics – guaranteed the regeneration of Christian families.

The family – the traditional ancient family, children and all – remained a core value for the monks of late antique Egypt. This chapter examines the phenomenon of holy people who heal children in *Sayings of the Desert Fathers*, evidence from Shenoute's monastery, and documentary sources from late antique Egypt. These diverse texts converge to present us with an account of Egyptian monasticism as an institution dedicated to the promotion and perpetuation of human society through the health and welfare of the child. Monasteries, in their care for children, acted as alternative, nonbiological family systems *and* as agents in the support and continuation

---

[3] Jacobs and Krawiec, "Fathers Know Best?"; Jacobs, "Let Him Guard Pietas"; Krawiec, "From the Womb of the Church"; Cooper, *Fall of the Roman Household*; Cooper, "Household and the Desert"; Vuolanto, *Children and Asceticism*; Vuolanto, "Early Christian Communities As Family Networks."

of traditional families. People brought their children to monks to be healed, and these communities of respected ascetics (who had in turn given up their children or their potential to have children) ensured the survival of the next generation of Christian families through their acts of healing and exorcising.

Healing and Exorcism in *Sayings of the Desert Fathers*

The two stories of healed or exorcised children in the Alphabetical Collection of the Greek *Apophthegmata Patrum* (*Sayings of the Desert Fathers*) exemplify the symbolic role of children as Christian society's future as well as the social role of monastic communities in sustaining both children and the institution of the family. These tales are attributed to two of the most revered monks in the tradition: Macarius the Great and Poemen. Like the accounts about other monks already discussed in this book, these texts cannot be taken as historically accurate biographies of their subjects, but they can be read as literary vehicles for monastic values and ideologies.

Both stories speak to the intense emotional effects an infirm child could have on the family. In each account, a weeping father brings his son to the monk for a miracle. The fathers' emotional outpourings may stem from grief due to personal attachment to their children or to the social and economic effect a disabled or dead child could have on the family, or both. Regardless, the message is clear: an infirm child could leave a family distraught. In the first story, which also appears in the Sahidic Coptic collection of *Sayings*, the weeping father brings his "paralytic son" to Macarius' cell and places the child on the doorstep. The father removes himself to "a good distance away" but does not abandon the child. The monk asks the boy, "Who brought you here?" When the child answers, "My father threw me down here and went away," Macarius instructs him to "Get up, and go back to him." The son arises, walks back to his father, and they return home together.[4] Macarius' miracle not only heals a child but also promotes family cohesion. The final tableau is of father and son traveling home together.

This account is particularly poignant given the story of Macarius' own entry into the ascetic community of Scetis, as recounted elsewhere in the

---

[4] *AP* Macarius the Great 15, in *PG* 65:269; trans. Ward, *Sayings of the Desert Fathers*, 130. For the Sahidic Coptic version: *AP* no. 224 in Chaîne, *Le manuscrit de la version copte*, 65. See the chart of the *AP* in multiple languages in Regnault, *Les sentences des Pères*, 222–23.

Greek alphabetical and Sahidic Coptic *Sayings*. A pregnant young woman accuses Macarius, an anchorite and solitary monk at the time, of fathering her unborn child. Publicly berated and humiliated, Macarius supports the woman throughout her pregnancy. She is unable to give birth at the appropriate time, however, and only bears the child after admitting her lie and acquitting Macarius of the charges. The monk only then flees the region for the monastic community at Scetis.[5] When faced with the prospect of a child needing paternal care, Macarius does not abandon the responsibilities imposed on him, even though in the context of the narrative, they are imposed unjustly. Thus the celibate anchorite does not actually renounce family or familial obligations either on a personal level or a conceptual level.

His actions are not just a matter of "doing the right thing" morally to a woman whose virginity he supposedly took. At least one other account in *Sayings* testifies to the financial and emotional distress placed upon families when the male breadwinner abandons his dependents. As discussed in Chapters 1 and 3 of this book, the Greek *Sayings* claim that when Carion became a monk, he left behind a wife, a daughter, and a son. During a famine, his wife comes to him, demanding he look after his children.[6] Such literary accounts of paternal social and economic responsibility have parallels in social reality, as we see from letters written by Egyptian women themselves. Women quite often capably handled the business of the household and trade (see, for example, the letter of Thermouthas, describing her handling of taxes, agriculture, and property leasing).[7] Nonetheless, in times of economic crisis, the absence of a husband or other male head of household could exacerbate financial hardship. During the Ptolemaic era, a woman named Isias writes to Hephaistion (her brother or husband), who had been "in detention in the Serapieion in Memphis" and subsequently released. Isias accuses him of staying away deliberately ("But you have not even thought about coming home") and reports that his "long" absence during "crises" has caused

---

[5] *AP* Macarius the Great 1, in *PG* 65:257–260; trans. Ward, *Sayings of the Desert Fathers*, 124–25. See also no. 101 in Chaîne, *Le manuscrit de la version copte*, 23; Regnault, *Les sentences des Pères*, 222–23.

[6] *AP* Carion 2, in *PG* 65:249–52; trans. Ward, *Sayings of the Desert Fathers*, 117–18. This text is not attested in the published surviving Sahidic and Bohairic Coptic *Sayings*, but it may have circulated in Coptic in antiquity; it was translated into Armenian. See the chart in Regnault, *Les sentences des Pères*, 220–21.

[7] *BGU* 3.822; trans. Bagnall and Cribiore, *Women's Letters from Ancient Egypt*, 191. See also the letter of another Thermouthis, from the Roman period, writing to her husband about family business: *SB* 14.11585; trans. Rowlandson, *Women and Society*, 326–27.

distress and difficulty for the whole household.[8] Dionysia of the
Heracleopolite nome writes to an official for legal recourse against
her estranged husband, who had abandoned her two years prior and
moved to Alexandria with another woman. She seeks the return of her
dowry and claims that in his absence, she and her child are clothed "in
rags" and "lack even basic nourishment"; her brother was supporting
her.[9] In the first century, a woman named Claudia Dionysia writes to
her brother or husband telling him about her extended illness and
requesting that he quickly send an "allowance" from the money gained
from the sale of various goods of hers.[10] Finally, a seventh-century
Coptic divorce petition records a demand for alimony owed to an
unnamed woman by her estranged husband, Paul, who had abandoned
her and the children and stopped paying the agreed-upon alimony.
The woman reports that she is ill and requires the funds for her basic
needs.[11] These letters and legal records demonstrate that in both
ancient and late ancient Egypt, women with children could find
themselves in precarious economic straits if abandoned by the head
of their household. Moreover, these women's letters highlight the legal
and social obligations they and their community expected of the men.
This context helps us understand the unspoken background to the
story in *Sayings* about Macarius. Macarius' commitment to the woman
expresses a social and financial commitment, one he makes due to
communal expectations and economic realities.

When Abba Poemen heals a child with a deformity caused by
demon possession, he too acknowledges the power and necessity of
familial relations. One of Poemen's relatives has a son whose face has
been turned backward, but the father fears approaching Poemen
directly for an exorcism and cure because Poemen has a reputation
for desiring solitude and isolation from the laity. The man has come to
visit Poemen previously, but whenever the Abba has heard about his
relative's visit, Poemen has driven him away. This father also weeps
over the fate of his child, and over the possibility that he will never be
healed. Another monk approaches Poemen on the man's behalf. The
other "old man" wisely first brings the child to the "lesser brethren,"
who all perform the sign of the cross over him. Then he turns to
Poemen, who at first is reluctant to do the same. Rather grudgingly,

---

[8] *UPZ* I.59; trans. Bagnall and Cribiore, *Women's Letters from Ancient Egypt*, 111.
[9] *BGU* 8.1848; trans. Rowlandson, *Women and Society*, 170–71.
[10] *SB* 5.7743; trans. Rowlandson, *Women and Society*, 343.
[11] Till, "Eine koptische Alimentenforderung," 71–78; trans. Rowlandson, *Women and Society*, 216.

after encouragement from the other holy men, Poemen stands over the boy, recites, "God, heal your creature, that he be not ruled by the enemy," and makes the sign of the cross. The child is cured.[12]

Poemen's apothegm neatly fits within the category of exorcisms and miracles that David Frankfurter and David Brakke characterize as "Christian narrative[s] of Christ's triumph over paganism."[13] The local populace in need of services from a "ritual expert" has turned from temple priest to Christian holy man. Moreover, the Christian "ritual expert" attributes his power to Christ or God, not to himself, the monk. This dynamic presents itself rather dramatically in Poemen's narrative. A lay Christian in desperate need of a healing turns to the most powerful holy man in his social network – his relative Poemen, who reluctantly delivers the cure but attributes the ritual power released in the performance of the sign of the cross to a source outside of himself and, in doing so, thus distances Christian miracle from pagan magic.[14] As Brakke argues, exorcisms were a significant vehicle for this cultural shift. "Exorcism was clearly the monastic gift of healing par excellence."[15]

Poemen's story exemplifies another equally significant cultural trend during this period of transition: the role of the institution of the family. Celibate monks who purportedly have renounced family ties nonetheless here affirm the social and emotional ties binding lay Christian families; moreover, the monks then enable these families to continue their legacy. *Sayings* thus portrays monks as crucial for the survival of the Christian family and the next generation of Christians in Egypt, alongside monks willing to sacrifice their own children (as discussed in Chapter 4). Albeit small in number, these narratives do more than depict a holy man as patron: a man (and for reasons that will become apparent later, I use the term "man" very deliberately) whose withdrawal signifies his intimacy with divine power and allows him to become the "focal point of religious transition" in late antiquity.[16] The role of children in these stories is striking given the fairly dominant anti-family rhetoric elsewhere in *Sayings*. These vignettes represent the monastic community, comprised of celibate individuals who often cut familial ties upon entry, as a vehicle for maintaining the stability of families and the health and welfare of children.

---

[12] *AP* Poemen 7, in *PG* 65:321; trans. Ward, *Sayings of the Desert Fathers*, 166. See also no. 229 in Chaîne, *Le manuscrit de la version copte*, 67–68; Regnault, *Les sentences des Pères*, 228–29.

[13] Brakke, *Demons*, 226; Frankfurter, "Perils of Love."   [14] Brakke, *Demons*, 229, 231.

[15] Brakke, *Demons*, 237.   [16] Brakke, *Demons*, 214.

A recently discovered manuscript also adds to our patchwork of sources on monastic exorcisms and healings of laity. Charles Hedrick identifies a codex fragment from Antinoe in Upper Egypt that describes an exorcism a monk named Herouoj performed upon a young girl.[17] The document dates to between the fourth and sixth centuries, the same period in which the stories in *Sayings* circulated and were collected. There are some indications that the account is a Coptic translation of an original Greek document. The manuscript recounts how a possessed girl was brought to Herouoj and his brethren. Herouoj stood in the middle of the other monks and prayed. A break appears in the text, and then it reports that Herouoj entered "the house of the man" (perhaps the child's father?), raised his hand over the girl, and exorcised her "in the name of Jesus."[18]

Each of these accounts presents holy people as central to the health of children and families alike. Moreover, they follow a trend found throughout late antique hagiography and the cult of the saints from the wider Mediterranean world. Across this period, lay Christian families sought out holy people to heal and exorcise infirm children.[19]

Monasteries and Children's Healthcare

Monastic involvement in the health of lay children is documented elsewhere in our sources from Egypt. Andrew Crislip's research has uncovered a medical codex at Shenoute's monastery, which contained remedies for "ailments one might not associate with monastic medicine, venereal ailments, and ailments of the breast." Although the codex postdates Shenoute's fourth- to fifth-century tenure by centuries, Crislip argues that "late ancient medicine maintained considerable continuity over time. ... So it is likely that the sorts of treatments therein reflect manuscript exemplars from earlier centuries."[20] The afflictions of the breast include swelling and difficulty lactating. As Crislip asks, why would a monastery need medical recipes to induce milk production? One answer is the nourishment of orphans at these communities; of course, these recipes could also simply form part of a larger medical corpus at the monastery, a part that remained unused. As Crislip remarks, Shenoute

---

[17] Hedrick, "Monastic Exorcism Text."

[18] The story seems patterned on *Sayings* because, at the end, Herouoj stands amongst his brothers and tells them everything that happened.

[19] Holman, "Sick Children and Healing Saints"; Holman, "Martyr-Saints and the Demon of Infant Mortality."

[20] Crislip, "Care for the Sick," 25–26.

himself banned monks from treating other men for genital afflictions and from treating women who were not members of his monastic communities – he calls them "women outsiders."[21] However, the very existence of this ban suggests that someone, somewhere in Shenoute's monastery, had treated or sought to treat female visitors, possibly even nursing mothers, who sought medical care from the monks. Thus, it may be that the text was not used in late antiquity, but it nonetheless raises a few possibilities for our understanding of monasteries in late antiquity, each of which involves the institution in the care of infants: monks treating lay women visitors, women at the monasteries serving as wet nurses, female monks entering with babies and children in tow, or even the large-scale treatment of women residing at the monastery during refugee crises (as occurred during Shenoute's tenure).[22]

Documentary sources testify to the phenomenon of lay Christians relying on the intercession of holy men for their health and healing, usually via a letter requesting prayers. Some specifically mention children or family. One woman references her status as the impoverished mother of a young child ("little Paniskos") in her request for prayers from Bishop Pisentius in Thebes; she wishes for him to pray to God to "lift up" her "ruined" eye.[23] In the mid-fourth century, a woman named Valeria writes to a monk named Papnouthis at the Hathor monastery asking for prayers for healing of an illness leading to "shortage of breath." She also seeks prayers for her daughters, husband, and household.[24] These prayer requests demonstrate the importance of the monastic community to the health of the lay community and also the importance of the health of the individual person (in these cases, the mother) for the well-being of the family. Pisentius' intercessory prayers on behalf of Paniskos' mother would, by extension, benefit the child as well.

Some of these interactions between monks and laity may have involved more tactile medical care, even if from a distance. We have at least one letter requesting the monk provide the letter-writer with some sort of medical or prayer regimen she herself can implement. A woman named Esther writes to a monk (probably a monk from the Monastery of Epiphanius at Thebes, where the letter was found), in distress over the deaths of her children. They have all died young. She asks the holy man for

[21] Crislip, "Care for the Sick," 26.

[22] See Shenoute, *Continuing to Glorify the Lord, Canons*, vol. 7, in Leipoldt, *Vita et Opera Omnia*, vol. 3, 69–74; Schroeder, *Monastic Bodies*, 93–94, 116–18.

[23] *O.CrumST* 360; trans. Bagnall and Cribiore, *Women's Letters from Ancient Egypt*, 240.

[24] *P.Lond.* 6.1926; trans. Bagnall and Cribiore, *Women's Letters from Ancient Egypt*, 205.

instruction and a "rule" she can follow to alleviate her situation.[25] Through prayer and other means, Egyptian holy people supported children and the continuity of lay Christian families through healing.

My final example of the relationships children forged between the monastic institution and the institution of the family comes from the famous child donation documents at Phoibammon's monastery near the city of Jême (in Western Thebes). These sources reveal a slightly different understanding of the monastery's commitment to children and their health. In these texts, the monastery often *replaces* the traditional Christian family unit by becoming the legal guardians (or perhaps owners) of the healed children. Moreover, some of these children come to the monastery after the monks or patron saints have cured them. The papyri thus document as a social phenomenon something portrayed in literary (and less historical) sources: parents who bring children to the monastery for healing.

Several papyri record contracts between the monastery and the parents, who promise their healed child to the community. According to one document, a mother, Tachel, gives birth to a premature boy, only to renege on her agreement to dedicate him to Phoibammon's monastery after he returned to health. When he falls ill again, she interprets his sickness as a punishment for failing to abide by her original promise, and so she reaffirms her commitment to dedicate her son, as the document states.[26] Other papyri record similar contracts, including one account of a boy brought back from the brink of death.[27] Although it is difficult to draw generalizations about Egyptian monasticism as a whole from this one set of unique documents, it is important to note that the practice at Phoibammon's monastery – local families taking their sick children to the monks for healing – conforms with social practices narrated in *Sayings* and hagiography.[28] The Phoibammon papyri, as documentary sources for contracts between the monastery and genuine historical individuals, confirm the established social practice of lay Christian families taking their sick children to monks for healing. At least at the monastery of Phoibammon, and possibly at other coenobitic communities, these children then were donated to the monastery.[29] Thus this practice both preserves the

---

[25] *O.Mon.Epiph.* 194; trans. Bagnall and Cribiore, *Women's Letters from Ancient Egypt*, 247.

[26] *P.KRU* 86.17–32; trans. Rowlandson, *Women and Society*, 299.   [27] *P.KRU* 91.7 and 100.21.

[28] On hagiography and saints' healing shrines, see also now Schenke, "Healing Shrines."

[29] For more on these documents, see Wilfong, *Women of Jeme*, 99–104; Richter, "What's in a Story?"; Papaconstantinou, "Notes sur les actes de donation d'enfants"; Schroeder, "Children in Early Egyptian Monasticism."

traditional family and also contributes to the reproduction of the monastic family.

Where Are the Holy Women?

Women, affiliated in modernity with children and domesticity, do not commonly appear in the late antique Egyptian monastic sources as ascetic healers of children. I have been unable to find a story or apothegm of an Amma or holy woman in Egypt who is approached for the healing or exorcism of a child. This stands in contrast to medical tradition in Roman Egypt, where women – whether in their capacity as midwives, nurses, wet nurses, or family members – cared for the health of other women and infants during and after childbirth.[30] The literary absence of holy women healers in Egypt also stands in contrast to the Cappadocian *Life of Macrina*, for example, where Macrina miraculously heals a young girl with a severe eye infection. The child's parents – a lay Christian woman and her husband, a soldier and lay Christian – visit her monastery (called a "school of virtue" in the text). Macrina holds the girl in her arms, kisses her eye, and promises them a drug to heal her ailment. After the family departs without receiving the medicine, the girl experiences a miraculous healing.[31] This parallel account of the healing of a lay Christian child by a holy *woman* follows the pattern of the literary portrayals of Egyptian holy *men*: a celibate holy person in a community of celibate Christians heals the ill or possessed child of a lay family, restoring the child's future and restoring the family to wholeness.

The ascetic women of hagiography and *Sayings* were known for their gender-bending proclivities. As David Brakke has argued, women with reputations as great demon fighters (such as Syncletica) are culturally coded as men. The famed Syncletica represented "the triumphant manliness engendered in demonic combat."[32] The one monastic woman depicted in the later wall paintings at the cave church of the Monastery

---

[30] Draycott, "Approaches to Healing," 142–48; Parca, "Wet Nurses of Ptolemaic and Roman Egypt"; *P.Grenf.* 1.61, *P.Lond.* 3.951, *P.Mich.* 3.202; trans. Bagnall and Cribiore, *Women's Letters from Ancient Egypt*, 229, 265, 359–60.

[31] Gregory of Nyssa, *Vita S. Macrinae*, in *PG* 46:996–98; trans. Corrigan, *Life of Saint Macrina*; Corrigan, "Saint Macrina"; the latter is available free online as Corrigan, "Life of Macrina, by Gregory Bishop of Nyssa." See the discussion of this text and other healing accounts, including those by non-Egyptian female martyr saints, in Holman, "Sick Children and Healing Saints," 251–52.

[32] Brakke, *Demons*, 212.

of Saint Paul is Marina, who dressed as a man.[33] The ascetic women of Egypt are not typically represented *as women* when they tend to sick or possessed children. Traditions about two cases of women monks attending to children (Marina and Hilaria) present cross-dressing women saints as caretakers and healers. In other words, these women appear as men to the audiences for their miracles and caregiving. (Neither of these traditions *in Egypt*, however, can be securely dated to the primary period of our study.)[34] Marina, according to tradition, joined a male monastery with her father while a teenager; she cut her hair, dressed like a man, and enrolled as a man. After being (falsely) accused of impregnating a woman, Marina is expelled from the monastery and raises the child herself, all while living as a man. The other cross-dressing monk, Hilaria, reportedly lived in Scetis as the man Hilarion. Originally the daughter of Emperor Zeno, as the story goes, Hilaria/on exorcised a demon from a lay Christian child sent to Scetis – Hilaria/on's younger sister. While these literary traditions cannot be securely dated to late antiquity, they nonetheless reflect the trend we have seen in other literary texts about holy people healing children: in the Egyptian context, the holy person presents as male.

Thus, in sources about or from Egypt, either due to the gender ideology of our sources, our relative lack of extant evidence about late antique women, or actual social practice (or some combination thereof), these healings seemed to have been presented as the domain of holy *men*.

Conclusions

In the ways I have described, late antique Egyptian male monks supported the institution of the family or took the place of the institution of the family by healing and exorcizing Christian children. Despite the strong ascetic imperative to renounce family, practice celibacy, and avoid children

---

[33] Lyster, "Reviving a Lost Tradition," 225–26. Three other holy women (including one mother depicted with her adult son) appear in the program, but they are martyrs (Lyster, "Reviving a Lost Tradition," 220, 223).

[34] Patlagean, "La femme déguisée"; following Patlagean regarding Marina and Hilaria, see also Davis, "Crossed Texts, Crossed Sex," 4, 8; Vogt, "The Woman Monk," 142. The surviving manuscripts of the Coptic *Life of Marina* date to the tenth and eleventh centuries, and they contain narrative elements that do not appear in the Latin, Greek, and Syriac recensions (Hyvernat, "Vie de Sainte Marine," 137). Thus, it is difficult to date the Coptic *vita* securely to the fourth to sixth centuries. For text and translation of the Coptic *Life of Hilaria*, see Drescher, *Three Coptic Legends*. The primary manuscript of the Coptic *Life of Hilaria* dates to the ninth century, and there seems to have been no Greek original *vita* that predated the Coptic (Drescher, *Three Coptic Legends*, iii–v; Depuydt, *Catalogue of Coptic Manuscripts*; Pierpont Morgan Library, "M 583 Curatorial").

in our textual sources, an equally important countervailing trend emerges from this material. Instead of being antisocial and anti-cultural, early monasteries in fact functioned to promote the social, cultural, and familial reproduction of late antique society through caring for the health of children and their families.

PART III

A Social History

CHAPTER 6

Making New Monks
Children's Education, Discipline, and Ascetic Formation

The Pachomian corpus reports a heart-rending episode in which hungry children plead for more food. When Pachomius visits one of his many monasteries, he is welcomed by a boy who complains that he and the other children at the monastery have not been fed cooked vegetables or porridge since Pachomius' last visit, even though the monks were supposed to serve cooked food every Saturday and Sunday. The monastic leader admonishes the cook, who avers that the food was not being eaten because the monks were so ambitious in their asceticism. The cook had chosen to make mats rather than prepare wasted food. Pachomius responds by burning the man's mats and instructing the monk to care more for his brothers, for two reasons: first, one must prepare food so that monks have something to renounce; second, children and sick monks need more sustenance. Chiding the cook, Pachomius asks, "Or do you not know that boys especially are not able to continue in virtue unless they are granted some relaxation or small comfort?"[1]

Monks' attitudes toward the children in their midst were complex. As this vignette demonstrates, children were in some ways a special, protected class. The text in which it appears, the *Life of Pachomius*, is hagiography, designed to extol Pachomius' sanctity. Narratively, the tale reveals Pachomius' virtues and leadership when he recognizes, acknowledges, and accommodates children's vulnerability. Yet, without the wisdom of Pachomius, in his absence, the other monks have neglected their small charges, allowing them to go for weeks without cooked food. The *Life* thus also presents a tale of monks who have subordinated the children's needs to their adult ambitions.

---

[1] Pachomian *Paralipomena* 15, ch. 8; ed. and trans. Veilleux, *Pachomian Koinonia, Volume Two*, 36–38. According to Veilleux (*Pachomian Koinonia, Volume Two*, note on 68), "There is no indication in the Rules that the cooked meals were restricted to Saturdays and Sundays."

At every monastery for which evidence survives of children's presence, young people lived at this crossroads: in some ways protected from the harsh realities of the poverty-stricken world outside the monastic walls, in other ways still vulnerable to the whims, desires, and ambitions of the adult monks around them – monks who fully endorsed the late antique social and familial hierarchies in which children stood squarely on the lower rungs. Above the enslaved, but well below free adult men, children even in the monastery found their standing and status subject to negotiation. Valued and perhaps even loved, children were in many ways a gift; caring for them was regarded as a sacred duty commanded directly by God. Their many needs and challenges, however, remained secondary to those of their adult caregivers.

This chapter and the following one take the perspective of the child in these early communities. Using primarily monastic rules and letters, but also some hagiography, they reconstruct the life of the child to as much of an extent as possible. Shenoute's corpus provides the majority of our sources for this endeavor, with the Pachomian corpus as our second most important resource. Due to the complexities of the terminology for children in Shenoute's monastery, I have applied a distinctly conservative interpretive methodology to his corpus. As Chapter 2 has proven, not all mentions of "children" or "little ones" (*šēre šēm, šeere šēm, koui*) refer to minor children, especially in Shenoute's corpus. In these chapters, I examine the context of monastic writings about these classes of monks; only when the context indicates that the group *must* involve minors do I interpret the sources to be about children specifically rather than both children and adult junior monks. Throughout this chapter, when translating and analyzing Shenoute's writings in particular, I indicate which monastic population I am discussing, whether minor children or low-status monks of any age. The polysemic resonance of these terms in ancient Coptic culture makes the vocabulary linguistically distinct from our modern terminology of childhood. We must imagine that ancient monks found it as easy to distinguish between the *šeere šēm* of a young girl and the *šeere šēm* of a new adult *monachē* as it was for them to distinguish between a spiritual father and biological or adoptive father, or spiritual sister and biological sister. Material from papyri, inscriptions, hagiography, *Sayings*, and travel literature supplements the Shenoutean and Pachomian documents. Although much of children's lives remains shrouded from view, this analysis seeks to reorient our own perspective on ancient monasticism to see it from the eyes of a child.

This chapter focuses on the explicit shaping of monastic children into monks.[2] The next chapter presents what we can glean of the daily life of the monastic child based on the rules concerning their behavior and treatment.

Education and Discipline

A boy in the Pachomian communities received education and nurturing aimed at fashioning him into a future monk, according to the hagiographies. Girls, however, earn almost no mention in the entire Pachomian corpus. To assume that they received the same education, training, and care as boys would be to view the ancient monastery anachronistically, ignoring the ancient privileging of men over women in education and literacy. Nevertheless, at the same time we reconstruct the educational experience of boys, we can present some historically grounded hypotheses about girls in Pachomian and other coenobitic communities (such as Shenoute's monasteries) based on our knowledge of ancient childhood and education as well as the responsibilities of adult women in those communities.

Both the First Greek *Vita* and the Tenth Sahidic *Vita* portray a Pachomius who believed that caring for children in the monastery and raising them to be ascetics was a sacred task, one decreed to the monks by God. Caring for "children" and the "little ones" constituted a monastic obligation in accordance with God's will. Utilizing hagiography as a transparent witness to social history is problematic, but the sources can shed light on monastic life at the time the *vitae* were written (the late fourth and early fifth centuries) and on the basic social context of monasticism even in an earlier stage. Each *Vita* evinces a predominantly respectful attitude toward youth; children were valued for their potential as future ascetics.

But as the account of hungry children intimates, adult monks' attitudes toward the young may not always have been positive. The Pachomian sources express a multiplicity of views, some even paradoxical, toward children. On one hand, monks were expected to renounce their own families upon joining a monastery, eschewing both procreation and the ongoing care for family and children that could detract from a life of ascetic dedication. On the other hand, people who joined the monastery as children were believed to become better monks as adults; these children

[2] An important recent contribution to our understanding of prospective and new monks is Dilley, *Monasteries and the Care of Souls*, 21–96.

required care and supervision from the adult monks. The First Greek *Life of Pachomius* encapsulates this point. Pachomius, speaking of the gift of clairvoyance, asserts,

> It is easier for children to reach this degree, that, being obedient from their earliest age, they may eagerly strain ahead to the things that are before [Phil. 3:13] until they reach perfection [Eph. 4:13], like Samuel in the Temple [1 Sam. 2:18, 26]. For ground that has been cleared is ready to be planted with vines step by step, but fallow land can scarcely be planted with good seed after it has been cleaned with great toil.[3]

Children are a bit of a "blank slate," ready to be formed into little monks with divinely sanctioned instruction. Like new ground ready to receive and nurture the seed, they bear fruit more readily than those who come to the monastic life as adults. The latter are fallow land, requiring greater "toil" to cultivate holy fruit.

The Pachomian community thus shared a widespread ancient view of children, one most lucidly expressed by the Stoic philosopher Epictetus: "For what constitutes a child? Ignorance. What constitutes a child? Want of instruction; for they are our equals so far as their degree of knowledge permits."[4] Adults viewed children as bundles of potential, waiting to be formed into living fulfilments of adult expectations. Worthy of respect, but stripped of individual agency and choice, monastic children could look forward to an education and training designed to mature them into new versions of the adults around them.

The perfection that children were anticipated to "eagerly strain ahead" to achieve required diligent training and oversight. Frequent and intense education greeted them in the monastery, according to the Tenth Sahidic *Life*:

> [Pachomius] set a little one in the midst of his disciples saying, "'Anyone who shall receive a young child such as this in my name receives me [Matt. 18:2, 10:42, 18:5].' But as for other little ones who have acquired an evil bent in their [youth] . . . [the manuscript breaks off for a few words] . . . [as Solomon] says, 'Anyone who lives wantonly from his youth shall become a slave [Prov. 31:21].' And so my brothers, every young child as well as those who are older whom the Lord has brought to us for the rebirth, let us be zealous . . . many times, let us teach them."[5]

---

[3] *V. Pach. G*[r] 49; ed. and trans. Veilleux, *Pachomian Koinonia, Volume One*, 331.

[4] Epictetus, *Discourses* book 2, ch. 1; trans. Higginson, *Works of Epictetus*, http://data.perseus.org/citations/urn:cts:greekLit:tlg0557.tlg001.perseus-eng2:2.1

[5] *V. Pach. S*[10] Fragment 2, in Lefort, *S. Pachomii Vitae Sahidice Scripta*, 33–34; ed. and trans. Veilleux, *Pachomian Koinonia, Volume One*, 451–52.

Although hagiography rather than a monastic rule, this text encapsulates the values of the Pachomian *koinonia* with respect to children. The Pachomian monastery prioritized the education and ascetic formation of its newest members from childhood on. A child in the community was valued, albeit not in the way a contemporary American adult might express her or his appreciation for children, as autonomous beings in and of themselves who have their whole futures ahead of them to be determined. The Pachomian *koinonia* valued children, but specifically as potential ascetics.

Children progressed through a precise and graduated educational program in the monastery.[6] This monastic *paideia* extended to the youth and to people who had joined the community as adults. First, they were taught that God was the creator of humans as well as "heaven and earth, the sun and moon" (a cosmological detail that may be a nod to the Origenist controversy or other heresiological debates).[7] Then they were to learn to bless God "without ceasing," either aloud or in their hearts. After this basic level of theological understanding came the pursuit of more specific educational goals, which matched the traditional spiritual practices of monks in Egypt. They should learn scripture and specifically memorize the Psalms.[8] Then they progressed to several stages that would implement the proper (in a monastic sense) interpretation and application of their previous knowledge. They learned "what is pleasing to God, and his will from his law," followed by the rules of the monastery and the imperative of the "golden rule" to "love their neighbor as themselves." Additionally, they learned to discern authentic scripture from heresy. The ultimate goal of this educational program was to nurture a spiritual development that worked in concert with ascetic bodily discipline, "so that, if they keep their body pure from their youth up, they may become temples of the Lord and the Holy Spirit may dwell in them."[9] (The passage uses both common Coptic terms for boys or children: *koui* and *šēre šēm*.)

Boys certainly advanced through this educational program as they matured. Girls, who are neither explicitly included nor specifically excluded from this curriculum, were probably schooled similarly. The

---

[6] Dilley's recent work on cognition and monastic *paideia* in Egypt should also be consulted (*Monasteries and the Care of Souls*, esp. 110–47).

[7] On the role of astrology and charges of "astral determinism" in the Origenist controversy, see Clark, *Origenist Controversy*, 166–67, 177–78, 198–201, 218–19, 231.

[8] Goehring, "New Frontiers," 181.

[9] *V. Pach. Sʰ* Fragment 2 in Lefort, *S. Pachomii Vitae Sahidice Scripta*, 33–36; ed. and trans. Veilleux, *Pachomian Koinonia, Volume One*, 451–52.

women's communities in both the Shenoutean and Pachomian federations were closely guarded, with restrictions on visits from men or to the men's community. Consequently, girls were not educated alongside boys, but they probably received some sort of instruction within the women's monasteries. Typically, neither impoverished girls nor impoverished boys received advanced education beyond training in the family's vocations or manual labor. Girls, especially those from wealthier families, received additional education; both the famous mathematician and philosopher Hypatia and the ascetic teacher and biblical translator Melania the Younger testify to the possibility for elite pagan and Christian women to progress beyond even an advanced education in grammar and rhetoric to philosophical or theological training.

Monastic children, along with illiterate adults, must have received instruction in reading and writing. Thus far, no literacy program specifically for children has been found among the Pachomian and Shenoutean sources. The Pachomian rules stipulate that memorization of scripture was required for all monks, though the curriculum may have relied as much on listening and recitation as on reading or writing. The regulations also report that illiterate new monks were nonetheless trained to read, regardless of their own desire to learn:

> And if he is illiterate, he shall go at the first, third, and sixth hours to someone who can teach and has been appointed for him. He shall stand before him and learn very studiously with all gratitude. Then the fundamentals of a syllable, the verbs, and nouns shall be written for him and even if he does not want to, he shall be compelled to read. There shall be no one whatever in the monastery who does not learn to read and does not memorize something of the Scriptures.[10]

Children, in all likelihood, were not exempt from this requirement. As Raffaella Cribiore has argued, the educational program for Egyptian children did not differ from adult instruction: "Since ancient society considered children miniature adults without tastes and talents of their own, it is no surprise that with very few exceptions, not only the formats but also the contents of books and instruction were identical to those offered to an adult public."[11] Quite possibly girls as well as boys learned to read and write in coenobitic monasteries. A tradition

---

[10] Pachomius, *Precepts* 140–41, in Boon, *Pachomiana Latina*, 50; ed. and trans. Veilleux, *Pachomian Koinonia, Volume Two*, 166.
[11] Cribiore, *Gymnastics of the Mind*, 178.

of providing school education to girls existed in Egypt, and some Christian scribes were girls or women.[12]

Reading, writing, and even book production were fundamental practices in late antique monasticism. The library and scriptorium of Shenoute's monastery, in particular, were famous in that region of Egypt, not only for the collection of manuscripts but also for distributing texts. The bishop of Alexandria wrote to Shenoute requesting he translate and distribute a letter about Origenism throughout the area, and the monastery's numerous manuscripts have provided a trove of source material for the modern scholar studying the Coptic Bible, Coptic liturgy, Coptic literature, and of course Coptic monasticism.[13] Even in the absence of direct evidence, we should from indirect evidence imagine that the monastery had an educational program, for the monks had to be literate in order to produce the kind of library it possessed. Hopefully, a program at Shenoute's monastery will emerge with the publication of critical editions of the materials. In the meantime, we should imagine that boys, and perhaps even girls, received instruction in literacy and penmanship.

At Shenoute's monastery, children were assigned caregivers and teachers who were expected to be neither frivolous nor idle. The rules suggest, however, that some guardians took ample time to joke and play with their charges, causing Shenoute concern.

> As for men who have boys who were entrusted to their care, if it is of no concern to them that they live self-indulgently, joking with them, and sporting with them, they will be removed from this task. For they are not fit to be entrusted with children. It is in this way also with women who have girls entrusted to them. But if they are children who grew up and they have reached the age of majority, then it will be done to them as it is written for us. If they are disobedient and they do not learn to be wise, they shall be cast out from us.[14]

From Shenoute's perspective, the senior monks appointed to care for the youth must take their duties seriously, not spending all their time playing or whiling away the days. If they do not teach children the serious ways of monasticism, then the children will grow up to be disobedient and foolish

[12] Cribiore, *Gymnastics of the Mind,* 85–87, 95–99; Haines-Eitzen, "Girls Trained in Beautiful Writing."

[13] Thompson, "Dioscorus and Shenoute"; Orlandi, "Library of the Monastery of Saint Shenoute."

[14] Shenoute, *Canons,* vol. 9, MONB.DF 186–87, in Leipoldt, *Vita et Opera Omnia,* vol. 4, 105–06; see excerpts and their translations in Layton, *Canons of Our Fathers,* 268–69. Alternatively, "men" and "boys" could be translated as "people" and "children." Thanks to H. Behlmer for assistance with the passage.

monks. Shenoute's expectations may be austere, but the fact that he articulates such a warning also suggests that even in his monastery, children indeed played with their tutors and guardians. Once the children reached the age of majority, they would be subject to the same rules and regulations as regular monks. Those who had not learned the ways of the monastery would be judged and banished.

Shenoute's concerns about contributing to the delinquency of a child through play may seem strict or even extreme by modern standards, since play resulted in severe punishment for the caregivers. But his concerns arise out of the same constellation of values and expectations expressed in the Pachomian sources; precisely because this category of monastic residents was valued for their potential as future monks, they needed to be raised with diligent care. Elsewhere in Shenoute's writings, children are protected from outright misconduct by their caregivers. In Volume 9 of the *Canons*, Shenoute calls out monks who avoid their own tasks but beat children to force them to work.[15] He also may call for the expulsion of monks who lead children (*šēre šēm*) to sin.[16] Elsewhere in his writings, Shenoute speaks about the moral agency of children and contends that children's own will does lead them astray even if first tempted by a demon; once they learn about "the judgment of God," they will "choose the good" for themselves.[17] Thus, the education of children is important.

Likewise, the first Greek *Life of Pachomius* shares Shenoute's belief that childrearing is a serious matter. Only the most advanced ascetic should be charged with the care of children, and even he must lean heavily on God: "As for the manner of keeping [the children], there is no need to say many words; one word is sufficient. The man who cleanses his own conscience to perfection [Heb. 9:14, 2 Cor. 7:1], in the fear of God and in truth, he it is who can keep the little ones with the Lord's help – for he needs his help."[18]

The regulations governing teachers and caregivers are stringent for two implicit reasons, reasons illuminated by the other passages about young

---

[15] Shenoute, *Canons*, vol. 9, MONB.YX 56, in Amélineau, *Contes et romans de l'Égypte chrétienne*, 280–81; trans. mine; see also excerpt and trans. in Layton, *Canons of Our Fathers*, 228–29.

[16] Shenoute, *Canons*, vol. 9, MONB.DF 178, in Leipoldt, *Vita et Opera Omnia*, vol. 4, 98; see also excerpts in Layton, *Canons of Our Fathers*, 260. Cf. an alternative translation and interpretation in Layton, *Canons of Our Fathers*, 261. Layton divides this passage into two separate rules.

[17] Shenoute, *As We Began to Preach*, *Discourses*, vol. 4, in Chassinat, *Le quatrième livre*, 80; trans. Brakke and Crislip, *Selected Discourses of Shenoute the Great*, 189–90. Note: what is translated as "young people" more literally means "concerning those who belong to the age of childhood" (David Brakke, personal correspondence, January 2016).

[18] *V. Pach. G¹* 49, in Halkin, *Sancti Pachomii Vitae Graecae*, 32; ed. and trans. Veilleux, *Pachomian Koinonia, Volume One*, 331.

people in the corpora. The Pachomian sources share with *Sayings* an anxiety about children's presence among adult monks, examined in the first part of this book. Both the Pachomian and Shenoutean rules prohibit one-on-one (and thus potentially sexual or intimate) contact between adults and children as well as between children themselves, as this chapter describes in more detail in what follows. The hagiographical Pachomius' insistence on appointing *only* a monk who has already achieved ascetic perfection is suggestive; such a monk would be the most trustworthy guardian of the children's sexual purity and of his own. The second reason is pedagogical: to ensure that they attain spiritual maturity, children require guidance from the most accomplished of mentors. As the quotation from the Greek *Life of Pachomius* cited earlier explains, such children, "obedient from their earliest age," more easily achieve "perfection." Such responsibility, the *Life* continues, requires an esteemed monk, and even he can only fulfill his duties "with the Lord's help."[19]

In this way, according to the Pachomian materials, people educated in the ascetic life as children become the most holy monks. These excerpts tell us something about the theory of asceticism in the monastery and about the perceived role of children; they were not all considered temporary residents. Shenoute similarly expects that the children will become monks, bound by the rules that regulate all in the community once they reach adulthood. Assiduous care must be given to their education and upbringing, to ensure that they reach their full ascetic potential.

Extant sources about the discipline of children in Egyptian monasteries are scant.[20] At Shenoute's monastery, where we know that male monks received beatings on their body and female monks on the soles of their feet, we find at least one surviving reference to the corporal punishment of *šēre šēm*. Children (and perhaps novice monks) may be punished with beatings from their superiors, even without Shenoute's prior authorization. For all other monks, male and female, corporal punishment requires the approval of either Shenoute or his "Elder" (the man who ranks second in the monastery, after Shenoute). Children and novices remain the exception. Shenoute writes in a letter to the women's community about punishment for disobedience:

> But rather take care, O (you) wretched souls, lest – as you have cast from off yourselves submission to your brothers, so that they do not rule you by their instruction and their teaching in your domain in accord with the rules of

---

[19] *V. Pach. G¹* 49, in Veilleux, *Pachomian Koinonia, Volume One*, 331.
[20] On monasticism more broadly, see Hillner, "Monks and Children."

divinity from the first until now and forever – you submit in your domain rather to many masters, which are the demons and every sort of evil thing, and God becomes angry with you and brings on you a wrathful condemnation, because you submitted to your enemies, the demons, and their designs, which are full of every kind of wickedness, and (because) you have rather cast off from yourselves submission to your brothers and their good advice, when they know from God that there is a great injury and there is a great condemnation on everyone among us who will do anything for themselves on their own by their own authority without (approval by) the elder in our domain, whether man or woman, whether old (*noc*) or young (*koui*), including him who will deal one in our domain or in your domain a blow with a rod or a slap, with the exception of boys (*šēre šēm*) and girls (*šeere šēm*).[21]

In this way, the monastery resembled the ancient household or school, in which parents, teachers, and tutors could beat their minor children, pupils, or charges without permission from the *paterfamilias* for every specific incident. The authority to beat adult full monks is held solely by Shenoute (the father) and his Elder. According to Shenoute, the immediate superiors have the right to subject the lower-status residents to beatings. The supervising monks serve as the teachers and tutors and thus hold the power (via Shenoute's generic proxy, issued here in this text) to beat them.

This passage is grammatically complex for a couple of reasons, making the translation and interpretation of this important rule about children confusing. The passage bears the hallmarks of the typical Shenoutean style in which the relationship between clauses is not always obvious: what precisely is the "exception" for boys and girls? The passage could be taken to mean that children were not allowed to be beaten at all; in this interpretation, the "exception" of boys and girls would mean that they are not to be beaten at all "with a rod or a slap." My translation and interpretation reach quite the opposite conclusion, however, because of the placement of the clause. The exception concerns not who can be beaten but under what authority a monk can be beaten. No one can be beaten without Shenoute or his associate's authorization, except for children (who can be beaten without their approval). Another complication is that the terms for "boys and girls," as we have seen, are multivalent; it is possible that "boys and girls" here means not children but the monastery's lowest rank of spiritual children – novices or junior monks.

---

[21] Shenoute, *Canons*, vol. 4, MONB.BZ 326–27, in Young, *Coptic Manuscripts*, vol. 1, 92–94, trans. Young, mod.

The tradition of corporal punishment in Egypt and the wider Mediterranean also suggests that my interpretation is the correct one. Unlike in the traditional household, free adults in a monastery could be beaten.[22] In Shenoute's federation, the immediate supervisors of children and/or junior monks have permission to beat their novices, just as teachers, tutors, and mothers in the Greco-Roman world had permission to beat their students or children. The monastery thus mirrors both the late antique family and the late antique grammar school. The rights of *patria potestas* lie solely in the hands of Shenoute and his second-in-command; as the monastery's *paterfamilias*, Shenoute outlines the rights consigned to his deputy as well as the lower-level house leaders and supervisors, which include the rights to beat novices or children in the course of regular discipline and instruction, as one would see in a school. As Cribiore has demonstrated, corporal punishment was standard in the lower-level schools of Greco-Roman Egypt; beatings lessened (though did not disappear) only as the male pupils advanced to the age at which they were expected to learn how to be the dominant person of the household, in other words, how to be the one who meted out punishment rather than endured it.[23] At Shenoute's monastery, only Shenoute or his delegate, acting in the role of the head of household, could increase or lessen punishments originally established by the community's father/*pater*, Shenoute. This policy has a gendered dimension. In the past, the women at Shenoute's monastery were responsible for more of their own discipline. The "mother" of the community determined who should be punished and how. During his tenure as leader of the federation, Shenoute expanded his authority and thus constrained some of the women's community's self-determination.[24] This realignment of power was indeed gendered and gendered in such a way that the authority of the monastic superior more closely resembled paternal authority in Greco-Roman families. This rule, as applied to adult novices, exemplifies the way in which the novitiate represented socially (not just linguistically) an extended childhood.

Children As Monks

At the Shenoutean and Pachomian federations as well as the later Naqlun Monastery, children and adolescents lived in the communities with the expectation (at least on the part of their adult compatriots) that many

---

[22] Hillner, "Monks and Children," esp. 783–84.   [23] Cribiore, *Gymnastics of the Mind*, 69–71.
[24] Krawiec, "Role of the Female Elder"; Krawiec, *Shenoute and the Women*, 53–54.

would become monks upon reaching adulthood. Some scholarship on monastic childhood presumes that the children in early monastic communities resided there temporarily and would likely have left upon reaching the age of adulthood. This hypothesis assumes boys as the paradigm for children and follows from the laws and customs of late antique Egypt, which allowed men in particular more independence upon reaching maturity. It also draws on the example of Basil's monastery in Cappadocia. Young women would have required the support of family or friends outside the monastery in order to leave (much as the "runaway bride" discussed in this book's introduction fled her husband and sought refuge in the household of a Christian family).[25] Certainly young male adults would have had the option to leave, but a close reading of the surviving documents suggests that many likely did not. Moreover, in Cappadocia, some boys were apprenticed to tradespeople outside the monastery, but even there, others were expected to become monks; if they so chose, they could take the monastic vow only upon reaching the age of majority.[26] I have found no evidence for such outside apprenticeships in Egyptian monasteries of the fourth through fifth centuries.

Before examining the Egyptian textual evidence more closely, let us consider the social and economic status of these young adults and what options remained open to them. These children had grown up in a monastery because their families also lived in the monastery or they had no family on the outside able or willing to care for them. Thus, most of the young men had no family to whom they could return upon leaving the community – no family business or farm at which to work, no family trade to learn and with which to apprentice, no family household in which to live while developing a trade or occupation. Most of the young women would have had no family household in which to live, no guardians to provide a dowry upon marriage, no relatives concerned enough to arrange a marriage. Exceptions surely existed, but it seems more likely than not that these new adults had little to no social network upon which they could rely after leaving the monastery. Even if the men had developed trade skills while working in the monastery, they would have still had to find people to hire or apprentice them or figure out ways to establish their own shops. Studies of contemporary children in foster care demonstrate that the attainment of legal adulthood brings significant challenges along with liberatory independence. Children who age out of foster care face increased

---

[25] *O.Lips.Copt.* 24; see also the discussion in Cromwell, "Runaway Child Bride."
[26] Vuolanto, *Children and Asceticism*, 102–04; Miller, "Charitable Institutions," 623.

risk of homelessness and other challenges.[27] Young adulthood in late antique Egypt, of course, differs dramatically from contemporary America, but foster children who age out of the system do share a number of characteristics with children who lived in monasteries: the absence of a household to shelter and support them during a transition; lack of parental figures or other adults to provide or finance education and training; and an expectation that they can support themselves as adults. Arguably, children who have aged out of foster care have a few advantages over their ancient analogues: they have had access to the same educational system as other children; they have developed friendships, social networks, and professional networks which are not circumscribed by the walls of their foster families' households. And yet many of these young adults struggle without the household and social support of their foster families as they launch into adulthood.

Children who "aged out" of late antique Egyptian monasteries chose to remain as monks, as a variety of textual evidence suggests. The Pachomian *vitae*, while they do not provide testimony from the perspectives of the children themselves, describe a community in which children are raised to be monks and indeed continue on in the community. The rules from the Naqlun Monastery to the north, examined further in the next chapter, also indicate that youth lived there with the expectation they would become monastics themselves; one of the regulations about interactions between monks and adolescents singles out young men who have not yet donned the monastic habit. The one ritual for joining a monastery or becoming a monk that is common among multiple communities is the donning of the monastic habit or cloak.[28] Thus, the rule's identification of adolescents who have not yet participated in this ritual means that some of the resident young people indeed did become monks as mature adults.

At Shenoute's federation, children may have been subject to some special regulations or exemptions when compared to the adult monks, but they were clearly regarded as living under the authority of the same overall monastic "Rule," even if more loosely or to a lesser degree than adults. Children were not placed outside the bounds of the rules but were seen as maturing into monastic tradition (and its rules) as they aged. Both Shenoute and his successor, Besa, write of this trajectory for children in the

---

[27] Dworsky and Courtney, "Homelessness"; Lee, Courtney, and Hook, "Formal Bonds"; Stott, "Placement Instability and Risky Behaviors"; Vaughn, Shook, and McMillen, "Aging Out of Foster Care and Legal Involvement"; Cunningham and Diversi, "Aging Out"; Scannapieco, Connell-Carrick, and Painter, "In Their Own Words."

[28] See note 37 in Chapter 4.

White Monastery Federation. Shenoute's charge to the monks supervising and educating children, discussed earlier, makes this clear: once children reach adulthood, "it will be done to them as it is written for us. If they are disobedient and they do not learn to be wise, they shall be cast out from us."[29] In other words, children receive education in the monastic rules so that they act in full obedience to those rules – as monks – as adults. Shenoute's admonishment also implies that many children do not go on to become monks; they refuse to be bound by the rules when they reach maturity and either leave or are forced to leave. (Moreover, as I discuss in the next chapter, children *before* the age of majority and novices were also subject to expulsion for a variety of reasons.)

Children who joined the monastery with their parents could be uprooted from their homes a second time if their parents broke the rules of the community. One entire family was expelled on account of the alleged misdeeds of the father. Although the monk's children seem to be blameless, they, along with his wife, share in the man's condemnation. Shenoute writes of the incident in Volume 4 of the *Canons*: "This one also whom we stripped of his monastic cloak, and his son, and his wife, and his daughter, whom we cast out immediately from the congregations of our fathers – you know all his hypocrisy and his pride and his lies and his false words and all his other evil deeds."[30] The son and daughter may be adult children rather than minors. However, elsewhere in the *Canons*, Shenoute carefully reminds monks that they are all brother, sister, father, son, mother, daughter to each other, regardless of the legal and biological ties they held prior to joining the community. Consequently, it seems possible that the son and daughter are underage – young children still legally tied to their guardians, minors who could not be separated from their parents without consequences for Shenoute and the monastery.

Accusations of just such a scandal swirled around Shenoute's successor, Besa. In a text in which he defends himself from accusations of various crimes (including murder), Besa attempts to refute an accusation that he is holding a child at the monastery against law or tradition. He writes,

> Do not think, brethren and men such as they are, that we have kept this little one until today, because of things that will perish, or because of matters such as we have heard that many have said. I tell you, and I declare before God

---

[29] Shenoute, *Canons*, vol. 9, MONB.DF 186–87, in Leipoldt, *Vita et Opera Omnia*, vol. 4, 105–6; see excerpts in Layton, *Canons of Our Fathers*, 268. Thanks to H. Behlmer for assistance with the passage.

[30] Shenoute, *Why O Lord, Canons*, vol. 4, MONB.BZ 59, in Leipoldt, *Vita et Opera Omnia*, vol. 3, 141.

and our Lord Jesus, that there is no such thing in my heart; but I fear God for the little innocent's sake, lest he be dragged to perdition, and lest sin before God be on our heads because we neglected a sinless soul; and we say that when he learns wisdom and knows good and evil, he is responsible, and there shall be no sin. He was given to God, and for that reason we have striven for him. But restless and wicked men who have progressed in evil, who err and who lead others astray [cf. 2 Tim. 3:13], are responsible because they have seized him by force against the will of God and against our will.[31]

Whether this child who had been "given to God" was an orphan, a runaway, or a child donated by living parents or guardians, we do not know. But Besa's language envisions a monastic future for the boy if the events he describes had not intervened. Apparently, the child has been removed from the monastery by outsiders (the "restless and wicked men"). Besa does not quote directly from the accusations laid against him, but he intimates that these people and their family, friends, or allies have accused him of kidnapping the child or holding him in the monastery either against the child's will, the family's will, the law or against social custom, and for less than holy purposes ("because of things that will perish, or because of matters such as we have heard that many have said"). Besa firmly asserts the most righteous of intentions and denies any wrongdoing. He admits that had the child remained in the monastery, he could have chosen to leave the community upon reaching the age of majority (when "he is responsible"). Besa insists, however, that the community's responsibility was to take him in and raise him, "lest sin before God be on our heads because we neglected a sinless soul." The phrase "given to God" to describe the child suggests that, in Besa's eyes, the boy was not at the monastery simply to be raised, educated, and then released back into the world. He was there to become a monk.

The Monastery of Phoibammon at Thebes constitutes our most ambiguous case regarding the status and future of children living in monasteries, since a number of papyri documenting child donations to the monastery or a healing shrine at the site have survived.[32] These papyri date to the eighth century, later than most material considered here; nonetheless, they lead us to ask questions about our earlier material. While we have extensive documentation of child donations, the language in the papyri indicates

[31] Besa, *Fragment 33*, in Kuhn, *Letters and Sermons of Besa*, vol. 1, 112–13; trans. vol. 2, 109. The text continues into *Fragment 34*.

[32] *P.KRU* 78–114; German trans. in Till, *Die koptischen Rechtsurkunden aus Theben*, 149–88; English trans. of some documents in MacCoull, "Child Donations and Child Saints," MacCoull, *Coptic Legal Documents*, and Schenke "Healing Shrines."

the children may *not* have been monks-in-training. These papyri were legal contracts in which the parents, who according to law and custom had absolute legal authority over their children, gave possession of the children to the monastery. As some papyrologists have noted, the legal force of the document is on the ownership of the child and the child's future production.[33] Arietta Papaconstantinou advocates for translating the Coptic term for these children's new status in the monastery (*hmhal* or *caouon*) as enslaved person or *hierodule* (enslaved temple servant).[34] Tasia and Pesynte's agreement regarding their son Panias indeed bears all the hallmarks of a contract: the obligations of both parties, names of witnesses, and an oath to God to honor the contract. The document stipulates that the monastery could decide in which capacity the child was to serve. Reflecting a terminology that was typical of documentary papyri from the region, it uses the word *topos* ("place") to refer to the institution of the monastery itself. The contract reports,

> We went to the *oikonomos*, who is the superior of the holy *topos*, Apa Surus, and said: The God of the *topos* has given the boy the gift of being healed. Do you wish that he come to the holy place and serve in it? God and you shall command it. Or do you wish that he hand over his labor to the holy place? We will give him in the way that you impose upon all the boys of the holy place.[35]

The family could choose to place their son in the monastery or pay the monastery earnings the child garnered. Typically the contract lasted into perpetuity, though some papyri specifically mention that the children could leave the monastery, either of their own free will or when expelled by the monastic superior.[36] In either case, the donated child (even as an adult) was required to give earnings to the monastery each year. The contracts include religious language, sometimes even a religious obligation. One child was specifically donated to "your [God's] altar."[37] Another donation document lists tending the altar lamps (a ritual duty) among the child's future responsibilities, in addition to the menial task of sweeping.[38] Other documents describe additional duties related to ritual

---

[33] Papaconstantinou provides a thorough survey of the field of scholarship on the child donation papyri in "Notes sur les actes de donation d'enfants." See also Wipszycka, "Donation of Children," 918–19, and Schenke, "Healing Shrines," 511.

[34] Papaconstantinou, "Notes sur les actes de donation d'enfants," 92–93 and 102.

[35] *P.KRU* 91; trans. MacCoull, "Child Donations and Child Saints," 410–11, mod.

[36] *P.KRU* 80, 96; see the discussion in Richter, "What's in a Story?" 240.

[37] *P.KRU* 79; trans. Wilfong, *Women of Jeme*, 102.

[38] *P.KRU* 80. See discussion and partial translation in Schenke, "Healing Shrines," 508–09; on tending lamps as a ritual duty, see Wilfong, *Women of Jeme*, 100.

or charitable tasks.[39] All the documents contain significant religiously inflected narration.[40]

Considerable scholarly debate has occurred over the status of the children: were they enslaved, oblates, or something else? The inclusion of religious language does not mean these children were *not* enslaved, property of the monastery; neither does the focus on labor preclude the children becoming monks. As we know from the Pachomian sources, Shenoutean sources, and other papyri about daily life in a monastery, manual labor in agriculture, mat production, and other fields constituted the bulk of a monk's duties. A monastery's economic survival depended on the monks' work. As Tonio Sebastian Richter has summarized, scholars have proposed four different ancient practices under which these child donations might be classified, none of which fully accounts for the evidence in the papyri: oblates, enslaved temple servants (*hierodoule*), child exposure, sales of dependents as enslaved people.[41] Richter instead proposes we consider these children as wards of the monastery. Most were sick, leading Richter to posit that they were children whose care posed a burden to their parents (due to illness, injury, demon possession, etc.); the boys were neither monks nor enslaved but rather people for whom family or community care was challenging and who were therefore entrusted to the monastery. In return, they performed rudimentary tasks but were not in training to become monks.[42] This hypothesis is based on a premise that chronically ill or disabled people were not accepted into the monastery as novices, an assumption that requires some further investigation; certainly monks already in the community who became sick, disabled, or mentally ill received care.[43] More recently, Gesa Schenke has argued that the children performed ritual and other labor as dedicated servants to a cultic healing shrine (a phenomenon attested more widely in late antique Egypt beyond this site). In this analysis, the children are neither monastic initiates, nor enslaved laborers for the monastery, nor disabled wards. Rather the children dedicate themselves to maintaining and serving the healing shrine of Saint Phoibammon, located at the monastery.[44] In sum, the status of the children is contested. Nevertheless, the language and circumstances of the documents indicate that the donated children,

---

[39] *P.KRU* 79; trans. Wilfong, *Women of Jeme*, 102. See Chapter 7 in this book for more on the duties of the donated children.

[40] Richter, "What's in a Story?"; Richter, "Pleasant and Unpleasant Emotions."

[41] Richter, "What's in a Story?" 246–54. [42] Richter, "What's in a Story?" 260–61.

[43] Crislip, *From Monastery to Hospital*; Crislip, "Care for the Sick."

[44] Schenke, "Healing Shrines," esp. 510–14.

whether monastic initiates or not, formed a special class within the community that performed ritually and economically significant labor.

Thus, at the most well-documented coenobitic monasteries of late antique Egypt, children lived in the community (at times with their guardians, at times without). In many cases, children were raised to become monks who would be knowledgeable in their communities' rules as well as in scripture, theology, reading, and writing. Some circumstances could result in their expulsion, but in many ways, they constituted a distinct class of residents (albeit a class integrated into the overall monastic hierarchy and social system), with exemptions from various regulations and expectations. Upon reaching the age of majority, children at communities like the White Monastery Federation could choose to stay, bound by the rules of their monasteries as monks themselves. The rules and life experiences of these children and adolescents are the subject of the next chapter.

CHAPTER 7

Breaking Rules and Telling Tales
Daily Life for Monastic Children

The previous chapter argued that children resided in some of the earliest monasteries in Egypt as a population that was both integrated into the fabric of monastic life and also set apart as special, since one of the prevailing ascetic theories in early monastic culture dictated that monks who began their training as children could become the most promising ascetics as adults. Such expectations for monastic children in turn shaped the education and ascetic formation monastic leaders developed for them. This chapter examines daily life in these monasteries, examining rules and narrative accounts to reconstruct the lives of these children. Many, many gaps remain, of course, and the nature of our sources means that this study represents a suggestive scholarly beginning rather than a comprehensive analysis. Yet the suggestions are enlightening, because these rules and narratives map for us the difficult terrain minor children navigated within a monastery. On one hand, the community offered a fairly stable home with food, healthcare, and educational opportunities for a lifetime. (Though, as we see in what follows, even children could be ejected from the monastic residence.) On the other hand, children were regarded as a challenge, even a danger, to adult monks, who often prioritized adults' needs and power over children's well-being. This chapter looks at these complexities with respect to sexuality, food, labor, health and disability, and even death.

Sexuality

As we saw in Chapter 3, the story in *Sayings of the Desert Fathers* about Zacharias wading into natron to mutilate his body after reaching adolescence places the expectation of sexual restraint and the blame for lustful indiscretion squarely on the youth. Children in coenobitic monasticism also faced regulations designed at times to protect them from adults' advances, at others to prevent their interactions with each other from going too far, and at still others to protect the adult monks' vow of celibacy while in the presence of sexually maturing youth.

Shenoute's monastery, which has the most detailed material about children as a whole, was governed by the most meticulous rules regarding children and sexuality. A few rules protect boys or girls from adults, but most presume that the child is the problematic element, someone who will inspire lust in others and thus must be constrained. Other rules acknowledge the challenges children face controlling their own desires. Adult monks are specifically prohibited from kissing a child with desire and from washing or anointing a child without prior permission.[1] One rule seems to anticipate (or respond to?) an excuse a monk might offer if caught red-handed with a youth: "Cursed is anyone who will defile and touch a child (*šēre šēm*) saying, 'I shall know whether he has come of age.'"[2] These rules may protect either party but definitively punish the adult or senior monk. Children themselves are prohibited from (and cursed for) engaging in activity with each other that might lead to sexual contact or desire, namely shaving each other or pulling a thorn out of another child's foot.[3] All of these restrictions appear in a list of rules at the beginning of Shenoute's first letter, an epistle written before he rose to leadership over the monastery. (Because of the reference to underage children specifically, I have translated the relevant terms in this section of Shenoute's works as words denoting minors: "child," "boy," and "girl."[4]) These regulations appear amidst other rules prohibiting sexual relations, masturbation, sexual touching, and passionate embraces by anyone of any age, rank, or gender.[5]

Shenoute also forbids those who supervise "boys and girls" from moving them to the front during prayer, because when one prays, one's face is too close to their feet and bodies. He orders a one-cubit distance between the monks and "boys and girls" and condemns anyone who causes the children and novices to move to the front. In the same passage, he also forbids embracing "boys and girls."[6]

---

[1] Shenoute, *Letter 1, Canons*, vol. 1, MONB.XC 7–8, in Schroeder, "Early Monastic Rule," 34–35; see also excerpts in Layton, *Canons of Our Fathers*, 92–96.

[2] Shenoute, *Letter 1, Canons*, vol. 1, MONB.XC 7–8, in Schroeder, "Early Monastic Rule," 34–35; see also excerpts in Layton, *Canons of Our Fathers*, 92–96.

[3] Shenoute, *Letter 1, Canons*, vol. 1, MONB.XC 7–8, in Schroeder, "Early Monastic Rule," 34–35; see also excerpts in Layton, *Canons of Our Fathers*, 92–96.

[4] See the discussion of *šēre šēm* and *šeere šēm* in Chapter 2.

[5] Shenoute, *Letter 1, Canons*, vol. 1, MONB.XC 7–8, in Schroeder, "Early Monastic Rule," 34–35; see also excerpts in Layton, *Canons of Our Fathers*, 92–96.

[6] Shenoute, *Canons*, vol. 9, MONB.DF 145–46, in Leipoldt, *Vita et Opera Omnia*, vol. 4, 95–96; see also excerpts in Layton, *Canons of Our Fathers*, 259.

Some regulations at Shenoute's monastery as well as those in the Pachomian *koinonia* and the rules at the semi-coenobitic, semi-anchoritic monastery of Naqlun express more concern for the purity and responsibility or maturity of adults than for protecting the children. Just as he admonishes caregivers to take their childrearing duties seriously (as we saw in the previous chapter), Shenoute also expresses concern that the monks supervising children and novices watch over them carefully in order to prevent them from engaging in desire-inducing activities. Girls and female novices as well as adult female monks should be prevented from peering through the barriers separating them from the male monks and priests visiting the women's residence for a funeral.[7]

The surviving rules from the Pachomian federation also prohibit intimate relations between monks and children, although they are less detailed. Jerome's translation of the rules requires adult monks to establish clear boundaries between themselves and the children, in order to prevent the formation of inappropriate relationships:

> If someone among the brothers is caught easily laughing and playing with boys and having friendships with those of tender years, he shall be admonished three times to withdraw from their intimacy and to be mindful of honesty and of the fear of God. If he does not desist, he shall receive the very severe punishment he deserves.[8]

The language of forbidden "friendship" in monastic literature typically serves as code for sexual, same-gender relationships.[9]

At Shenoute's monastery, it is possible that some sort of sexual relationship or encounter between a male monk and a child or novice was one of the catalysts leading to the leadership crisis in the community that eventually propelled Shenoute to the position as father of the federation. The manuscripts are fragmentary, making the social history difficult to reconstruct. Moreover, multiple incidents seem to be at issue. But one reading of the surviving texts points to an encounter involving sex with a child or novice, which Shenoute believed the monastic father at the time failed to address sufficiently. Such a sin may be part of the constellation of events

---

[7] Shenoute, *You God the Eternal, Canons,* vol. 5, MONB.XS 358–59 and MONB.XL 194, in Leipoldt, *Vita et Opera Omnia,* vol. 4, 63; see also excerpts in Layton, *Canons of Our Fathers,* 179, 181.

[8] Pachomius, *Precepts and Judgements* 7, in Boon, *Pachomiana Latina,* 66; ed. and trans. Veilleux, *Pachomian Koinonia, Volume Two,* 177.

[9] Wilfong, "Friendship and Physical Desire"; Behlmer, "Koptische Quellen"; Schroeder, "Prophecy and Porneia."

that led Shenoute to write his first two letters to the community, criticizing his monastic father for weak leadership.[10]

The rules at the Naqlun Monastery in the Fayyum, likely compiled later than the Shenoutean or Pachomian rules, attempt to disrupt all possible interactions between monks and children, alluding to the problems of sexual temptation inherent in such encounters.[11] In this community, adolescent boys could expect to be regarded as problematic, potentially disruptive. Their very membership in the community was at risk if adult monks engaged in relations with them. Some of the Naqlun rules are vague about the issue at stake, prohibiting situations that might lead to intimacy without necessarily invoking sex specifically. One prohibition charges monks never to speak with a boy, explaining that he will be a stumbling block. Another forbids conversing with a boy or young man. One regulation specifically alludes to homoeroticism, charging that discussions with children and adolescents lead to familiarity or friendship. Another authorizes the expulsion of any young man who has not yet donned the monastery's habit and has caused a "scandal." As mentioned in Chapter 1, this rule indicates that the young man in question would be living at the monastery to prepare for the ascetic life – a monk-in-training – rather than as a temporary lay visitor. Thus, at the Naqlun Monastery, concerns about sex motivated strict regulations of interactions between adult men and underage males.

The ubiquity of these rules combined with the traditions attested in *Sayings of the Desert Fathers* suggests that a child in the community faced sexually charged attention from his or her elders, especially as he or she reached puberty. In some monasteries, children could expect protection from sexual advances by adults but could also expect blame for such incidents. In others, like Naqlun, an adolescent would receive the brunt of the punishment and could even be expelled. Sexual contact *between* children or teens also faced scrutiny and incurred punishment.

Food

A child in either the Pachomian or Shenoutean federation could expect to receive food more frequently than the adult monks. One regulation in Shenoute's *Canons* specifically allows children to eat twice a day and gives

---

[10] Emmel, "Shenoute the Monk"; Schroeder, "Prophecy and Porneia"; Schroeder, *Monastic Bodies*, ch. 1.

[11] Wipszycka, "Apports de l'archéologie," 68–70; Derda, "Polish Excavations at Deir El-Naqlun," 124–30. The rule itself is published (with a Latin translation) in *PG* 40:1065–74.

Shenoute's Elder the authority to determine the mealtimes. Adult monks were typically allowed one meal a day in this federation, making two meals a generous allotment by the standards of the community. This section of Volume 5 of the *Canons* also allows old men and old women to eat twice a day.[12] Likewise, the sick (particularly monks with fevers) and those weary or injured from work may partake of additional food and water at the discretion of the male Elder. "Children" here probably means minor children, not novices, because in this section of the text Shenoute specifically singles out *physically* needy populations – the elderly, children, the sick, and the weary or injured.

I suspect that in addition to the two meals a day, children in Shenoute's monasteries regularly received a bit of extra food, probably bread, when hungry. This certainly seems to be the case at the Pachomian monasteries, where two texts record the care afforded to hungry children. In one hagiographical fragment (examined at the opening of Chapter 6), Pachomius chastises the adults, and especially the cook, for failing to feed prepared food to the children, admonishing them in this way: "Or do you not know that boys especially are not able to continue in virtue unless they are granted some relaxation or small comfort?"[13] Children need not, in fact should not, fast like adults. Moreover, adequate food and nutrition are foundations for the children's advancement in asceticism. Likewise, a rule in the regulations attributed to Horsiesius allows only children to eat some extra bread, as long as they take it out of the sight of other monks who are not eating: "Let no one, great (*noc*) or small (*koui*), eat before the signal is given to eat. If a little one (*koui*) wishes to eat, he may not eat at all in the oven-room or among the brothers who are not eating; rather let him be given bread and let him go elsewhere to eat by himself."[14] The Pachomian monasteries thus make accommodations for hungry children.

At least at Shenoute's monastery, however, extra bread is forbidden during the Lenten fast. This rule applies to all in the community, "whether male or female, whether great (*noc*) or small (*koui*)," but the "small" in this case likely refers to monks of junior rank or lower status in the community,

---

[12] Shenoute, *Canons*, vol. 5, MONB.XS 319 in Leipoldt, *Vita et Opera Omnia*, vol. 4, 53–54; see also excerpts in Layton, *Canons of Our Fathers*, 158.

[13] Pachomian *Paralipomena* 16, in Halkin, *Sancti Pachomii Vitae Graecae*, 140; ed. and trans. Veilleux, *Pachomian Koinonia, Volume Two*, 36–38.

[14] Horsiesius, *Reg.* 41, in Lefort, *Oeuvres de S. Pachôme*, vol. 1, 93; ed. and trans. Veilleux, *Pachomian Koinonia, Volume Two*, 210–11.

not minor children specifically.[15] We have no reason to believe that children were expressly included in this seasonal, ritual restriction of the diet; and although the rule does not explicitly exempt children, it seems geared primarily toward the adult population, given what we already know about exemptions from monastic fasting practices for the young, the elderly, the sick, and the weak.

Labor

In late antiquity, child labor was widespread, and children (like the adult monks) certainly worked at physically exerting tasks. Minor children were excluded from certain types of physical work at Shenoute's monastery, and Shenoute himself seemed particularly concerned that adults or established monks in the community not foist their own labors onto children. Junior monks (and possibly children) also had tasks designated for them (although not exclusively for them) in this monastic federation. Few examples of such rules survive, giving us only a tiny glimpse into the labor of children, but they are illuminating nonetheless. Some duties were carved out specifically for adults and senior monks, with another group designated as appropriate for children and junior monks with supervision.

Shenoute prohibits adolescents (*lelou šēm*) from one very specific task: the gathering of fruit, especially dates from the palms, either from the trees or from the fronds that have fallen to the ground. Such work is not "children's work," he says, especially with all the running to and fro involved. He also mentions cutting involved in the task; perhaps it was considered too dangerous for children, or they were frequently injured from the sharp palm fronds.[16] (Another passage in Shenoute's writings for monks identifies "plucking palm fronds" and "pulling out date-palm fibers" as particularly laborious.)[17]

---

[15] Shenoute, *Canons*, vol. 5, MONB.XL 185, in Leipoldt, *Vita et Opera Omnia*, vol. 4, 58–59; see also excerpts and different translation ("whether male, female, old, or young") in Layton, *Canons of Our Fathers*, 168–69.

[16] This rule appears twice in Volume 9 of the *Canons*: MONB.XK 198–99, in Amélineau, *Oeuvres de Schenoudi*, vol. 2, 516; MONB.DF 48, in Crum, *Catalogue of Coptic Manuscripts*, 84. These are not different copies (in different codices) of the same passage in the same place in the text in each codex; rather, the rule appears in a different place in the text in each codex. More work on Volume 9 of the *Canons* (including an edition and translation) is desirable.

[17] Shenoute, *Canons*, vol. 5, MONB.XS 319, in Leipoldt, *Vita et Opera Omnia*, vol. 4, 54; see also excerpts and trans. in Layton, *Canons of Our Fathers*, 161.

Monks who beat children and novices under their care in order to force them to work and yet are lazy themselves earn a censure from Shenoute: "Some people among us who strike and who beat children/novices (*ehenšēre šēm*) so that they do their work in the gathering (*synaxis*), but they themselves neglect to do it, though they are able – they are not upright."[18] Additionally, those who "forget" their work are "wicked," unless they do so because they are ill.[19] It is unclear whether the monastic leader is concerned about the children's welfare or the hypocrisy of their supervisory monks. He says nothing about children or novices being overworked, neither does he condemn the striking of children and novices per se. Nonetheless Shenoute deems the corporal punishment unfair and corrupt, because the monks punish those in their charge for the infractions they themselves commit (avoiding work) and possibly even are forcing the children to do labor assigned to adults.

In Shenoute's federation, children or novices are charged with at least two specific gender-segregated tasks related to religious ritual. Whenever the monks gather, the house director or his "second" should come with one or two other monks to distribute soaked reeds (materials for weaving mats).[20] Boys or male novices may fulfill this duty two at a time only if a senior, respected monk (lit. "a great/old man who fears God") accompanies them. Likewise, girls and female novices have a parallel regulation: they may light lamps for their gathering also only under the supervision of a house director, her second, or a senior, respected monk (lit. "a great/old woman who has fulfilled her faith and fear of the Lord"). The same rule also allows girls and female novices to distribute wool for the women in the place where they gather to work (presumably to spin, weave cloth, or sew garments).[21] The requirement of supervision applies to this task as well.

---

[18] Shenoute, *Canons*, vol. 9, MONB.YX 56, in Amélineau, *Contes et romans de l'Égypte chrétienne*, 280–81; trans. here is mine. See also excerpts and additional trans. in Layton, *Canons of Our Fathers*, 229.

[19] Shenoute, *Canons*, vol. 9, MONB.DF 64 (unpublished), in FR-BN 130⁵ f. 69v, online https://gallica .bnf.fr/ark:/12148/btv1b100904808/f142.image.r=130%20Copte, accessed December 4, 2019: ⲁⲩⲱ ⲉⲩϩⲓⲟⲩⲉ ⲉϩⲉⲛϣⲏⲣⲉ ϣ[ⲏ]ⲙ ⲉⲧⲣⲉⲩⲣ̄ⲡⲉⲩϩ[ϣ ...] ϩⲛ̄ⲧⲥⲩⲛⲁϫⲓ[ⲥ ...] ⲉⲩⲁⲙⲁⲗⲉⲓ ⲇⲉ ϩ[.?]ⲟⲩ ⲉⲁⲁϥ ⲉⲟⲩⲛ[.?]ϭⲟⲙ ⲙ̄ⲙⲟⲟⲩ ... ⲁⲩⲱ ⲟⲩⲡⲟⲛⲏⲣⲟⲛ ⲛⲉ ⲛ̄ⲛⲉⲧⲛⲁⲟⲃϣⲟⲩ ⲉⲁⲁϥ ⲕⲁⲧⲁⲧⲉⲛⲧⲟⲗⲏ ⲭⲱⲣⲓⲥ ϣⲱⲛⲉ. The fragment is damaged.

[20] Shenoute, *Canons*, vol. 5, MONB.XS 353, in Leipoldt, *Vita et Opera Omnia*, vol. 4, 60; see also excerpts and trans. in Layton, *Canons of Our Fathers*, 174–75. See also Crislip, *From Monastery to Hospital*, 134–35.

[21] Shenoute, *Canons*, vol. 5, MONB.XS 353–54, in Leipoldt, *Vita et Opera Omnia*, vol. 4, 60–61; see also excerpts and trans. in Layton, *Canons of Our Fathers*, 174–75. On creating clothing in Shenoute's monastery, see Krawiec, *Shenoute and the Women*, 19–20; Krawiec, "Garments of Salvation."

Labor, in the form of tasks in support of the monastery's ritual or
charitable deeds, lies at the heart of the eighth-century documents about
children found at the Monastery of Phoibammon near ancient Jême
(Thebes). Several papyri record the donation of children to this monastery,
as discussed in Chapters 1 and 5. Let us recall one contract with characteristic language about the social conditions facing the donated child:

> We went to the *oikonomos*, who is the superior of the holy *topos*, Apa Surus,
> and said: The God of the *topos* has given the boy the gift of being healed. Do
> you wish that he come to the holy place and serve in it? God and you shall
> decide. Or do you wish that he hand over his work obligation to the holy
> place? We will give him in the way that you see to all the boys of the holy
> place.[22]

As an economic contract, this document records the obligation the boy
owed the monastery; either he himself has to go to the monastery and
"serve" with his own labor or he has to give them the fruit of his labor.
The nature of the service, should Panias live at the monastery, remains
unstated. Certainly, the rules at Shenoute's monastery indicate that
monks performed a variety of kinds of manual labor for the community. The economics and legalities of landownership and management
had changed by the eighth century, but we do not know how much
monastic labor had changed. Another child's parents likewise promise
their offspring as a "servant" (or "enslaved person," *cauon*) to the *topos*,
and if he is not "able to be an enslaved person (*cauon*) of the
monastery where he was healed, he is to give to the monastery everything from his manual labor."[23] The nature of the work is left unde-
fined, and the emphasis is on the boy's labor as a commodity and
service. The child does not necessarily become a monk. He is required
to turn over all the fruits of his labor to the monastery. As
Papaconstantinou has noted, in many cases, the monastery explicitly
became the "master" of the child.[24]

The children mentioned in these documents typically had been ill
before their donation; as discussed in the previous chapter, they may
have been charitable wards of the monastery, rather than initiates.
Regardless of their role, they labored either in or on behalf of the
community. Some papyri list particular forms of work the children
would perform. One task mentioned more than once is the lighting of

---

[22] *P.KRU* 91.23–26; trans. MacCoull, "Child Donations and Child Saints," 410–11, mod.
[23] *P.KRU* 100.59–61; trans. MacCoull, "Child Donations and Child Saints," 412, mod.
[24] Papaconstantinou, "Notes sur les actes de donation d'enfants," 93–94. See *P.KRU* 79 and 81.

lamps, a ritual duty.[25] (Later Byzantine monastic *typika* also identify lamp lighting as a particular activity for children, including orphans.)[26] Boys are tasked with the "lamp of the altar" and the "holy illumination." Other contracts mention tending to the water basin and dealing with bread given to "passing strangers."[27] Some duties are menial, perhaps with no ritual function.[28] Other documents reference craftwork.[29] No matter the official status of the children, their labor was a primary asset they brought into the community.[30]

Thus, at the later Monastery of Phoibammon, children labored in modes of production economically advantageous for the community, as well as in support of the monastery's ritual and charitable tasks. While the earlier monastic material, especially from the White Monastery Federation, cautions against overworking free (non-enslaved) monastic children, the evidence from the Phoibammon community leads us to question whether such safeguards were commonplace and whether, even as early as the fourth and fifth centuries, enslaved children labored in coenobitic monasteries.

Health, Sickness, and Physical Vulnerabilities

As the food regulations show, children are classified along with the elderly and the sick as a physically vulnerable class of people. At times, children or novices are treated the same way as full or adult monks, including when members of both groups are sick. In a section of the *Canons*, Volume 5, Shenoute discusses special accommodations for the ill. Any monk in the infirmary can request some oil when sick. So too may a sick monk receive extra wine, if he or she requires it (whether the monk is male or female, *šēre šēm* or *šeere šēm*). The truly sick need it and should receive it; the caregivers, however, must take care not to be deceived into giving monks more wine than necessary.[31]

---

[25] Wilfong, *Women of Jeme*, 100. See *P.KRU* 93.32 ("lamp of the altar"), *P.KRU* 92.14 ("holy illuminations").

[26] E.g., the twelfth-century *Typikon* of Emperor John Komnenos for the Monastery of Christ Pantocrator in Constantinople. Thomas and Hero, *Byzantine Monastic Foundation Documents*, vol. 2, 725, 754.

[27] See *P.KRU* 93.32–34 (the "basin," "lamp of the altar," bread), *P.KRU* 92.14 ("holy illuminations"); *P.KRU* 81.21ff. ("lamps"), *P.KRU* 99.13ff. ("illumination of the altar"); discussion and partial trans. in Richter, "What's in a Story?" 244–45.

[28] "Sweeping" and "sprinkling" in *P.KRU* 79, 80, 93; see Richter, "What's in a Story?" 244n21.

[29] *P.KRU* 96; trans. in Richter, "What's in a Story?" 263.

[30] Some children or families were also required to pay an annual fee (Richter, "What's in a Story?" 244–45; Papaconstantinou, "Notes sur les actes de donation d'enfants," 102–05).

[31] Shenoute, *You God the Eternal, Canons*, vol. 5, MONB.XS 325–26, in Leipoldt, *Vita et Opera Omnia*, vol. 4, 55–56; see also excerpts in Layton, *Canons of Our Fathers*, 163–64.

Sick children, specifically, receive special aid and assistance at Shenoute's monastery. Shenoute assigns caretakers for them, so they are not left alone during the weekly Sabbath gathering. He writes of *šēre šēm* who are "small" and have not yet matured to the point where they can determine if they are sick, or how sick they are. These children, then, must be minors, not adult novices. Ill young children cannot be left alone when the monks assemble for their weekly prayer gathering. Whether in their houses or in the infirmary, they require a guardian or caretaker of some kind to remain with them. If the children are not too sick to attend, they are carried to the assembly and allowed to sleep there if necessary.[32]

Another regulation carves out an exemption for other physically vulnerable groups but specifically *not* for children, even though they are still developing physically and emotionally.

> If someone urinates in a narrow-necked vessel or in a jar or in anything else like these ones, who was not commanded by the Elder – except for those in the infirmary alone, and the elders who are very advanced in their years and these others who seek out the Elder, and if it is necessary for some among us to act this way, so that they relieve themselves in some vessel like this due to a wound or an impediment on their leg, so that they are not able to walk outside, they shall ask the Elder. And apart from these ones (I have just mentioned), if some children (*šēre šēm*) or other people defecate in any vessel of this sort, they shall be cursed.[33]

All monks will receive punishment if they relieve themselves anywhere other than the designated locations. Only the sick, the elderly, and the injured are shown lenience. As in the previous example about food, this rule identifies people who may have physical reasons for requiring an exemption. However, here Shenoute specifically mentions children as a class of people for whom this rule applies. This passage has a small lacuna in an awkward place, before *šēre šēm*. If the reconstruction in Johannes Leipoldt's edition of Shenoute's works is correct, Shenoute is stating that the rule must apply to children. (If Leipoldt is mistaken, it is possible that "children or other people" are part of the exception, but Leipoldt's reading is most likely correct.) Thus, Shenoute specifically singles out children in this rule, and he does so in a way that differs from the standard formulary

---

[32] Shenoute, *Canons*, vol. 9, MONB.DF 184, in Leipoldt, *Vita et Opera Omnia*, vol. 4, 103–04; see also excerpts in Layton, *Canons of Our Fathers*, 264.

[33] Shenoute, *A22*, *Canons*, vol. 3, MONB.YA 421, in Leipoldt, *Vita et Opera Omnia*, vol. 4, 124–25; trans. here is mine; see also excerpts and additional trans. in Layton, *Canons of Our Fathers*, 130–31. This sentence is rather long and complicated. I thank Heike Behlmer for her assistance with this passage.

he typically uses to emphasize that what he says applies to the entire community, regardless of age, rank, status, or gender (e.g., "whether male or female, whether great or small," or all monks "from the least to the greatest"). In other words, Shenoute seems to be calling out *minor children* specifically for this rule. Considering the tendency of children (either by accident or mischievous intent) to misuse the lavatory, this rule provides an interesting window onto the lives of children and the ways in which their physical and emotional development might impinge on the orderliness of a monastery.

The Expulsion of Children

At both the Naqlun community and Shenoute's federation, minor children – and at the latter monastery, adult novices as well – faced expulsion. Such an act was controversial at Shenoute's monastery, indicating that these rules illuminate the liminal space in which children existed in communal monasticism, as neither fully monk nor fully lay person.

At Naqlun, as we have already discussed, children (likely adolescent boys) could be removed from the community for causing a "scandal." The rule seems designed to protect the reputation of adult monks – even those who may have been equally involved in, or even mostly responsible for, such an entanglement.

A few accounts survive of the expulsion of children or adult novices from Shenoute's community, each of which seems to have sparked controversy in the community. According to *Is It Not Written* in Volume 6 of Shenoute's *Canons*, Shenoute weathered a crisis in confidence in his leadership precisely because he exiled a number of *šēre šēm*. He defends his own judgments by asserting that they pale in comparison to the final judgment, which is a substantially more dramatic fate awaiting people who commit the same misdeeds as the expelled monks: "If you are amazed at what this man [Shenoute or the Elder] does or what we do to the bad novices whom we excommunicate because of their defilements and also their estranged hearts, then had you seen those people whom the earth opened and swallowed (Num. 16:31b), similar to these of this (present) time, how greatly you would be amazed."[34]

Children or novices who have left the monastery or who were expelled risk being ostracized from friends or relatives in the monastery. People who

---

[34] Shenoute, *Canons*, vol. 6, MONB.XM 157–58, in Young, "Fourth Work of Shenoute's *Sixth Canon*," 95–96; trans. 99–100, mod.

have been expelled, Shenoute argues, justly face punishments for their crimes.[35] He urges those remaining in the monastery not to be "soft-hearted" or harbor any regrets about these people, whether "they are great (*noc*) men or great (*noc*) women or they are boys (*šēre šēm*) or girls (*šeere šēm*)." In this passage, Shenoute uses the language of youth and age for emphasis, warning the community not to feel pity for *any* monk who has left or who has been expelled.[36] As I have argued elsewhere, the penalty of expulsion appears more commonly in the documents by Shenoute from the White Monastery than in the Pachomian materials.[37] Here, Shenoute underlines that anyone, regardless of rank or status, could face this punishment. The question of age, and whether *minor* children could face this consequence (not simply adult junior monks), remains unanswerable at this time. As discussed in Chapter 1, we do know of one case in which Shenoute expelled an entire family due to the actions of the father, but in that case, Shenoute provided no evidence for wrongdoing on the part of the monk's children; they were all simply thrown out together.[38] Given family law in the Roman Empire, it seems unlikely that minor children with relatives also in the monastery could be ejected on their own. The fate of errant orphans remains a question.

Death and Burial

Children lived and died in Egyptian monasteries. Both archaeological and literary evidence reveals that children were buried in these communities. We may never know the full details about all of the young people interred at monasteries. Likely not all of them had lived there. Some of them may have been relatives of adult monks or important patrons, had been visiting on pilgrimage at the times of their deaths, or had sought healing or medicinal care from the monks.

Our earliest monastic rules say little about funerary regulations for dead children and child monks. Only Shenoute's corpus reveals particular burial customs for youth and junior monks. In Volume 5 of the *Canons*, Shenoute describes the traditions at his monastery, which differentiate between adult monks or full monks, on one hand, and children or junior monks (*šēre/šeere šēm*) on the other. (Context does not dictate whether these "children" were

---

[35] Shenoute, *Canons*, vol. 9, MONB.DF 185, in Leipoldt, *Vita et Opera Omnia*, vol. 4, 104–05; see also excerpts in Layton, *Canons of Our Fathers*, 266.
[36] See discussion in Chapter 2.   [37] Schroeder, *Monastic Bodies*, 55–59, 77–82.
[38] Shenoute, *Why O Lord, Canons*, vol. 4, MONB.BZ 59, in Leipoldt, *Vita et Opera Omnia*, vol. 3, 141. See discussion of this passage in chapter 1, 46.

minors or adult junior monks, so the rule may have applied to both.) Children could not expect to be clothed in burial shrouds upon their interment:

> As for every one who will die among us at any time, whether male or female, three pairs of burial shrouds and two burial cords[39] shall suffice for them, according to the ordinances of our Fathers. They shall not be decreased or increased, except in the case of boys (*šēre šēm*) or girls (*šeere šēm*). Burial garments shall not be provided for them.[40]

The burial shrouds allotted to the adult or full monks were typically plain linen sheets used in pairs to wrap the body. In later adult monastic burials at the Epiphanius Monastery near Thebes, the cords or ribbons (*kerea* or Greek *keiriai*) were woven through the shrouds or placed on the outside.[41] The excavation of monastic burial sites in recent years has been limited, due to the sensitive nature of exhuming graves. The relevant archaeological evidence, however, indicates that not all monasteries followed the same traditions as Shenoute's. Shenoute asserts that this rule predates him, that the burial practices were established prior to his own leadership of the monastery and were thus old customs. His reference to the "Fathers" might also be a rhetorical embellishment designed to bolster the authority of his own rule, regardless of the true history of the tradition.

Both textiles and bones testify to the death and burial of children in monasteries but not to the reasons for their presence. Richly embroidered child tunics have been unearthed in the Panopolis-Achmim region, where Shenoute's monastery was located.[42] The poor documentation of the excavations (in which textiles and other grave goods were removed without recording much detail about their provenance) means that we do not know if these garments came from lay Christian burials or monastic sites. One child's grave has been discovered recently in the late antique layer of the cemetery at the Deir el-Bachit Monastery.[43] The boy was buried in a colorfully embroidered tunic, which has led one of the archaeologists to speculate that the child may have been a monk in training; an enslaved person or servant would not have been buried in such a fine tunic. Indeed,

---

[39] From the Greek *keiriai*: ribbons or bands at times placed on the outside of the burial shrouds. See Winlock and Crum, *Monastery of Epiphanius I*, 48, 184. Layton translates this term as "candles" (*Canons of Our Fathers*, 177).

[40] Shenoute, *You God the Eternal, Canons*, vol. 5, MONB.XS 355, in Leipoldt, *Vita et Opera Omnia*, vol. 4, 61; trans. is my own; see excerpts and alternate trans. in Layton, *Canons of Our Fathers*, 177.

[41] Winlock and Crum, *Monastery of Epiphanius I*, 47–49, 184.

[42] Forrer, *Die Graeber- und Textilfunde von Achmim-Panopolis*.

[43] Lösch, Hower-Tilmann, and Zink, "Mummies and Skeletons."

although Shenoute's rule forbids burial garments for children, it does convey a stratification of monastic status that extends to the grave. All monks in Shenoute's monastery receive the same burial goods regardless of gender but not all monastic residents regardless of status or rank. The status of the boy at Deir el-Bachit remains speculative, but any conjecture must take monastic hierarchies into account; a child novice is one among several possibilities.

It is tempting to turn for context to the sixth-century monastery of Saint Stephen in Palestine, where the bones of children were found among the bones of adults in a large ossuary. The remains are numerous, indicating a large number of skeletons. Many show signs of disease. These children, therefore, were likely patients at a monastic hospital or infirmary for laity, rather than child monks or children living in the monastery as their permanent residence.[44]

Although the resurrection promised the reunion of Christians within the heavenly body of Christ, death itself guaranteed one last rupture of familial ties between children and their loved ones in Shenoute's monastery. At the funerals, girls were not allowed to participate in the rituals honoring their deceased mothers, or mothers their deceased daughters. Since members of the men's community would travel to the women's to officiate at and participate in the ceremony, these rituals gave rise to a bevy of rules as Shenoute sought to restrict contact between the two genders. None of the dead women's colleagues could join the procession to the desert grave except for the female Elder and six elderly, senior female monks. These seven women represented the entire grieving women's community, even the deceased's female relatives. These designated representatives were required to process a discreet distance behind the men.[45] Thus, a mother could not accompany her dead daughter's body out to the burial site. Neither could a daughter witness her mother's interment. Women and girls were also forbidden to witness the funeral service in the monastery for their mothers, daughters, and sisters. To prevent the stirring of passion upon seeing the men who performed the service, Shenoute prohibited all women of any status or age – whether "great women" (*noc nshime*) or girls/"little daughters" (*šeere šēm*) – from even peeking through the doors of the room in which the others had gathered.[46]

[44] Leyerle, "Children and Disease."

[45] Shenoute, *You God the Eternal, Canons*, vol. 5, MONB.XS 355–56, in Leipoldt, *Vita et Opera Omnia*, vol. 4, 62; see also excerpts in Layton, *Canons of Our Fathers*, 178.

[46] Shenoute, *You God the Eternal, Canons*, vol. 5, MONB.XS 358–59 and MONB.XL 194, in Leipoldt, *Vita et Opera Omnia*, vol. 4, 63; see also excerpts in Layton, *Canons of Our Fathers*, 180.

The lives and even deaths of children in early Egyptian monasteries were highly regulated. At times, the goals of adult ascetic formation were perceived as working hand in hand with the physical and spiritual needs of children (as when Shenoute castigates monks who beat children or junior monks in order to coerce them to perform labor the adults will not do themselves). At other times, however, the lives and needs of children are subordinate to those of the adults. Additionally, the use of the terms "boy" and "girl" to sometimes designate minor children, and, at other times, possibly a category of people at the monastery who were "junior" monks (including adults), speaks loudly about hierarchies within the monastery even for adults. New or junior adult monks classified as "little sons" and "little daughters," like children in a household, were subject to the decisions and authority of their parents, especially their fathers. As we see in the next chapter, leaders of monasteries drew upon the "familial" ties in this new monastic family to shame and persuade the men and women under their authority or influence. They also leveraged family ties between a monk and her or his natal family to advocate for themselves.

CHAPTER 8

The Ties That Bind
Emotional and Social Bonds between Parents and Children

The rhetoric of familial renunciation, especially the renunciation of one's biological or legal children, pervaded early ascetic literature, as Chapter 4 demonstrated. The same discourse applied in the opposite direction. Monastic literature also depicted sons and daughters renouncing their biological or legal parents upon joining a community. The Greek *Life of Pachomius* provides one such example. Young men came to Pachomius wishing to join his community and learn from him. Once Pachomius decided to receive these young men, he instituted a particular ritual of initiation addressing the bonds between children and their parents: he "test[ed]" both the prospective monks and their parents, whom he required the young men to "renounce" (along with "the whole world" and "themselves").[1] Monastic rules, handbooks, and literary texts testified to the distractions and even the dangers of maintaining familial attachments within the monastery.

Nonetheless, familial bonds were tenacious. The travails of a fifth-century woman monk named Aphthonia illustrate these conflicts. Aphthonia lived in the women's community of the White Monastery Federation and, at some point, wrote to her parents complaining of her treatment. In her letter home, Aphthonia accuses her superiors of fighting with and abusing her. The leader of the White Monastery at the time, Besa, wrote her a letter reprimanding her. Only Besa's letter survives, which quotes from Aphthonia's letter briefly (e.g., "Most of all when you sent to your father and your mother: 'they fought with me,' or 'they abused me'").[2] As a result, we have only a one-sided account of this conflict. Besa accuses Aphthonia of lying about the abuse. He claims she misled

---

[1] *V. Pach. G¹* 24, in Halkin, *Sancti Pachomii Vitae Graecae*, 14–15; ed. and trans. Veilleux, *Pachomian Koinonia, Volume One*, 312.
[2] Besa, *Aphthonia* 1.5, in Miyagawa et al., ed. urn:cts:copticLit:besa.aphthonia.monbba, Coptic SCRIPTORIUM; Engl. trans. in Miyagawa and Zeldes, urn:cts:copticLit:besa.aphthonia.monbba, Coptic SCRIPTORIUM.

her parents about the nature of the conflict, that the abuse and fighting were merely ordinary monastic discipline: a reprimand for having broken the monastery's rules. In other words, in Besa's version of the story, Aphthonia has embellished or outright lied about a time when she was justly punished. He claims she had received an unauthorized care package from her natal family, for which her spiritual (monastic) mother accordingly punished her.[3]

In writing to Aphthonia, Besa not only promotes his version of the story over and against hers but also endeavors to shame the woman into reorienting her social and emotional allegiances to her monastic family and away from her biological family. Instead of turning to her *biological* parents, he argues, she should have aired her grievances with her *spiritual* mother. That she wrote home demonstrates that her "heart" (Coptic *hēt*) was not fully pledged to her new monastic mother.[4] Besa also reminds Aphthonia of the social and economic mutual dependencies in the monastic kinship network. Like a household, the monastic family provided for a person's basic needs: "What is it that you asked for or needed and were rejected, or you weren't given it?" he demands.[5] Furthermore, throughout the letter, Besa deploys the vocabulary of emotion and affect, cloaking Aphthonia with negative and shameful emotional discourse.[6] She committed evil or greedy acts;[7] she inappropriately felt afflicted and aggrieved;[8] she was foolish (lit. "without heart or mind"), boastful, prideful, and bitter;[9] she threw shame on her

---

[3] Besa, *Aphthonia* 1.5–6, in Miyagawa et al., ed. urn:cts:copticLit:besa.aphthonia.monbba, Coptic SCRIPTORIUM.

[4] Besa, *Aphthonia* 2.2, in Miyagawa et al., ed. urn:cts:copticLit:besa.aphthonia.monbba, Coptic SCRIPTORIUM. A citation from Matthew 15:8, which itself quotes from Isaiah 29:13, follows: "As it is written: 'This people honors me with their lips, but their heart is distant far away from me.'" See also Behlmer, "Our Disobedience Will Punish Us."

[5] Besa, *Aphthonia* 1.6, in Miyagawa et al., ed. urn:cts:copticLit:besa.aphthonia.monbba, Coptic SCRIPTORIUM; Engl. trans. in Miyagawa and Zeldes, urn:cts:copticLit:besa.aphthonia.monbba, Coptic SCRIPTORIUM.

[6] Emotional discourse in Coptic literature is extremely undertheorized, especially when compared to scholarship on Greek literature. In what follows, I identified words that referred to emotions, feelings, or affect in a word list generated from the letter to Aphthonia in the Coptic SCRIPTORIUM online corpus. I initially identified the words out of context and then went back into the text to analyze how they functioned contextually. Terms I identified included: *at-hēt*, *boone*, *thmko*, *lupei*, *mnt-babe-rōme*, *mnt-rmn-hēt*, *mnt-jasi-hēt*, *mokh*, *mton*, *rmn-hēt*, *r-hote*, *siše*, *tcaie*, *phthonei*, *šoušou*, *hise*, and other compounds or combinations including *hēt*.

[7] Coptic "*boone*," which means evil with the valence of greed or envy, in Besa, *Aphthonia* 2.5, in Miyagawa et al., ed. urn:cts:copticLit:besa.aphthonia.monbba, Coptic SCRIPTORIUM.

[8] *thmko* and *lupei* in Besa, *Aphthonia* 2.2, in Miyagawa et al., ed. urn:cts:copticLit:besa.aphthonia. monbba, Coptic SCRIPTORIUM.

[9] *at-hēt*, *mnt-rmn-hēt*, *mnt-babe-rōme*, *mnt-jasi-hēt*, *siše* in Besa, *Aphthonia* 1.4, 2.4, 2.3, 2.3, 2.4, in Miyagawa et al., ed. urn:cts:copticLit:besa.aphthonia.monbba, Coptic SCRIPTORIUM.

monastic sisters;[10] she persisted in pointless suffering that led her astray.[11] In a play on Aphthonia's very name, Besa accuses her of disgracing and reviling (*phthonei*) no one but herself.[12] He urges her to move herself from an emotional state to a state of equanimity through monastic compliance. Although she has failed to please her *monastic* parents, Besa writes, she can put *his* heart to rest by obeying her superiors; these actions, he argues, will make her satisfied as well.[13] In Coptic, what I translate as "satisfied" literally means "to be of an agreeable heart or mind"; thus Besa posits a connection between compliance and emotional equanimity. He also slams Aphthonia for failing to exhibit good emotion, namely reverence or fear of God.[14] In contrast, Besa depicts himself as unswayed by improper emotion; he is not afraid of her letter to her parents and expresses only justifiable fear – namely, that she will be ensnared by the devil.[15] Thus Besa paints two affective portraits in this letter: one of composed, emotional equanimity (himself), the other of distressed, affective disorder (Aphthonia).

Besa tells us that Aphthonia hails from a prominent local family; he addresses her in the letter's opening as "daughter of the Comes Alexander."[16] It seems that during the course of events preceding his letter, Aphthonia has threatened to leave the monastery and join a new one. Given Aphthonia's social and economic status, her threat holds water. Her departure could bring prestige to another monastery while damaging Besa's monastic federation socially. Her move might also have financial consequences; if her family has sent her little gifts, perhaps they donated capital to the monastery or could do so in the future. Besa replies with

---

[10] *tgaie* (shame, disgrace) in Besa, *Aphthonia* 1.2, in Miyagawa et al., ed. urn:cts:copticLit:besa. aphthonia.monbba, Coptic SCRIPTORIUM.

[11] *hise* in Besa, *Aphthonia* 1.3, in Miyagawa et al., ed. urn:cts:copticLit:besa.aphthonia.monbba, Coptic SCRIPTORIUM.

[12] Besa, *Aphthonia* 1.3, in Miyagawa et al., ed. urn:cts:copticLit:besa.aphthonia.monbba, Coptic SCRIPTORIUM.

[13] Various usages of *mton* (rest) and *hēt* (heart, mind, belly): *arti-mton*; *tarepenhēt mton* in Besa, *Aphthonia* 3.4, in Miyagawa et al., ed. urn:cts:copticLit:besa.aphthonia.monbba, Coptic SCRIPTORIUM. See also section 3.5, where Besa insists that her submission will put all their hearts at ease (*penhēt namton tērn hiousop*).

[14] *r-hote* in Besa, *Aphthonia* 3.1, 3.3, in Miyagawa et al., ed. urn:cts:copticLit:besa.aphthonia.monbba, Coptic SCRIPTORIUM. On cultivating the "fear of God" in monastic discipline, see Dilley, *Monasteries and the Care of Souls*, 148–85.

[15] *r-hote* in Besa, *Aphthonia* 1.6, 3.1, in Miyagawa et al., ed. urn:cts:copticLit:besa.aphthonia.monbba, Coptic SCRIPTORIUM.

[16] Besa, *Aphthonia* 1.1, in Miyagawa et al., ed. urn:cts:copticLit:besa.aphthonia.monbba, Coptic SCRIPTORIUM. Thanks to David Brakke, Malcolm Choat, Brice Jones, and Roberta Mazza for helpful comments on the term and office of "Comes" in this period.

a threat of his own: gossip designed to tarnish Aphthonia's status and reputation. He alludes to an inappropriate relationship she had with another woman, thus implying that perhaps she would not be welcome anywhere else. He then warns of further punishment if she does not retract her accusations and ultimatum.[17] With this letter, Besa uses gossip and the rhetoric of affect to shift the balance of power in this relationship between monastic father and spiritual daughter. He attempts to create a reality in which Aphthonia needs the monastery more than it needs her, and where she remains vulnerable to his authority and power.

The account of Aphthonia's clash with Besa testifies to the enduring nature of familial bonds and the threat they posed to uniform obedience to monastic authority. As monastic father, Besa reasserted paternal authority over his spiritual daughter by seeking to sever her ties with her natal family and reinforce her social and emotional ties to her monastic family; to do so, he used emotional rhetoric to shame and persuade her. As this chapter demonstrates, his strategies appear in many other sources about parents and children in monastic settings. Besa's call to Aphthonia to replace filial piety to her natal parents with monastic piety to her mother "in this place" was not unique. Augustine, in his rules for nuns, obliged the women to obey their superior "as a mother," including honoring her.[18] Likewise, the mother superior should treat the women monastics under her as her daughters, caring for them physically and emotionally as if she were their biological mother.[19]

In Roman Egypt, as elsewhere in the ancient world, filial piety of daughters and sons was a social expectation, one strand of the mutual obligations of family members to each other and a publicly visible duty that affected a person's status in the wider community.[20] Some of the ties children had with their parents were emotional. As Cornelia Horn and John Martens have observed, the Gospel of Luke captures the joy of a mother giving birth to a healthy baby in its accounts of Mary and Elizabeth.[21] Many of the essays in *Becoming Byzantine*, the proceedings

---

[17] Besa, *Aphthonia* 2.6, Besa, *Aphthonia* 1.6, 3.1, in Miyagawa et al., ed. urn:cts:copticLit:besa.aphthonia.monbba, Coptic SCRIPTORIUM.

[18] "Praepositae tanquam matri obediatur, honore servato." Augustine, *Ep.* 211, 15 in *PL* 33:964; accessed via Corpus Corporum, http://mlat.uzh.ch/?c=2&w=AugHip.Episto36.

[19] "Perseverate in bono proposito, et non desiderabitis mutare praepositam, qua in monasterio illo per tam multos annos perseverante et numero et aetate crevistis; quae vos mater non utero, sed animo suscepit." Augustine, *Ep.* 211, 4 in *PL* 33:959; accessed via Corpus Corporum, http://mlat.uzh.ch/?c=2&w=AugHip.Episto36.

[20] Huebner, *Family in Roman Egypt*, ch. 3, especially 80–91.

[21] Horn and Martens, *"Let the Little Children Come to Me,"* 76–77.

of the 2006 Dumbarton Oaks Symposium on children, explore the extensive representations of affective bonds between parents and children in
hagiography and other literary sources. Sabine Huebner's analysis of letters
between parents and children reveals some of the feelings wrapped up in
correspondence ostensibly about legal or financial matters.[22]

As our account of Aphthonia's fight with Besa illustrates, representations of emotions and other familial bonds in early Christianity need
further theorizing and contextualization. This chapter examines the emotional ties between adults and children specifically in monastic and ascetic
contexts, paying close attention to the ways in which familial bonds are not
purely "emotional" but rather a dense web of social, economic, and
affective interdependencies. Such bonds are formed, renegotiated, and
challenged by the reconfiguration of familial relationships in all kinds of
communities throughout Roman Egypt.[23] Communities that privilege the
ascetic family over biological and legal kinship networks add further stress
and complexity to these relationships. Some late antique monastics, like
Aphthonia, left biological kin behind. Other children joined monasteries
along with their parents. Yet others forged relationships with adults in their
communities to whom they were unrelated.

Especially in texts about children, where we read "emotions," late
antique readers may have read something different or perhaps something
more. The question is not *whether* early Christians loved and grieved over
their children but *how*, and what meaning was ascribed to these feelings.[24]
Tonio Sebastian Richter, in his study of Coptic child donation papyri from
the Monastery of Phoibammon, has asked whether emotions are "culturally encoded," and if emotions expressed by individuals are in fact drawing
on more broadly understood and communally defined collective
emotions.[25] In other words, are emotions culturally constructed and contingent? And how can one navigate the complex terrain of emotions
expressed in texts with genre expectations (epistolary conventions, narrative tropes, etc.), "authentic" emotions experienced by individuals, and
cultural expectations of emotional expressions by those individuals?

Research on emotions over the past two decades suggests that Richter is
on to something: not just emotional expression but also emotions themselves are culturally contingent. As David Konstan has argued, the

---

[22] Huebner, *Family in Roman Egypt*, 66–72.   [23] Huebner, *Family in Roman Egypt*.
[24] Golden, "Did the Ancients Care When Their Children Died?"; Doerfler, *Jephthah's Daughter,
Sarah's Son*.
[25] Richter, "Pleasant and Unpleasant Emotions"; Richter, "What's in a Story?" See my analysis of these
papyri in Chapters 1 and 6.

emotions of the ancient Greeks differed from contemporary conceptions of the emotions, in both the "individual" and "systemic" realms.[26] Differences in language and social environment mean that the emotional world of the ancients does not map seamlessly onto ours.[27] Even in modernity, emotional expression and interpretation vary across diverse cultures.[28] Emotional discourse in ancient sources must be interrogated to be understood. The language of love, loss, and grief indicates authentic human emotion, but also emotion expressed within a particular cultural and literary context. Societal expectations regarding the roles of children and parents are strong and frame the way parents and children write about and to each other; they also shape the way early Christian authors describe such relationships. The emotional dimensions of family bonds cannot be neatly bracketed from a community's or family's economic relations and social networks. All the figures discussed in this chapter – be they the authors, recipients, or subjects of these texts – operate in a milieu with particular cultural expectations about the expression and meaning of emotions. Moreover, they might express and interpret emotions differently in particular local "emotional communities" (e.g., family, monastery, civic square) within their own social networks.[29]

This chapter analyzes the role of emotions between parents and children in the formation of monastic communities, ascetic households, and ascetic identities in a variety of sources, focusing primarily on the writings of Cassian, Shenoute, and Jerome. I first explore the influence of three intersecting cultural matrices on parent-child relationships: ancient theories of emotion, biblical discourses, and ascetic renunciation. This chapter attends to the particularities of each author's "emotional communities" while also tracing cultural trends and similarities that span the fourth- and fifth-century Mediterranean. Barbara H. Rosenwein coined the phrase

---

[26] Konstan, *Emotions of the Ancient Greeks*, 4–5.

[27] Konstan, *Emotions of the Ancient Greeks*, 6–12, 22.

[28] LeVine, "Human Variations," 57; Konstan also relies on research in psychological anthropology (*Emotions of the Ancient Greeks*, ch. 1); LeVine, in contrast, believes that a "universal meta-language" of emotions or "common framework for all humans" can be discerned (LeVine, "Human Variations," 58).

[29] Rosenwein, "Worrying about Emotions"; see also Rosenwein, *Emotional Communities*, where she expands upon and applies this notion. As Geoffrey Koziol notes in his review (Review of *Emotional Communities*, by Barbara H. Rosenwein), Rosenwein draws heavily on William M. Reddy's concept of "emotives" in *Navigation of Feeling*. Reddy critiques social-constructivist theories of emotions as obscuring the role of human agency. Reddy seeks to bridge the gap between individual authenticity, societal influences, and the historiographer's historical distance with his concept of "emotives." Rosenwein does not wholly reject social constructivism but rather adapts Reddy by turning to the hyper-local to resist sweeping periodization arguments about the social construction of emotions.

"emotional communities," defining it as a hyper-local social group in a certain time and place; one individual may belong to many "emotional communities" (monastery, family, friendship network) and express and value emotions differently in each. Likewise, multiple "emotional communities" can exist at one point in the timeline of human history, even in the same city or geographic region.[30]

This chapter seeks to untangle some of the societal influences and expectations that shaped emotional encounters while also remaining sensitive to the notion that individual emotional expression, in public or private, has authenticity. Moreover, the analysis does not bracket social and economic factors in relationships but rather considers them fundamental to understanding familial bonds, including affective bonds. Ancient theories of emotion (in either concentrated or diluted forms), gender, and social status all influenced the ascetic negotiation of emotional relationships, the representations of emotions, and the strategic deployment of emotional language in our sources. Local "emotional communities" were forged in larger societies with deep histories; understanding them requires examining both the social construction of emotions in particular times and places and the claims to individual authenticity or agency. Writings on parents and children bring these discourses to the fore.

Reading Early Christian Emotions

Ancient Theories of Emotions

Early Christian authors composed their letters, sermons, and saints' lives in a world with a variety of cultural influences. Pervading theories of emotions were no exception. Our sources exhibit the influences of classical and late classical understandings about feelings and affect. In particular, they adopt classical notions about the limits of public displays of emotion and about the relationships between judgment and affect regarding events that inspire feelings. As we saw in Besa's letter to Aphthonia, he critiqued her emotions as inappropriate affective as well as excessive responses to the events they concerned. Likewise, Cassian's, Jerome's, and Shenoute's ascetic writings on parents and children betray the influences of both classical and biblical emotional frameworks.

This chapter examines two aforementioned elements of classical theories of emotion at work in the monastic writings: the connection between

---

[30] Rosenwein, *Emotional Communities*, 2, 4–5, 191.

emotional display and rhetoric or persuasion, and the cognitive definition of an emotion as stemming from a judgment. Traces of these elements date back to Aristotle, as David Konstan has observed. Aristotle defined emotions as "those things 'on account of which people change and differ in regard to their judgments.'"[31] In the Roman Empire, the first element is pervasive. Control and self-mastery were prized in public oratory. Affect and emotional authenticity were considered essential for the successful rhetor, because of the expectation that the speaker have a sensory and sentimental effect on the audience's affective state.[32] For example, for Quintilian, affect was cultivated, constrained, and publicly recognized as sincere because of this deliberative cultivation of the self.[33]

The second element, the understanding of emotions as results of judgments, is sometimes attributed primarily to the Stoic school of philosophy. As Konstan has argued, however, this framing is widespread in classical Greek literature and philosophy.[34] Some components of this concept are indeed intrinsic to Stoic emotional theory – the notion that feelings arise in a person in reaction to objects and events, and specific ways of classifying feelings into good and negative categories. But certainly by late antiquity, these elements are so ubiquitous that an author need not be considered "Stoic" to share in them. Moreover, some of Stoicism's philosophical principles influenced Christians, from the apostle Paul onward.[35] Stoicism's effects on late antique asceticism can be seen in Christian theorizing about the nature of virtue, that "[w]hat is ethically relevant is what man [*sic*] can control."[36] Ascetic discipline – to train body and mind to react virtuously, especially in the presence of temptation to do otherwise – shares this core value with the Stoic understanding of virtuous moral agency.[37] Thus, in tracing these broader elements of ancient emotional theory (judgment and emotion, and persuasion and affect) in ascetic writing about the emotional bonds between parent and child, I do not propose that Cassian, Shenoute, and Jerome were fluent in Stoic moral philosophy. Rather, I argue that classical influences on Christian culture in

---

[31] Konstan, *Emotions of the Ancient Greeks*, 27, citing *On the Soul*.

[32] Gunderson, *Staging Masculinity*, 90–91, 95–96; Konstan, *Emotions of the Ancient Greeks*, 30–32.

[33] Gunderson, *Staging Masculinity*, 94–96.   [34] Konstan, *Emotions of the Ancient Greeks*, 20–21.

[35] Anderson, *Second Sophistic*, 133–35, 215–16; Colish, *Stoic Tradition*, vol. 2; Rasimus, Engberg-Pedersen, and Dunderberg, *Stoicism in Early Christianity*. On influences into modernity, see Nussbaum, *Upheavals of Thought*.

[36] Colish, *Stoic Tradition*, vol. 1, 44; Brunt, "Morality and Social Convention," 111–14; Clark, "Foucault, the Fathers, and Sex."

[37] For a historical analysis in early medieval Latin authors, especially ascetics, see Colish, *Stoic Tradition*, vol. 2. On late antique Egyptian monasticism, see Brakke, *Demons*, 39, 40, 52–57.

late antiquity, particularly after the Second Sophistic, are widespread and profound, at play even in the writings about parents and children.

The cognitive aspect of ancient emotional theory has a number of interlocking parts. In the next pages, I outline some of the fundamentals of Stoic emotional theory and then move to describing how these principles, in a more diffuse form in late antique culture, operate in early asceticism.[38] As Margaret Graver has argued, the ancient Stoics understood the perfect person not to be someone who feels nothing but to be someone who experiences appropriate feelings. They thus distinguished between feelings (affective states of the human condition) and emotions. Emotions were defined as improper stirrings of the self in response to an event, responses that accompanied erroneous judgments about those events.[39] One tries to fend off feelings that stem from erroneous judgments. Stoics determined the propriety and rationality of affective responses in part by looking to the objects that inspired feelings.[40] Affect results not because some thing or event is inherently good or evil but from evaluating whether a thing the person had already classified as good or evil was present or about to be present.

Erroneous judgments about present good events tend to lead to delight (*hēdonē*), prospective good events to desire (*epithumia*), present evil events to distress (*lupē*), and prospective evil events to fear (*phobos*).[41] The primary *pathē* or emotions to be deflected consist of these four (*hēdonē*, *lupē*, *epithumia*, and *phobos*). Due to his or her character, each person already has a preestablished evaluation about the appropriate feelings for a situation. These prejudgments (resulting from the character of a person, developed over time through education, upbringing, and life experience) form the matrix or framework in the psyche that determines a person's affective response to an event. The psyche is activated by the event or sense of an impending event and physically responds by moving, shifting, or changing, which is why emotions often manifest physically. A person with a strong psyche does not respond to potential triggers or can use reason to respond instead of emotion; a weak psyche is susceptible. Emotions, according to the Stoics, "imply false judgments" about these events.[42] So the perfect person does not feel distress at an impending

---

[38] The following pages are an abbreviated version of a longer excursus on affect theory and Stoicism appearing in Schroeder, "Perfect Monk." In some places the wording is identical.

[39] Graver, *Stoicism and Emotion*, ch. 1, especially 4–5.   [40] Graver, *Stoicism and Emotion*, 37.

[41] See the chart in Graver, *Stoicism and Emotion*, 54.

[42] Graver, *Stoicism and Emotion*, 5. The judgment is based not on the determination of something as good or evil but on whether an already established good or evil thing is present or about to be

negative event (such as a looming battle), because he knows before ever foreseeing this event that such is a time for action, not anger or fear.[43]

Some feelings are good and "proper" for their context: joy (at good present events), wish (for good prospective events), and caution (including shame and reverence).[44] The perfect person feels not emotions (*pathē*) but good feelings (*eupatheiai*), such as the love bond between friends or a parent and child, because they are appropriate responses to a good object (the friend or child).

The wise sage or perfect person uses reason to prevent pre-emotions – initial movements of the self, such as tears that well upon hearing of the death of a friend – from leading to inappropriate emotion, such as extended or dramatic public grief.[45] The Stoics shared their views of some emotional responses with the wider ancient world. Contempt for excessive mourning, for example, was not limited to the Stoics. In the words of Konstan, for classical authors ranging from Homer to Pliny, Seneca to Plutarch, "Grief, then, was reasonable and necessary in its proper place, or rather, in its proper moment. It is persistent, unrelenting grief that the ancients are unanimous in discouraging."[46]

In early Christianity, a prominent expression of this emotional ideal was the notion of the virtuous or good death of the martyr, who faced death "fearlessly, even joyfully."[47] The transmission of these classical ideals to later authors, such as our ascetic writers of the fourth and fifth centuries, may be a product of direct classical *paideia* or a wider diffusion of these elements in late antique culture, perhaps even through the New Testament itself.[48]

Biblical Discourses

Early Christian authors of all stripes reckoned with the implications of their cultural inheritance of classical *paideia* and biblical tradition. Late

---

present. There are several levels of judgments and assessments: whether something is good or evil (a classification the person has already made, before that thing appears on the scene), and a determination of the appropriate response for situations (a predetermined judgment, as well – one that occurs over time as a result of education and character formation). Graver, *Stoicism and Emotion*, 36–40.

[43] Graver, *Stoicism and Emotion*, 36–40, the example of Agamemnon on 42–43, and the summary on 55.
[44] Graver, *Stoicism and Emotion*, 54–55, esp. fig. 3.
[45] Graver, *Stoicism and Emotion*, 76–78, 90–101.
[46] Konstan, *Emotions of the Ancient Greeks*, 256.
[47] Denzey, "Facing the Beast," 185; Schroeder, "Exemplary Women," 54–56, 60.
[48] Luckritz Marquis, "Perfection Perfected."

antique writings about family, children, and emotion are no exception, and one of the remarkable examples of late antique hybridity is the way in which classical *paideia* is in fact transmitted through the Christian Bible and biblical interpretation.[49] In fact, postbiblical Christian authors, including figures not traditionally associated with classical philosophy, such as Shenoute, may have absorbed principles of Stoic moral philosophy through their readings of Paul and the apologists. Some scholars have even gone so far as to argue that Stoicism may have influenced Christian origins more than Middle Platonism.[50] For example, Stoic principles lie behind Paul's appeal to "love" (*agapē*) as "the highest form of virtue" for believers to practice with each other in Romans 12–15.[51] Thus, classical philosophy influenced earliest Christian discourse about emotional bonds within a "familial" community – Paul's community of brothers and sisters in Christ. The apostle's turn to emotion to persuade his audience toward desirable behavior (namely, certain liturgical practices) and his character-ization of fraternal love as a *eupatheia* leading to moral virtue are entirely consistent with classical emotional theories, including Stoicism.[52]

While biblical texts, especially Paul's letters, may have transmitted classical *paideia* to later Christian authors, fourth- and fifth-century ascetic writers also shaped the reception of the Bible through their ascetic inter-pretations. In the words of Elizabeth A. Clark, "For ancient commentators, all Scripture was revealed truth relevant to present Christian experience, not merely historical narration, and was to be aligned with their endorse-ment of asceticism's superiority."[53] Ascetic exegesis thus crafted a discourse of familial renunciation that claimed to be grounded in biblical authority. Among the three primary authors featured in this chapter, Jerome is perhaps the most extreme in his advocacy of the value and rewards of ascetic life over lay Christian piety. Yet each monk privileges asceticism, including the renunciation of family, over all other walks of life. Cassian, Shenoute, and Jerome explicitly engage biblical exemplars and scriptural interpretation to formulate their ascetic theories, including their ascetic theories on parent-child relations and the attendant emotional bonds. All

---

[49] Rasimus, Engberg-Pedersen, and Dunderberg, *Stoicism in Early Christianity*; Brown, *Body and Society*, 137; MacCormack, *Shadows of Poetry*; Chin, *Grammar and Christianity*; Elm, *Sons of Hellenism*.

[50] Rasimus, Engberg-Pedersen, and Dunderberg, *Stoicism in Early Christianity*, vii.

[51] Thorsteinsson, "Stoicism As a Key," 21–23; Denzey, "Facing the Beast."

[52] Konstan, *Emotions of the Ancient Greeks*, 169–84; Graver, *Stoicism and Emotion*, 173–90; Nussbaum, *Therapy of Desire*, 164–65, 542–43. For classical authors, the *eupatheia* of love was *philia*; Paul used *agapē*; Cassian, as we see in what follows, sometimes used *caritas*.

[53] Clark, *Reading Renunciation*, 9.

three invoke Jesus' directives to become eunuchs for the kingdom of heaven (Matt. 19:12) and to renounce or hate their family in order to be a disciple (Mark 10:29–30, Matt. 19:29, Luke 14:26).[54] Shenoute's biblical discourse also draws heavily from the Prophets as models for parents turned monks and as a model for his own self-fashioning as an author and leader who guides his flock in proper asceticism.[55]

Emotional Discipline and Cassian's Ascetic Sage

John Cassian, who founded monasteries for men and women in what is now Marseilles, France, wrote what would become foundational books for monks in later Europe. Cassian crafted the literary persona of an ascetic shaped by his years as a monk in Egypt, where he trained before establishing the monasteries in Gaul. Because he presents a stylized version of Egyptian monasticism as a model for Gaul, Cassian's work is both an important comparanda for our study of Egyptian authors and also an expression of the influence of Egyptian monastic ideologies of children and family. For Cassian, ascetic discipline culminates in the creation of a Christianized, asceticized sage. Askesis trains the body and psyche to express feelings volitionally and subject to religious authority (the *logos* of biblical tradition and theological authority standing in for – but not entirely replacing – the *logos* of reason in the philosophical world). It trains the body and psyche not to submit to the movements of negative emotions but to assent to the expression of good feelings. Cassian was embedded in the classical rhetorical and philosophical tradition to such a point that Marcia Colish has argued that Stoicism, in particular, finds among early Christian authors its fullest expression in Cassian, who "achieved a sensitive combination of [Stoicism] with Christianity."[56] His most explicit embrace of Stoicism appears in his ethics: virtue comes from the mind, and its development depends upon attitude and judgment. Cassian's ascetic perfection consists of *tranquilitas animi*, which is the monk's objective through monastic practice, prayer, and contemplation. It seeks no "complex extirpation of feeling" but rather to produce a monk with virtuous affect. For Cassian, this state is attainable, albeit

---

[54] Cassian, *Conferences* 24.26, in Petschenig, *Collationes*, 704–05; trans. Ramsey, *Conferences*, 847. Shenoute, *God Is Holy, Canons*, vol. 7, MONB.XU 100–01, in Amélineau, *Oeuvres de Schenoudi*, vol. 2, 153. Jerome, *Ep.*108.3.2, in Cain, *Jerome's Epitaph on Paula*, 44.

[55] Krawiec, *Shenoute and the Women*, 136–42; Brakke, "Shenoute, Weber, and the Monastic Prophet"; Schroeder, "Prophecy and Porneia."

[56] Leyser, "*Lectio Divina, Oratio Pura*"; Colish, *Stoic Tradition*, vol. 2, 115.

impermanent; during one's temporal lifetime, it will never be "an immutable psychic state."[57]

We can see this view of ascetic perfection in Cassian's explication of the emotional life of the monk, which involves feelings but not inappropriate emotions. The climax of ascetic renunciation is one of profound depth of feeling, which binds monks to each other and to God. Ascetic renunciation of property and family operates hand in glove with open expressions of affect; monks "will even in this life receive love (*caritatem*) a hundred times more precious from his brothers."[58] This love creates a spiritual bond between monks that is both stronger and "a hundred times sweeter and nobler (*sublimior*)" than familial or sexual love. Similarly, replacing the "pleasure" of owning a "field and house," the monk will "possess as his own" and "enjoy a hundred times more all the riches (*centuplo maiore divitiarum gaudio perfruetur*)" of God.[59] Ascetic renunciation of family does not require the renunciation of love. Rather, monastic love and delight resemble the eupathetic love cherished by Cassian's philosophical predecessors.

Cassian frames this emotional theory in biblical terms, through an exegesis of Matthew 19:29. Prior to the aforementioned passage on love, he cites Jesus in the Gospels: "Everyone who leaves house or brothers or sisters or father or mother or wife or children or fields on account of my name shall receive a hundredfold in the present age and shall possess eternal life."[60] Adopting the monastic life requires renouncing legal or biological family and inherited property. Such ascetic renunciation, however, does not require people to sever affective bonds. Through askesis, the monk will exchange carnal love for the deeper and more binding happiness of monastic companionship.[61] Cassian's happiness (*gaudio*) is the feeling of joy, which figures positively in Stoic thought.[62]

For Cassian, the disciplined monastic eschews sexual relations and replaces them with more enduring and joyful relations between monks. In Book 7 of the *Institutes* Cassian in some ways "out-Stoicizes" the Stoics by advocating for a conquering of the "natural" sexual impulse (which the

---

[57] Colish, *Stoic Tradition*, vol. 2, 116–17, 120.
[58] Cassian, *Conferences* 24.26.2, in Petschenig, *Collationes*, 705; trans. Ramsey, *Conferences*, 847.
[59] Cassian, *Conferences* 24.26.2–4, in Petschenig, *Collationes*, 705–06; trans. Ramsey, *Conferences*, 847–48. Also see the conclusion to this volume.
[60] Cassian, *Conferences* 24.26.1, in Petschenig, *Collationes*, 705; trans. Ramsey, *Conferences*, 847.
[61] Cassian, *Conferences* 24.26.3–4, in Petschenig, *Collationes*, 705–06; trans. Ramsey, *Conferences*, 848; see also Colish on Cassian's view of friendship as Stoic (*Stoic Tradition*, vol. 2, 120–21).
[62] Graver, *Stoicism and Emotion*, 59; Gaca, *Making of Fornication*, ch. 3.

Stoics did not).[63] As Kate Cooper and Conrad Leyser have argued, Cassian's construction of ascetic masculinity was radical in demanding sexual abstinence but nonetheless in keeping with traditional elite Roman sensibilities on manhood: "[Cassian] endorsed the traditional premise that the problem of sexual desire was one of excess and its regulation," and in so doing presented an asceticized version of "civic masculinity."[64] Thus in addition to his philosophically inflected writings in the *Conferences* on abstinent, monastic relationships as "spiritual gladness and the joy of a most precious love," Cassian also defines sexual abstinence itself in traditional terms of excess and regulation.[65]

Cassian's harmonizing of Stoic psychological and emotional theory with ascetic exegesis is also evident in Book 4 of the *Institutes*, which narrates a particularly brutal incident of monastic hazing. Cassian recounts a story of a certain Egyptian Abba Patermutus, who joined a monastery with his eight-year-old son. The monastic father separated the two, placing them in different cells under the authority of separate superiors, expressly in order to break the father-son bond between them, "lest the father think, from constantly seeing the lad, that of all the goods and carnal feelings (*affectione carnali*) of his that he had renounced and cast aside, at least his son was still his."[66] The ties that bind cannot so easily be broken by distance, however, and so the monastic superior escalated the situation, precisely to test Patermutus' emotional maturity – his feelings, and the objects of those feelings. "In order to find out more clearly whether he [the father] made more of his feeling for his kindred (*affectione sanguinis*) and of his own heart's love or of obedience and mortification in Christ (which every renunciant ought to prefer out of love for him)," the child was "purposely neglected," "clothed in rags," covered with "filth" (*foedatus*), and randomly beaten by a variety of people until the boy cried.[67] Cassian reports that Patermutus nonetheless remained "stern and unmoved out of love (*amore*) for Christ and by the virtue of obedience (*obedientiae*)." These virtues (love and obedience) replace familial love, and Patermutus "no longer considered as his son the child whom he had offered to Christ along with himself, nor did he

---

[63] Cassian, *Institutes* 7.1.1 and "naturali" and "naturam" in 7.3.1–2, in Petschenig, *De institutis*, 130–31; trans. Ramsey, *Institutes*, 169–70.

[64] Cooper and Leyser, "Gender of Grace," 544, 547.

[65] Cassian, *Conferences* 24.26.5, in Petschenig, *Collationes*, 706; trans. Ramsey, *Conferences*, 848.

[66] Cassian, *Institutes* 4.27, in Petschenig, *De institutis*, 65–66; trans. Ramsey, *Institutes*, 92.

[67] Cassian, *Institutes* 4.27, in Petschenig, *De institutis*, 66; trans. Ramsey, *Institutes*, 92–93.

worry about his present sufferings." Instead he "rejoiced (*exsultabat*), because he saw that they were not being borne fruitlessly."[68] The monastic father then, "with a view to testing his strength of mind to the utmost," ordered Patermutus to throw the child in the river. He acceded immediately, grabbing his son and running to the riverbanks, where other monks who had been stationed there by the monastic superior ahead of time prevented him from killing the child. Having proven himself a true imitator of Abraham in complete obedience to the will of another, he soon became the next leader of the monastery.[69] This account obviously bears resemblance to the accounts in *Sayings* examined in Chapter 4 on child sacrifice motifs. In this chapter, with respect to the *Institutes*, I wish to focus on affect and the parent-child bond.

Cassian's emphasis on obedience and his open comparison of Patermutus with the biblical patriarch Abraham masks his own manipulation of traditional elite theories of fatherhood and emotions. This passage has much to say about the social institutions of fatherhood and paternity, which I address in the next chapter, but it also has much to say about psychology and emotional development. The abba tests Patermutus' "strength" and "steadfastness" of "mind." The perfect ascetic thus has a "strong" mind whose will prevents inappropriate emotion. It is not merely that the father does not display *pathē* physically; he no longer feels them – he is "unmoved." The abba subjects Patermutus to renunciatory discipline whose result is one of the *eupatheiai*, joy (his rejoicing), not distress. Arguably, other ancient writers, including Stoics, might balk at the abuse of the child and urge that compassion and empathy were truer responses to his pain. But for Cassian, love bonds between parent and child are vulnerable to corruption and must be subordinated to the will. Cassian thus asceticizes the Stoic good feelings for monastic ends, effectively recategorizing even the attachment between parent and child as among the *pathē* in the local "emotional community" of the coenobium.

The emotional and psychological theory at work stretches but does not reject classical emotional theory; Cassian places biblically sanctioned familial renunciation on a psychological spectrum defined by classical principles. Richard J. Goodrich has argued that Cassian positions himself in opposition to an ascetic paradigm founded on elite philosophical study: "The true monk was not an aristocrat who had taken up the study of

---

[68] Cassian, *Institutes* 4.27, in Petschenig, *De institutis*, 66; trans. Ramsey, *Institutes*, 93.
[69] Cassian, *Institutes* 4.27, 4.28, in Petschenig, *De institutis*, 66–67; trans. Ramsey, *Institutes*, 93.

Christian *philosophia*. The true monk detached himself from the world and became a slave for the sake of the Gospel."[70] The requirements of complete and utter submission to authority (the monk as enslaved) are on vivid display in the story of Patermutus. Yet Cassian's commitment to monastic obedience, specifically the submission of body, will, and whole self to monastic authority, stands not in opposition to but in creative tension with an ascetic vision crafted as Christian *philosophia*, even if it is not named as such. Patermutus represents the monk as a reconfigured philosopher-sage for whom the biblical commands to renounce marriage, family, and property stand in harmony with classical emotional and psychological theory. Cassian does this all the while overtly identifying himself not as an imitator of classical philosophers but rather as a pupil of the Egyptian desert fathers, a group of figures traditionally positioned outside Greek and Roman *paideia*.[71] As Rebecca Krawiec has shown, Cassian "uses the paradoxical figure of the learned illiterate monk" to create a monasticism steeped in classical culture and rhetoric while simultaneously privileging the practices of the foreign, "exotic," and purer Egyptian monk, who through prayer and contemplation possesses a greater knowledge of biblical wisdom than the elites in his own circles.[72] Surrendering authority is also ascetic imitation of Christ, who, according to Philippians 2:7, became enslaved to save humanity. In this way, Cassian presents monks like Patermutus as Stoic models as well as enslaved people: men who depict the qualities of the sage without ever having opened a philosophical treatise, a rhetorical handbook, or a letter of Cicero. In Cassian's monastic handbooks, a biblically based model of asceticism is not only harmonized with the classical ideal of the sage, it is the most perfect expression of that sage.

Emotions, Persuasion, and Social Control in Shenoute

Despite his well-known appeals to familial renunciation as the bedrock of monasticism, Shenoute draws on the emotional bonds between parents and children as well as the social responsibilities inherent in these relationships in order to persuade his community. Like the other authors studied in this chapter, Shenoute's rhetoric of affect is informed by theories of biblical interpretation and classical theories of emotions. As I have argued

---

[70] Goodrich, *Contextualizing Cassian*, 31.
[71] See also Leyser on Cassian's monastery in the *Conferences* as a *coenobium* of letters, "a hybrid institution." Leyser, "*Lectio Divina, Oratio Pura*," 92–95.
[72] Krawiec, "Monastic Literacy," 782.

elsewhere, "Stoic views on emotions and the proper way men in particular should handle emotions and the objects and events that could possibly trigger emotions contribute to Shenoute's understanding of how the ideal monk should act in the world."[73] Other classical influences include gendered views on affect and public displays of affect, as we see later in this chapter. In Shenoute's writings specifically on bonds between parents and children, however, elements of ancient philosophy are less obvious than the general influences of ancient Mediterranean culture after the Second Sophistic. Often passages about familial bonds concern social control in the monastery or wider community.

Often Shenoute's rhetoric uses the bonds between parents and children as a metaphor or simile for something else. For example, a naughty child who hides from his father functions as a metaphor for the relationship between humanity and God; do not sinners, he asks, likewise hide in shame from their creator?[74] Shenoute also acknowledges the depth and strength of emotional bonds between parents and their children, bonds that often surface as grief. He claims that the desolation and grief he feels when a monk sins rivals the devastation felt by a father over an errant son, a mother over her daughter, brother over brother, or friend over friend.[75] By comparing his relationship with the monks in his community to the local "emotional community" of a family or household, Shenoute validates the power of familial emotional ties.

Occasionally, he even promotes the maintenance of traditional familial bonds, albeit strategically, and typically to persuade the monks to submit to his own authority as monastic leader. In Volume 2 of his *Canons* for monks, he uses the language of familial love, particularly between mothers and their children, in order to urge the women to repent, change their behavior, and recognize Shenoute and his rules as their authority. His argument is one familiar to readers of ascetic literature; indeed, we see Jerome make the very same case in his letters: the promise of eternity together in heaven should soothe the pain of separation here and now.

> For if you shall be separated from your children and your brethren and all your people in this dwelling-place and shall also be separated from them in unending eternity, then why did you separate from them? And if you shall

---

[73] Schroeder, "Perfect Monk," 181–93. On Shenoute and emotions, also see Crislip, "Emotion Words in Coptic," 45–56.

[74] Shenoute, *This Great House, Canons*, vol. 7, MONB.XU 308–9, in Amélineau, *Oeuvres de Schenoudi*, vol. 2, 8.

[75] Shenoute, *This Great House, Canons*, vol. 7, MONB.XU 310, in Amélineau, *Oeuvres de Schenoudi*, vol. 2, 9.

not have the satisfaction of your children and your brethren and your menfolk and all your people, then why did you depart from those who are of your kin? And if you shall not find the saints that you may be with them in heaven, and if you shall not find a resting-place, then why did you forsake them?[76]

In this text, the women seem to be complaining that they have not seen their children or husbands for more than a month. Shenoute retorts by asking them to imagine how painful it will be to be separate from them for eternity if they continue to undermine their own salvation by demanding to spend more time with their relatives, in defiance of the community's rules separating men and women – even male and female family members. Why, Shenoute asks, are they jeopardizing the rewards they will receive (namely, a heavenly reunion with their family) for their earthly renunciation of family? To maintain a structure of monastic relationships that is *not* based on preexisting family relationships, he leverages their familial intimacy, urging them to delay the emotional gratification of time spent among loved ones.

In Volume 4 of his *Canons*, Shenoute likewise appeals to the women's attachment to their relatives, especially their children, to encourage their submission. He describes visits to the women's community by a man who is second only to Shenoute in rank in the monastery. This man, whom Shenoute calls "the old man" or "the Elder," delivers Shenoute's letters, reports back to Shenoute about events in the community, and carries out various commands of his:

He is for his part a wise person in his deeds. And he will pray with you and come to us in peace, and we shall be reassured in our domain, we and all the elders, along with your children, your parents, your brethren, and all your relatives after the flesh, and all the brothers who pray for this, so that they may hear good news of you, for frequently they hear me (say) that I am grieved over you.[77]

Here, Shenoute speaks not of the monastic family but of the fleshly family (*kata sarx*). He affirms the women's attachment to their relatives, their children, parents, and others who were family to them before they ever joined the monastery. As Krawiec has documented, the women in Shenoute's monastery at times resisted the visits and instructions from

---

[76] Shenoute, *Canons*, vol. 2, MONB.XC 228–30, in Kuhn, *Letters and Sermons of Besa*, vol. 1, 121–23; trans. vol. 2, 117.

[77] Shenoute, *Why O Lord*, *Canons*, vol. 4, MONB.BZ 351–52, in Young, *Coptic Manuscripts*, vol. 1, 106–07, 113.

the Elder. And, as Shenoute alludes in this passage, he and the women were "frequently" at odds. Here, he takes advantage of their familial bonds and appeals to the women's emotions in order to persuade them to accept his emissary (the Elder) and the accompanying commands.

In Volume 7 of his *Canons*, Shenoute reminds the monks twice of the magnitude of the personal sacrifice that familial renunciation entails. The emotions of relatives – between fathers and sons, mothers and daughters – are examples of the strongest and most binding forms of love. Children take the extraordinary act of abandoning their families for the life of God in their monasteries, Shenoute argues, only then to see their monastic companions sin. Shenoute thus uses the power of these now lost familial bonds to shame sinners. Many people have forsaken relationships with their parents or children to become monks in his monastery, and so, he argues, it is a travesty when other monks disrespect and disregard this sacrifice by sinning with impunity:

> Did the parents not love their children or the children not love their parents or a man not love his wife or the woman not love her husband, especially a young man and his bride? And it is a wonder that many are the children who renounce their parents and the parents their children and men their wives and women their husbands because of their love for God and his blessed son, and they are ashamed of those who do these things, especially some extremely unclean men and some extremely pestilential women who love things contrary to nature.[78]

Shenoute cites familial *love* as the crux of this bond between family members. He continues, emphasizing that *only* love for God can supplant the love parents and children share; those who exchange parental love for illicit love incur shame.[79]

Shenoute also attempts to harness the power of familial bonds to push his monks toward desired actions, such as repentance. In Volume 7 of his *Canons* for monks, Shenoute writes about the effects of regional conflicts with people known as the Blemmyes, who have raided villages in his part of Egypt.[80] Writing about the casualties caused by these incursions, Shenoute

---

[78] Shenoute, *God Is Holy*, *Canons*, vol. 7, MONB.XU 100–01, in Amélineau, *Oeuvres de Schenoudi*, vol. 2, 153.

[79] Shenoute, *God Is Holy*, *Canons*, vol. 7, MONB.XU 101–02, in Amélineau, *Oeuvres de Schenoudi*, vol. 2, 153–54.

[80] The identity of the peoples called "the Blemmyes" in Roman sources is contested; this name may refer to multiple different tribes of people from Lower Nubia, as Jitse Dijkstra documents in "Blemmyes, Noubades and the Eastern Desert." Dijkstra, however, does not use Shenoute as a source; on Shenoute, the Blemmyes, and vol. 7 of his *Canons*, see Emmel, "Historical Circumstances"; Schroeder, *Monastic Bodies*, ch. 3; Grossmann, "Zur Stiftung und Bauzeit."

draws on his audience's shared definitions of legitimate, expected emotional responses to events. He acknowledges that they as a community will fear the Blemmyes' attacks and mourn relatives lost in the fighting. Shenoute's aim, however, is not compassion. People understandably grieve over the deaths of their loved ones, he acknowledges. They should, however, mourn over their living relatives' sins; such grief is more virtuous. In his sermon *This Great House*, Shenoute acknowledges the primacy of familial grief while simultaneously asking what the true and more authentic source of grief is:

> We filled the district. We filled the cities and the villages and the roads crying out because of fear of the barbarians, exclaiming, "Woe, woe." Some, "Because of my children." Some others, "Because of my parents and my siblings." Now where is the father, or where is the mother, or where is the brother, or where is the person who weeps and who mourns because his daughter fornicated and his son was impious and also his brother? If some are distressed because their children or their siblings sinned, then they are worthy of every honor.[81]

Shenoute thus invokes the very poignant image of public lamentation for lost children, parents, and siblings only to undercut it, to imply that such outpourings are emotional excess when compared to (what he considers) an even greater loss. He uses the shared, cultural understanding of emotional authenticity within his local emotional community to shame this community and argue for an even more authentic source of grief: sin.

This Great House depicts people crying out in the streets, the villages, and the cities – a very public form of lament. Public lamentation was part of Egyptian funerary culture since at least the New Kingdom, as documented by mortuary inscriptions of mourners at funerals. The images and texts depicted in these tombs may themselves have evolved from an older literary tradition of lament in Egyptian literature and expressions of grief (but not the uttering of lamentations) by figures in Old Kingdom tombs.[82] Although the figures publicly grieving or lamenting in these pharaonic

[81] Shenoute, *This Great House, Canons*, vol. 7, MONB.XL 279–80 (unpublished), in FR-BN 130⁴ f. 142 r/v, online, https://gallica.bnf.fr/ark:/12148/btv1b10090479w/f118.image, accessed December 4, 2019: ⲁⲛⲙⲉϩⲛ̅ⲧⲟϣ ⲁⲛⲙⲉϩ︤ⲛ̅ⲡⲟⲗⲓⲥ ⲁⲩⲱ ⲛ̅ϯⲙⲉ ⲙ̅ⲛ̅ⲛⲉϩⲓⲟⲟⲩⲉ ⲉⲛⲁϣⲕⲁⲕ ⲉⲃⲟⲗ ⲉⲧⲃⲉⲑⲟⲧⲉ ⲛ̅ϩⲉⲛⲃⲁⲣⲃⲁⲣⲟⲥ ⲉⲛϣϣ ⲉⲃⲟⲗ ϫⲉⲟⲩⲟⲓ̈ ⲟⲩⲟ̈ⲓ. ϩⲟⲉⲓⲛⲉ ϫⲉⲉⲧⲃⲉⲛⲁϣⲏⲣⲉ. ϩⲉⲛⲕⲟⲟⲩⲉ ϫⲉⲉⲧⲃⲉⲛⲁⲉⲓⲟⲧⲉ ⲁⲩⲱ ⲛⲁⲥⲛⲏⲩ. ⲉϥⲧⲱⲛ ϭⲉ ϩⲱⲱϥ ⲡⲉⲓⲱⲧ ⲏ ⲉⲥⲧⲱⲛ ⲧⲙⲁⲁⲩ ⲉϥⲧⲱⲛ ⲡⲥⲟⲛ ⲉϥⲧⲱⲛ ⲡⲣⲱⲙⲉ ⲉⲧⲣⲓⲙⲉ ⲁⲩⲱ ⲉⲧⲛⲉϩⲡⲉ ϫⲉⲁⲧⲉϥϣⲉⲉⲣⲉ ⲡⲟⲣⲛⲉⲩⲉ ⲁⲩⲱ ⲁⲡⲉϥϣⲏⲣⲉ ⲣ̅ⲁⲥⲉⲃⲏⲥ ⲁⲩⲱ ⲡⲉϥⲥⲟⲛ. ⲉϣϫⲉⲟⲩⲛ̅ϩⲟⲉⲓⲛⲉ ⲉⲩⲙⲟⲕϩ̅ ⲛ̅ϩⲏⲧ ϫⲉⲁⲛⲉⲩϣⲏⲣⲉ ⲏ ⲛⲉⲩⲥⲛⲏⲩ ⲣ̅ⲛⲟⲃⲉ. ⲟⲛⲧⲱⲥ ⲥⲉⲙ̅ⲡϣⲁ ⲛ̅ⲧⲁⲉⲓⲟ ⲛⲓⲙ.

[82] Enmarch, "Mortuary and Literary Laments," 97–99; *pace* Seibert, *Die Charakteristik*. Seibert argues that Middle Kingdom literary laments are rooted in historical funerals. Enmarch posits that funeral depictions in the New Kingdom and later were influenced by earlier literature.

sources include both men and women, women predominate. In New Kingdom tombs analyzed by Roland Enmarch, the wife or groups of mourning or "wailing" women speak the laments.[83] Women also feature in *liturgical* texts, such as the Old Kingdom Pyramid Texts, the Coffin Texts, and Greco-Roman liturgical papyri. (Here liturgical texts are distinguished from depictions of funerals within tombs.) The liturgical laments are often "spoken in the voices of Isis and Nephthys," the goddesses who mourn for their brother Osiris. According to Enmarch, in these texts, which are idealized formulations of words spoken at the embalming of a corpse rather than at a funeral, "The mythological figures of Isis and Nephthys, because they fulfil [*sic*] the abstracted role of mourners, are allowed to express far more directly their grief than the mourners in tomb captions, where it would perhaps have offended the decorum of tomb decoration in earlier periods to record too honestly the expressions of bereft relatives on tomb walls."[84]

Three aspects of Enmarch's work are important for our understanding of Shenoute's critique of public grieving. I have already mentioned the first: gender and the frequency of women as public or liturgical mourners and grievers in tombs and liturgical texts. Second is the attention to decorum, and the perhaps inappropriate nature of "excessive" public grief (however "excessive" might be defined) by human mourners. And, finally, is the acceptance of such "excessive" grief from deities or remarkable figures. In the texts examined here, Shenoute questions the propriety of the public lament of the Christians around him. Elsewhere, however, he himself adapts the persona of a leader or prophet, grieving and lamenting over the sins of his community; in one volume he uses emotional language writing about an illness he experiences and problems in the monastery.[85] He also attributes to God a fitting, even righteous, grief over lost souls.[86] Gender and power dynamics may contextualize Shenoute's seemingly divergent views on public grief and lament. As leader of his community, Shenoute asserts the authority to determine when, where, and how Christians express appropriate grief. The people he critiques – likely many of them women – have chosen an unauthorized outlet for their emotions, and one with a long tradition as a ritual of critiquing institutional authority. In defining the boundaries of appropriate emotional

[83] Enmarch, "Mortuary and Literary Laments," 91–93.
[84] Enmarch, "Mortuary and Literary Laments," 95.
[85] Brakke, "Shenoute, Weber, and the Monastic Prophet"; Shenoute, *Canons*, vol. 8, in Boud'hors, *Le canon 8 de Chénouté*.
[86] Schroeder, "Perfect Monk."

expression, Shenoute also circumscribes the authority of subordinates and lay Christians.

Emotional Askesis in the Letters of Jerome

While Shenoute's rhetorical moves are clearly influenced by biblical and Egyptian traditions, they also resemble those of the Latin church father Jerome, famous not only for his biblical exegesis and translations but also for his role as an advisor to many wealthy ascetic families. Like Shenoute, Jerome deploys emotional language in order to persuade. He often doles out praise for emotional propriety and opprobrium for emotional excess, in order to urge his correspondents to act according to his advice. Jerome also resembles Cassian in the way his rhetoric speaks particularly to an elite audience and strives to cultivate an emotionally disciplined Christian subjectivity within that audience.

Colish has argued that Jerome is a somewhat fair-weather Stoic – advancing Stoic principles when they suit him and lambasting them as "error" and "heresy" elsewhere.[87] I would call his adaptation of Stoic discourse strategic and gendered. The Stoic influences appear most conspicuously in his letters and biblical commentaries, where he accepts and applies to ascetic Christianity the ethical distinction between emotions and pre-emotions (*passio* and *propassio*) as well as the Stoic categorizations of feelings into *eupatheiai* and passions. (His rhetoric exhibits these influences despite an overt condemnation of Stoic philosophy in his critique of Pelagianism during the Origenist controversy.[88]) The Stoics usually classify passions or emotions into four groups: pleasure, pain, fear, and desire. They should for the most part be "overcome" by "virtue."[89] The exception is joy (*gaudium*), which Jerome classifies in different contexts as a *passio* (something to be extinguished) or as a *eupatheia* and gift of the Holy Spirit.[90] As Colish notes, Jerome diverges from classical writers when he contrasts "heavenly joys" and "earthly pleasures," but his structure (distinguishing an emotion from a good feeling) is traditional. Jerome's other key *eupatheia* is *pax* or the peace of Christ. It is "a gift of grace," but conceptualized "in Stoic terms" as tranquility, "a tranquil mind (*tranquilla mens*) undisturbed by any of the passions (*passionibus*)."[91] In

---

[87] Colish, *Stoic Tradition*, vol. 2, 70–73.
[88] Jerome, *Ep.* 133 1, in Hilberg, *Epistulae III*, 241–42; see also Clark, *Origenist Controversy*, 223–24.
[89] See also Colish, *Stoic Tradition*, vol. 2, 76.   [90] Colish, *Stoic Tradition*, vol. 2, 76.
[91] Colish, *Stoic Tradition*, vol. 2, 77.

other words, Jerome Christianizes, theologizes, and asceticizes classical
good feelings: joy and tranquility result from Christian askesis.

Jerome's treatment of the emotional ties between parents and children,
especially in ascetic families, appears in his correspondence. I examine here
Letters 39 to his patron and student Paula (on the death of her daughter
Blaesilla), 108 to Blaesilla's sister Eustochium (on the death of her mother,
Paula), and 107 to Paula's daughter-in-law, Laeta. While his emotional
theory cuts across both sexes – often applying to women as well as men – it
is also gendered. He expects ascetic women to renounce many of the
gendered expectations of their class, including what he considers to be
emotional indulgences.[92] Ascetic women reject their identities as mothers
and as such have a tenuous claim to affective bonds with their children. At
other times, Jerome paradoxically expects the parent-child bond to
strengthen women's asceticism. Thus, his articulation of the proper ascetic
affect for women varies depending on the goal of his argument and the role
of gender in achieving his objective. Stoic psychology, classical psychology,
primarily concerns men – not women. Women, albeit capable of virtue, are
typically considered more emotional.[93] Jerome at times concedes to this
late antique form of gender stereotyping and at others asserts that women,
by renouncing their femininity through asceticism, can transcend their sex,
including its emotive qualities.

Jerome uses the rhetoric of emotions, the parent-child bond, and the
Stoic expectations of virtue and propriety not only to console his recipients
but also to persuade them to follow his advice and instructions. He
employs two techniques: presenting his course of action as the most
reasonable, appropriate, and virtuous, and mentioning familial, affective
bonds to reinforce his own intimacy with and influence over these women.
Jerome's use of emotional discourse is strategic and gendered: at times he
applies classical principles of virtue and affect to women, and elsewhere,
when it suits him, he treats motherhood and daughterhood as entirely
different emotional paradigms.

Jerome writes *Ep.* 39 to his longtime friend, patron, and student in
asceticism, Paula, after her daughter Blaesilla has died, probably as a result
of excessive fasting under Jerome's tutelage.[94] The other elites in Rome are
outraged, Jerome is exiled, and Paula shockingly accompanies him to

---

[92] Clark, "Ascetic Renunciation and Feminine Advancement"; *pace* Colish on Jerome's feminism,
Stoic Tradition, vol. 2, 88–89.

[93] E.g., Graver's treatment of Philo in *Stoicism and Emotion*, 104.

[94] Cain, *Letters of Jerome*, 102–05; Clark, *Jerome, Chrysostom, and Friends*; Cain, *Jerome's Epitaph on
Paula*, 21.

Palestine. Jerome seeks to comfort Paula and to resuscitate his own reputation among the elites in Rome. He attempts to manipulate her maternal feelings and exploit her expectations of family bonds in order to console her on the death of her daughter as well as buttress her commitment to asceticism and to him.

Schooling her in the appropriate expression of feelings, he defines the boundary between natural mourning and unseemly grief. As examples of *proper* mourners, he provides himself and Paula's own dead daughter Blaesilla. He admits that he weeps over the girl's death – not for Blaesilla herself but rather for his own loss and the world's loss of her virtues (chastity, mercy, etc.). Thus, he frames his emotional response as natural and acceptable, since it is appropriate to mourn the departure of loved ones.[95] Likewise, he presents Blaesilla as a model of emotional propriety during her lifetime, when she mourned the loss of her own virginity more than the loss of her husband. In the framework of ancient emotional theory, Jerome is arguing that Paula's daughter exhibited the appropriate affective response to specific events – the loss of virginity (in Jerome's value system) being a greater danger than the loss of a husband. He accuses Paula, however, of impropriety upon the death of her daughter – of moving from the natural reaction of a mother's tears to emotional excess. He alleges that she fasts only to "gratify her grief (*doloris*)" and urges her instead to control her feelings.[96] He cites classical Stoic principles as guides, such as the use of reason to prevent emotion that exceeds what is natural.

> I pardon you the tears of a mother (*matris lacrimis*), but I ask you to restrain your grief (*dolore*). When I think of the parent I cannot blame you for weeping; but when I think of the Christian and the monk, the mother disappears from my view. . . . Yet why do you not try to overcome by reason (*ratione*) a grief which time must inevitably assuage?[97]

Citing her behavior at her daughter's funeral, he charges that tears that "know no limits" have overwhelmed Paula. Their excess renders them "detestable," "sacrilegious," and "unbelieving." She, however, has been tempted by the devil to believe that such displays are "pious."[98]

Jerome also seeks to manipulate Paula's feelings in service of his own reputation and the legacy of upper-class propriety in a Christian era. His

---

[95] Jerome, *Ep.* 39.1, in Hilberg, *Epistulae I*, 293; trans. in *NPNF 2*.
[96] Jerome, *Ep.* 39.3, 5, in Hilberg, *Epistulae I*, 298–300, 304–05; trans. in *NPNF 2*, vol. 6.
[97] Jerome, *Ep.* 39.5, in Hilberg, *Epistulae I*, 304; trans. in *NPNF 2*, vol. 6, mod.
[98] Jerome, *Ep.* 39.5–6, in Hilberg, *Epistulae I*, 305–7; trans. in *NPNF 2*, vol. 6.

portrait of emotional excess is distinctly gendered, and he subsequently uses his own theories on gender and asceticism to chart a more restrained and virtuous path for Paula. In the passage cited earlier, Jerome distinguishes Paula's identity as mother from her identity as a "monk" and "Christian." For Jerome, women's identities are frequently in conflict. Though askesis should trump womanhood, Jerome's women often resist his categorizations, as Paula seems to do here (as well as in Jerome's portrait of her in *Ep.* 108, which we examine later in this chapter). In *Ep.* 39, he provides the decorum of famed ascetic Melania the Elder as a model for Paula; one of Melania's sons died right after her husband, and according to Jerome, she neither shed a tear nor succumbed to intemperate public display: "Would you not suppose that in her frenzy she would have unbound her hair, and rent her clothes, and torn her breast? Yet not a tear fell from her eyes. Motionless she stood there; then casting herself at the feet of Christ, she smiled, as though she held Him with her hands."[99] Jerome privileges a Stoicized Christian askesis over traditionally gendered forms of women's grief. Although he camouflages his philosophy with scripture and offers in its place biblical and saintly models for mourning and steadfastness, his advice to Paula nonetheless bears classical traces.

Jerome also draws upon the classical framework of classifying emotions in part based on the event that triggers the feeling: is the feeling an appropriate response to that event? Grief is warranted only upon the death of one doomed to eternal hellfire.[100] Instead of mourning, Paula should "congratulate" her daughter upon being taken by God after renewing her vow of widowhood. Tears are appropriate after the death of one who dies unredeemed, and then "no tears shed for her would have been too many."[101] Jerome urges Paula to displace her inappropriate emotions with a more natural and productive feeling: reverence or fear of God. Paula's anger at Jerome and God for taking away her daughter is intermingled with her grief; she should instead fear God, who has claimed Blaesilla as his own daughter, and who, according to Jerome, eventually lays claim to us all.[102]

Similarly, in his eulogy of Paula in Letter 108, Jerome praises her for moments of affective discipline and critiques her for emotional excess concerning her family. In chapter 19, he commends Paula's use of prayer and scripture to control her grief:

[99] Jerome, *Ep.* 39.5, in Hilberg, *Epistulae I*, 305; trans. in *NPNF 2*, vol. 6.
[100] Jerome, *Ep.* 39.3, in Hilberg, *Epistulae I*, 298–99; trans. in *NPNF 2*, vol. 6.
[101] Jerome, *Ep.* 39.3, in Hilberg, *Epistulae I*, 299; trans. in *NPNF 2*, vol. 6.
[102] Jerome, *Ep.* 39.3, in Hilberg, *Epistulae I*, 299–300.

I know that she was informed by letter about the life-threatening illnesses of her children and especially of her Toxotius, whom she loved exceedingly. After stoutheartedly (*virtute*) fulfilling the verse: "I was troubled and I did not speak," she exclaimed: "Whoever loves his son or daughter more than me is not worthy of me," and she prayed to the Lord: "Protect the sons of the ones put to death who daily put to death their own bodies for your sake."[103]

Paula exhibits affective equilibrium at a trying moment for any mother; she rightly loved her children, as a Roman mother should.[104] But upon learning of their possible deaths, she maintains emotional self-mastery by quoting the Gospels and reminding herself and Jerome's audience of the power of ascetic discipline. In describing Paula's techniques of emotional self-control, Jerome substitutes scripture, prayer, and askesis for philosophy's reason and training. As Andrew Cain has argued, Letter 108 helps set the stage for the veneration of Paula as a saint within a few generations of her death.[105] The hotspot for this veneration would be the monasteries in Bethlehem, which she and Jerome had established, and which were near the Cave of the Nativity, where her body was interred.[106] In this epitaph for Paula, Jerome establishes norms for the local emotional communities of these monasteries by simultaneously depending upon and transforming the classical tradition.

Yet, according to Jerome, Paula's status as a mother proves pivotal, and ultimately fatal, for her journey to affective self-mastery. When one child after another dies, her grief overwhelms her. In all other realms of asceticism (renunciation of wealth, fasting, prayer, scriptural study), Paula proved herself a virtuoso. But according to Jerome, the emotional bond of mother and child remained too powerful when faced with her children's passing:

Indeed, when her husband and children passed away she nearly died herself, and even though she made the sign of the Cross on her mouth and stomach and thereby tried to alleviate a mother's anguish (*matris dolorem*), emotion (*affectus*) overwhelmed her and parental feelings threw her unsuspecting heart into upheaval. Although she had mastered her soul, she was mastered by the weakness of her body, which an illness once seized and dominated for a long period, making us anxious and imperiling her.[107]

---

[103] Jerome, *Ep.* 108.19.4, in Cain, *Jerome's Epitaph on Paula*, 72–73.
[104] See also Cain on Paula as a model for the ideal Roman mother who especially loves her son: *Jerome's Epitaph on Paula*, 354.
[105] Cain, *Jerome's Epitaph on Paula*, 24–30, 36.   [106] Cain, *Jerome's Epitaph on Paula*, 26–27, 36.
[107] Jerome, *Ep.* 108.21.4, in Cain, *Jerome's Epitaph on Paula*, 78–79, trans. mod.

Jerome's description reflects an important aspect of ancient emotional theories, that emotions are expressed in the body. Paula's body is literally sick from grief. Here Jerome implicates her gender, and especially her motherhood, for her inability to constrain her emotions. As Cain notes, some ancient authors, including the Stoic Seneca, depicted the death of close relatives as "traumatic" and containing affect, but Jerome portrays Paula's reaction as neither natural nor ideal.[108] His depiction of Paula's grief is a commentary on the limits motherhood places on the ascetic woman, not a commentary on the virtues of a mother's devotion to her children. Although in many ways the ideal ascetic, Paula fails in this one aspect of self-mastery. Her maternal feelings undermine her emotional equilibrium, because excessive grief goes hand in hand with motherhood.[109]

Jerome also attempts to manipulate the affective bond between Paula and her daughters by invoking Stoic expectations to expose the precarious nature of Paula's identity as ascetic mother. He positions Blaesilla as Christ's daughter as much as God's bride, causing divine fatherhood to usurp Paula's motherhood. He classifies Paula's grief (a potentially natural feeling) as instead anger at God (an inappropriate emotion) that is only masquerading as bereavement. He asks, "Have you no fear (*vereris*), then, lest the Saviour may say to you: 'Are you angry (*irasceris*), Paula, that your daughter has become my daughter? Are you vexed (*indignaris*) at my decree, and do you, with rebellious tears, grudge me the possession of Blaesilla?'" Her mourning, he asserts, is really anger and defiance at God; and she lacks the good feeling of reverence. Still speaking with the voice of God, he writes, "If you really believed your daughter to be alive, you would not grieve that she had passed to a better world. This is the commandment that I have given you through my apostle, that you sorrow not for them that sleep, even as the Gentiles, which have no hope" (1 Thess. 4:13).[110] Jerome uses scripture to camouflage his philosophical principles and employs logic to discipline her emotions. The rational thing to do, he argues, is not to grieve, for Blaesilla has moved on to a better life with God; reason, though, is proven by scripture.

---

[108] Cain, *Jerome's Epitaph on Paula*, 395; see also Jerome's discussion of Paula's "faults" in *Ep. 108* 21.5, in Cain, *Jerome's Epitaph on Paula*, 80–81.

[109] Compare to his description in *Ep.* 118 of the widower Julian, who has lost a wife and two daughters. Jerome praises Julian for quickly drying his tears of mourning. *Ep.* 118.5.4, in Hilberg, *Epistulae II*, 442.

[110] Jerome, *Ep.* 39.3.4–5, in Hilberg, *Epistulae I*, 299; trans. in *NPNF* 2, vol. 6.

Jerome portrays the ideal child-parent relationship in chapter 28 of Letter 108, where he describes Eustochium's devotion to Paula. His ideal daughter-mother relationship is one of heightened affect and quite properly so (in contrast to Paula's deep grieving for her children). In Jerome's portrait, at the end of Paula's life, she and Eustochium share a bond that has been *strengthened* by the ascetic endeavor. Mother and daughter have lived with each other in the monastery, practicing asceticism together. This bond has created a child who holds the utmost respect for her mother, cares diligently for Paula on her sickbed, and grieves extensively in anticipation of her death:

> During this bout of sickness, the exceptional devotion to her mother that the daughter Eustochium had always displayed was further affirmed by all. . . . As she ran back and forth between her bedridden mother and the cave of the Lord, she lamented bitterly and implored God that she not be deprived of such wonderful companionship, that she not outlive her mother, that their bodies be carried out on the same bier.[111]

Jerome has no harsh words for Eustochium's tears. What differentiates Eustochium's laudatory grief from Paula's faulty one? First, in this local emotional community, a daughter's reverence for her mother is both a *eupatheia* and a cultural expectation. Second, Eustochium stands in for the reader and the local emotional community of the monasteries. Within the text, Eustochium honors and grieves the dying Paula in a way that mirrors the experiences of the brothers and sisters in the community. The mother-daughter bond depicted here was forged in asceticism and exemplifies the devotion of all of Paula's spiritual children for their monastic mother.[112]

Similarly, on the benefits of monastic childrearing within biological families, we might also look to Letter 107, where Jerome writes to Paula's daughter-in-law, Laeta, with advice on raising her daughter little Paula (the elder Paula's granddaughter) to become a virgin dedicated to the church. Rearing an ascetic child, he argues, is too difficult for a lay mother; instead, the child should be sent to Paula's monastery to be raised as an ascetic with love from her grandmother and aunt.[113] According to Jerome,

---

[111] Jerome, *Ep.* 108.27.2–3, in Cain, *Jerome's Epitaph on Paula*, 88–91.

[112] Compare this view with Jerome's *Ep.* 107 to Laeta, Paula's daughter-in-law, in which Jerome implies that a lay mother is incapable of raising an ascetic daughter; the burden is too great. *Ep.* 107, in Hilberg, *Epistulae II*, 290–305; see also Doerfler, "Holy Households," 73–79.

[113] Jerome, *Ep.* 107.13, in Hilberg, *Epistulae II*, 303–05; trans. Wright, *Jerome*, 338–69. In a similar letter (*Ep.* 128), Jerome advises a man named Gaudentius how to raise his infant daughter Pacatula as a virgin. (Jerome, *Ep.* 128, in Hilberg, *Epistulae III*, 156–62; trans. Wright, *Jerome*, 466–81.) The

multigenerational asceticism heightens the attachment women feel for
each other, and likewise that attachment motivates them to advance in
their askesis.[114]

Jerome's mixed messages on the value and necessity of emotions can be
attributed in part to his views on gender. On one hand, he wishes them to
use reason and ascetic discipline to withstand overwhelming grief; on the
other hand, he seems to believe that such intense mourning is endemic to
womanhood, especially motherhood. Let us return to the passage in Letter
39, where Jerome writes to Paula, "When I think of the parent I cannot
blame you for weeping: but when I think of the Christian and the monk,
the mother disappears from my view." In other words, Paula's ascetic vow
negates her identity as a mother. Jerome urges her to imitate Job,
a righteous *man* who endured "great trials" and "still lifted up his eyes to
heaven, and maintained his patience unbroken." In comparison, he chides
that Paula is "over-delicate." If Job is too old a standard, he writes, she can
follow a contemporary model, the Roman matron Melania. In Jerome's
telling, Melania not only shed no tears upon the deaths of her husband and
son but also renounced motherhood completely by leaving behind her
surviving offspring soon after.[115]

Conclusions

The monastic authors I have examined here all wrote as ascetic authorities
for their own local emotional communities in three geographically distinct
locales: southern Gaul, Upper Egypt, and Bethlehem. For each community, emotional discipline is a fundamental component of the ascetic
discipline practiced in the monastery. Affective bonds between children
and parents prove to be some of the most contested relationships in the
community, which is further complicated by their being so intertwined
with economic ties and social bonds in late antiquity. In each of the
examples, the emotional relationships between children and parents cannot be disentangled from other questions and conflicts in their local
communities about authority, status, and property. These emotional ties

---

advice is very similar to *Ep.* 107, but in 128 Jerome does not suggest Gaudentius send Pacatula to
a monastery. Also see Katz, "Educating Paula"; Larsen, "On Learning a New Alphabet."

[114] Compare to *Ep.* 118, in which Jerome urges the widower Julian to join a monastery, disinherit his
one living child (a nonascetic daughter) and her husband, and to give his remaining wealth to the
church. (Jerome, *Ep.* 118, in Hilberg, *Epistulae II*, 434–45; trans. in *NPNF* 2, vol. 6.)

[115] Jerome, *Ep.* 39.5.4, in Hilberg, *Epistulae I*, 305; trans. in *NPNF* 2, vol. 6. On Melania and Jerome,
see Luckritz Marquis, "Namesake and Inheritance," 36; Doerfler, "Holy Households," 73; Darling
Young, "Life in Letters," 153.

also prove to be points of leverage, ways in which the leaders of these ascetic communities seek to increase their influence over their flocks.

The emotional discourses of all three of our authors exhibit varying degrees of influence from classical traditions regarding feelings and affect. Even Shenoute's and Jerome's discussions of ritual acts associated with grief (tears, public lament, etc.) are part of a larger, ancient Mediterranean discourse of emotional expression and social control. We discussed earlier in this chapter both Jerome's attempts to control Paula's and Eustochium's emotional expressions and Shenoute's shaming of Christians grieving over their injured, kidnapped, or murdered relatives. As Theodore de Bruyn has argued, debates over public lamentation were the site of power struggles between the church hierarchy and Christian women. Women's public lament in Greek societies expressed their "shared pain as mothers and laborers in a male-dominated society." They used their status as mothers to mediate between living and dead, male and female. Their piercing and public grief critiqued the social systems that led to the deaths of their loved ones.[116] The women also seized the moment of death to usurp the public square, displacing men from their traditional political and oratorical territory. As public *rituals*, women's lamentations possessed cultural authority, and their emotional intensity imbued their rituals with a deeper sense of authenticity from the audience than, say, the preaching of a bishop.[117] In fact, de Bruyn's research on the context of public lament in late antiquity suggests that the people Shenoute criticized for crying "Woe, woe" may have been women.

In each of this chapter's examples, men also shame, manipulate, or discipline people's feelings in order to assert paternal authority. In Cassian's writings, the monastic father's ascetic regime produces a model monastic Stoic sage (embodied by Patermutus), who properly regulates and directs his own feelings, and who properly submits to the monastic father as the community father. Jerome and Shenoute (like the bishop in de Bruyn's analysis) make mockery of women's emotions in order to reassert paternal authority. In the case of Jerome, an ascetic father asserted his own authority over his student, and he asserted the rights of a father (God) over and against the rights of a mother. In the case of Shenoute, we see an attempt to transform the deep-rooted cultural tradition of public lamentation into religious submission; grief over a relative's death is subordinated to grief over breaking the moral code of God, the scripture, and the monastery. Jerome and Shenoute also shift the locus of blame away from

---

[116] De Bruyn, "Philosophical Counsel," 175–76. [117] De Bruyn, "Philosophical Counsel," 177.

the institutions and authorities the lamentation implicitly indicts and instead blame the *mourners*. Both also use a kind of eschatological logic in their attempts to train the affective responses of others. In Shenoute's logic, only a great tragedy (sin) deserves a great mourning. And in Jerome's, death brings a reunion with God and thus presents no tragedy to mourn.

Each author privileges the emotional bonds between ascetic family members. Shenoute, Besa, and Cassian seek to strengthen the ties between spiritual parents and children at the expense of the ties between biological and legal family members. For Jerome, asceticism can *strengthen* natal familial bonds if families join monasteries together. He shares with the other monastic leaders a belief that ties between ascetic and nonascetic parents or children need to be broken.

These monastic leaders' adaptations of classical theories of emotion, often through ascetically inflected biblical interpretation, lay the groundwork for another impulse in fourth- and fifth-century monasticism. These leaders do not abandon emotional attachment between parents and children as a motivating social force; instead, they harness it. Their local emotional communities demand the subordination of emotional, social, and economic relationships with parents and children outside the communities while strengthening the emotional, social, and economic dependencies of monastic parents and children. This move goes hand in hand with a development in the next chapter: the understanding of the monastery as a multigenerational social institution with a genealogy of spiritual ancestors and future progeny.

Conclusion
Monastic Genealogies

Recent research into family in the Roman Empire has stressed the social and economic motivations for producing offspring across the economic spectrum: non-elite families birthed children and adopted heirs to ensure security in old age; elite families did the same to ensure continuity, even individual immortality, by preserving a legacy for their family name and property.[1] The key player in the scholarly narrative is typically the father, even though in this period some women – especially in Egypt – could own property and designate heirs. In his study of asceticism and family in late antique Christianity, Ville Vuolanto has argued that Christianity provided late antique persons with the sense of continuity they desired in terms of immortality (in the form of resurrection) and legacy (in communal memory), even for ascetics and their families. Vuolanto's research concerns primarily elites and proposes that even though people who chose asceticism as children or youths would not produce children – and thus would not provide themselves or their parents with perpetuity of name and property via heirs – they nonetheless provided perpetuity of legacy and *domus* in the form of an "imperishable patrimony" generated by God and the church.[2] Thus children who chose asceticism – or who had an ascetic future chosen for them by their guardian(s) – severed the genealogical line in one sense but in another sense provided a greater legacy of sanctity and status for their family. Vuolanto finds some evidence for differences between fathers and mothers: young Christians adopting asceticism more frequently came from households parented by widows than by fathers; fathers,

---

[1] Vuolanto, *Children and Asceticism*, 216–17; Huebner, *Family in Roman Egypt*, 175–96; Wiedemann, *Adults and Children in the Roman Empire*, 26, 34–35, 39.
[2] Vuolanto, *Children and Asceticism*, 217–18.

posits Vuolanto, showed more investment in traditional biological and legal means of ensuring familial continuity than mothers.[3]

In her book *The Fall of the Roman Household*, Kate Cooper examines the role of fathers as well, arguing that late antiquity witnessed a shift in the power of fathers over their children. She writes, "At the end of antiquity . . . the older vision of Roman family life based on the legal powers of the *paterfamilias* gave way to a new ideal."[4] Cooper is particularly interested in the way local social and political authority migrated from the head of household to the bishop, but she also argues that this trend has roots in internal family dynamics. This historical moment witnessed an inversion of the traditional Roman relationships of power that privileged age over youth. In late antique Europe and North Africa, due to complicated political and economic forces, "the aspirations of sons" were "given preference over the wisdom of their fathers," and a concept of the "moral independence of sons" from their fathers developed.[5] It became more socially acceptable to subvert the hierarchical relationships between fathers and sons, in which youth once automatically deferred to age.

Into this swirling transformation of the institution of family in late antiquity stepped another institution: the monastery. While Vuolanto has argued that ascetic Christianity developed successful strategies to advance itself as a path of familial continuity despite the obvious lack of offspring, he also has admitted that Christian asceticism touched few households, and producing children was still regarded as necessary for Christian society.[6] His conclusions are primarily limited to elite families and do not account for the increasing populations of both child and adult Christians living in monasteries, especially in Egypt. Late antique monasticism both participated in and disrupted familial networks of power in the Mediterranean world. As early as the fourth and fifth centuries, we see the monastery as an institution challenging the ancient household's position as the cornerstone of society's political and economic apparatuses. It aspired to become a political institution, with all the power and status of a Roman *familia*.[7] Monasticism also asceticized a key component of this institution – fatherhood – all the while maintaining that this anomaly – the celibate, ascetic father – was no innovation; the monastic father was but one node in

---

[3] Vuolanto, *Children and Asceticism*, 219–20.   [4] Cooper, *Fall of the Roman Household*, ix.
[5] Cooper, *Fall of the Roman Household*, 28.   [6] Vuolanto, *Children and Asceticism*, 218–19.
[7] Ariel G. López argues that Shenoute's monastery actively and deliberately challenged the estates of late antique Egypt as Shenoute advocated for the rights of the poor. López, *Shenoute of Atripe and the Uses of Poverty*.

a chain of fathers and sons stretching back into the biblical era and forward into eternity.

We know that by the seventh century, monasteries in Egypt had evolved into large estates, paying taxes and keeping complex economic staff and records.[8] Although documentation that would allow us to categorize a monastery as an estate does not exist in detail as early as the fourth and fifth centuries in Egypt, the monastic literature reveals that this institutional framing begins early in the development of the Christian monastery's institutional self-identity.[9] The Pachomian monastery of Thbew was founded on a family estate, and the monastery of Tabennese was paying land taxes in 367–368 CE.[10] Likewise, by the early Merovingian period (sixth to seventh centuries), monasteries and convents were well integrated into the political and economic systems of Frankish Gaul. And as in Egypt, we see in early fifth-century Gaul John Cassian establishing a monastery that contains the foundational elements of these later developments.

The 400s in both Egypt and Gaul were turbulent times theologically, socially, and politically. In Egypt, theological divisions ripped through the ecclesial and monastic networks. To name just two, the Christological debates (culminating but not ending in Chalcedon in 451) cleaved Egyptian churches from their Latin and Greek contemporaries, and the Origenist controversy alienated many Egyptian Christians from each other.[11] In Gaul, the local ruling class contended with barbarians of various stripes, heretical controversies, and economic crisis. Bishops rose to prominence as local leaders with a political capital that could not be ignored. Thus, as Raymond van Dam argues, "the conversion of the Gallic aristocracy in the fifth century can more properly be seen as the transformation of Christianity in order to conform with existing aristocratic structures of authority and ideologies of prestige."[12] The political players changed and the landscape transformed, but the coin of the realm remained the old traditions – redefined and remixed, for sure, but still traditions – of

---

[8] Clackson, *Orders from the Monastery of Apollo*; Winlock and Crum, *Monastery of Epiphanius I*; Crum and Evelyn-White, *Monastery of Epiphanius II*; Godlewski, *Le monastère de St. Phoibammon*. For a private estate, see Hickey, *Wine, Wealth, and the State*. Scholarly analyses of the role and function of estates in the late antique Egyptian economy are varied and sometime contentious. Papyri providing evidence for the economy of the estate of Apion in Oxyrhynchus, for example, increase dramatically in the latter sixth century, as does the level of detail and complexity in these sources compared to the fifth century (Hickey, *Wine, Wealth, and the State*, 5–7, 9–21).

[9] Wipszycka, "Resources and Economic Activities," 159–263; Goehring, "World Engaged," 48–49.

[10] *V. Pach. Bo* 56; ed. and trans. Veilleux, *Pachomian Koinonia, Volume One*, 77. See discussion in Rousseau, *Pachomius*, 153–55. Wipszycka, "Terres," 625–36; Goehring, "World Engaged," 49.

[11] Watts, *Riot in Alexandria*.   [12] Van Dam, *Leadership*, 156.

nobility and authority. "The values of the old aristocracy had become characteristic also of the new aristocracy of churchmen."[13] Cassian's coenobium, despite its ascetic and renunciatory premise, exemplified this phenomenon. His monasticism posed a direct challenge to the aristocracy in some ways, while simultaneously appropriating aristocratic traditions for its own institutional and theological ends.[14] In the words of Rebecca Krawiec, "Cassian's monastic spirituality used the language and replicated the values of the Latin elite audience he was writing for so that his presentation of a new, foreign way of life does not abdicate elite masculinity but guards it."[15] In Marseilles, Atripe, and elsewhere, monastic founders imbued their coenobia with enough historical heft and scriptural underpinnings to ground them firmly in what were regarded as eternal traditions of ancient Mediterranean society and biblical history. In doing so, they sought to create institutions stable enough to weather the vicissitudes of their generation and to carry on the social and cultural work required to ensure the next generation's future.

This chapter demonstrates the ways in which Christian monasticism as an institution positioned itself as both rival and heir to the classical tradition of *familia*. It usurped the societal foundations of family and legacy, transforming traditions of paternity, inheritance, and genealogy. Focusing on the monastic federation of Shenoute in Upper Egypt and the monastery of Cassian in Gaul, it demonstrates how the coenobium evolved and positioned itself as a "house" or *domus* in late antique culture – an ancient institution that included home, household, property, and family, and required the financial, religious, disciplinary, and educational management of all of those moving parts. As Kristina Sessa's research has demonstrated, the concept of *oikonomia* (stewardship, management, ordering) and the gendered nature of household management and authority were important aspects of the late antique family.[16] Stewardship of a *domus* (including its lands) remained an "elite ideal" and an aspiration into late antiquity.[17] In both Egypt and southern France, coenobitism displaced families but not *familia*, legacies but not *legatum*, projecting itself onto the late antique social and economic landscape. The monastery, be it in Atripe

---

[13] Van Dam, *Leadership*, 141; see also Goodrich, *Contextualizing Cassian*, 21.
[14] On Cassian's monasticism as a challenge to elite sensibilities, see Goodrich, *Contextualizing Cassian*, 31; on whether the "elites" of late antique Gaul constituted a distinct class, see Jones, *Social Mobility*.
[15] Krawiec, "Monastic Literacy," 795.
[16] Sessa, *Formation of Papal Authority*, 1–14, 35–62; though Sessa examines the *domus* in Italy, her insights are applicable as a frame for understanding some of the values and structures of the elite late antique household in the broader Roman Empire.
[17] Sessa, *Formation of Papal Authority*, 63–86.

or Marseille, displayed ambition rivaling that of the most elite family in Rome, demanding recognition and status and asserting an eternal lineage.

Paternity

From documentary papyri to hagiography, from *Sayings* to graffiti and dipinti in monastic cells, from Shenoute's letters to Cassian's *Conferences*, the student-teacher relationship in early monasticism is configured as one of a son submitting to the instruction of a spiritual father. The father's title – Abba ("the father," *peiōt*) – evokes in shorthand all the affective qualities of paternal relationship: the implicit authority of father over son, mutual responsibility, and a present (even if understated) love bond. The dimensions of power and emotion are intertwined, as Philip Rousseau describes in his discussion of monks' relationships to their ascetic teachers as represented in the Greek *Sayings of the Desert Fathers* and *History of the Monks of Egypt.* "Their attitude involved nothing less than a total surrender: 'Like sons bringing gifts to a loving father,' each one offered his soul."[18] In Shenoute's and Cassian's communities, fatherhood transcends the individual master-disciple dyad, becoming an institution within an institution, accruing to itself the rights and responsibilities of the late antique *paterfamilias*, and by extension, family and legacy.

In his first two letters (what is known as Volume I of his *Canons* for monks), Shenoute criticizes his own monastic father for lacking proper paternal stature.[19] Shenoute composed these letters in the early 380s, before himself becoming the third leader of the community, when the father of the monastery at the time is believed to have been a man named Ebonh.[20] Shenoute wrote the letters while in the midst of a dispute with Ebonh over his leadership, specifically his decision not to punish a certain group of monks whom Shenoute believed had sinned. Thus Shenoute began his career chipping away at the reputation of his superior by questioning his ability to carry out his role as *father.* He accuses Ebonh of speaking to him "hatefully" during a dispute, not "lovingly" in the way a father speaks to a son.[21] He thus makes an emotional appeal by invoking a sense of intimacy

---

[18] Rousseau, *Ascetics, Authority, and the Church*, 19–20.

[19] Some of the material in the following pages also appears in a more extended analysis of masculinity in Schroeder, "Perfect Monk."

[20] Emmel, "Shenoute the Monk"; Schroeder, *Monastic Bodies*, 24–53.

[21] Shenoute, *Letter 1, Canons*, vol. 1, MONB.YW 80 (unpublished), FR-BN 130² f. 2v, online, https://gallica.bnf.fr/ark:/12148/btv1b10089625k/f5.image.r=130%20Copte, accessed December 4, 2019: ⲉⲡⲉⲓⲇⲏ ⲁⲕⲭⲛⲟⲩⲓ̈ ⲇⲉ ϩⲛ̅ⲟⲩⲙⲓⲛⲉ ⲛ̅ϣⲁϫⲉ ⲉⲛⲧⲁⲟⲩⲉⲓ̈ⲱⲧ ⲁⲛ ⲧⲉ ⲉ4ϣⲁϫⲉ ⲙⲛ̅ⲡⲉ4ϣⲏⲣⲉ ϩⲛ̅ⲟⲩⲁⲅⲁⲡⲏ·

and responsibility between father and son. Even in dispute, the monastic father should treat his spiritual son with love (*agapē*). Implicitly, that love bond requires the father to respect and listen to his offspring.

Moreover, Shenoute uses his accusation of Ebonh's betrayal of that bond to justify his own disrespect of his father figure; Shenoute confesses that he spoke harshly in return, therefore admitting that he has acted as a son in a dishonorable way.[22] In this way, Shenoute provides evidence that the socially disruptive trend Cooper documents in Europe has penetrated Upper Egypt. Shenoute publicly and sharply shrugs off the cultural convention of deference to the father. Yet, even in this act of youthful rebellion, he does not invoke an alternative, countercultural set of moral principles but rather shames the father by reminding him of their shared values. Justifying his insolence with reference to those very cultural norms that would normally condemn him, Shenoute places the blame on the father, whom he accuses of mishandling his paternal role. The medium of exchange is the emotional bond of love intertwined with respect and responsibility in the father-son relationship. Shenoute's impudence serves some very traditional mores.

Similarly, the construction of the monastery as *familia* in Shenoute's federation both endorses and complicates ancient views on the social role of the household. The monk subordinates family of origin (family "according to the flesh" [*kata sarx*]) to monastic family. Familial ties that predate one's monastic commitment are supplanted by the ties monks forge between their new spiritual brothers, sisters, mothers, fathers, sons, and daughters.[23] The women in Shenoute's federation in particular resisted this restructuring of their identities and networks, often providing extra food or other resources to their relatives. Volume 4 of Shenoute's *Canons* contains a rule mandating the expulsion of anyone who gives more food to their relatives than to the others, listing fathers favoring their sons, mothers their daughters, siblings their siblings, and anyone favoring any member of their family of origin.[24] The regulation ultimately concludes by forbidding the sharing of food with any of one's colleagues, but the language, emphasizing family from the outset, indicates that family members maintained

---

ⲁⲗⲗⲁ ⲧⲁⲟⲩⲣⲱⲙⲉ ⲧⲉ ⲉⲩϣⲁⲝⲉ ⲙ̄ⲛ̄ⲡⲉⲧϩⲓⲧⲟⲩⲱϥ ϩⲛ̄ⲟⲩⲙⲟⲥⲧⲉ ⲉⲕϫⲱ ⲙ̄ⲙⲟⲥ ⲛⲁⲓ̈ ϫⲉⲙⲏ̄ ⲛ̄ⲥⲟⲟⲩⲛ ϩⲛ̄ⲟⲩⲱⲣϫ̄ ϫⲉⲛⲓⲙ ⲡⲉⲛⲧⲁϥⲣ̄ⲛⲟⲃⲉ.

[22] Shenoute, *Canons*, vol. 1, MONB.YW 81 (unpublished), FR-BN 130² f. 3r, online, https://gallica .bnf.fr/ark:/12148/btv1b10089625k/f6.image.r=130%20Copte, December 4, 2019: ϩⲛ̄ⲟⲩⲛ̄ϣⲟⲧ ⲉϥⲛⲁϣⲧ̄ ⲛ̄ⲑⲉ ⲛ̄ⲁⲙⲛ̄ⲧⲉ. See also Schroeder, *Monastic Bodies*, 33.

[23] Krawiec, *Shenoute and the Women*, ch. 8; Jacobs and Krawiec, "Fathers Know Best?"

[24] Shenoute, *Canons*, vol. 9, MONB.DF 187, in Leipoldt, *Vita et Opera Omnia*, vol. 4, 106; see also excerpts in Layton, *Canons of Our Fathers*, 270.

familial bonds within the monastery – especially parents and children, since parent-child pairs are mentioned twice. Monks should afford relatives no extra care or consideration, insists Shenoute. Moreover, elsewhere he goes further, arguing that they should cut themselves off from their lay mothers, fathers, sons, and daughters according to the flesh when they join the monastery.[25]

Shenoute articulates this same ascetic ideology in Volume 3 of the *Canons* through an exegesis of Luke 12:53, where Jesus declares that fathers will be divided from sons and mothers from daughters. Shenoute does not limit his reading of this passage to renunciation of one's family of origin. The good monk renounces originary kin (biological or adoptive relatives) as well as monastic kin who fail to adhere to the rules of the community. He urges female and male monks to break ties with fellow monks who sin. "For it is more perfect for the person to cut off himself from his brother or his son or his daughter or his father or his mother or any other relative because of God, if they sin against God, the one who created them."[26] Here, Shenoute quotes a passage often cited to justify ascetic renunciation and instead wields it to justify expulsion or other punishment of *ascetic* siblings.[27] Monasticism requires a double-renunciation: cutting oneself off from originary kin and then from sinful monastic kin.

John Cassian narrates accounts of Egyptian monks as models for asceticism in his monastery in Gaul, using these stories of a "foreign" and more "authentic" monasticism as justification for reconfiguring the Roman traditions of family and fatherhood for his community.[28] Cassian models his ascetic teachings in his two major works, the *Institutes* and the *Conferences*, on a representation of Egyptian monasticism. Let us return to the passage in Book 4 of the *Institutes*, wherein Cassian recounts the physical abuse of the son of a monastic initiate. Patermutus had joined a monastic community with his eight-year-old son, and Cassian tells of the monastic father separating the two, expressly in order to break their father-son bond. As we discussed in Chapter 8, one element of the bond was emotional; Cassian's language highlights the affective quality of the relationship and the monastery's role in demolishing certain paternal feelings and replacing them with others. But the passage also establishes the social rights and responsibilities of fathers and sons in the community and

---

[25] E.g., Shenoute, *This Great House*, Canons, vol. 7, MONB.XU 331, in Amélineau, *Oeuvres de Schenoudi*, vol. 2, 23.

[26] Shenoute, *A22, Canons*, vol. 3, MONB.YA 427, in Leipoldt, *Vita et Opera Omnia*, vol. 4, 128.

[27] For its use to justify ascetic renunciation, see Clark, *Reading Renunciation*, 100, 197.

[28] Goodrich, *Contextualizing Cassian*, 59, 63; Krawiec, "Monastic Literacy," 774–75.

cements the role of the monastic father – not the biological or legal father – as the child's *paterfamilias*:

> And when at last they were taken in, they were at once not only handed over to different superiors but even made to live in separate cells, lest the father think, from constantly seeing the lad, that of all the goods and carnal feelings of his that he had renounced and cast aside, at least his son was still his. Thus, just as he knew that he was no longer a rich man, so he might also know that he was not a father (*patrem*).[29]

Patermutus' identity as father was not broken so easily by distance, however, and so the superior escalated the situation: the child was "purposely neglected," "clothed in rags," covered with "filth," and randomly beaten by a variety of people until he cried. Patermutus, however, remained "unmoved" and "no longer considered as his son the child whom he had offered to Christ along with himself." When the abbot, John, ordered Patermutus to throw the child in the river, the monk (in imitation of the biblical patriarch Abraham) took his son and heir to the water, where other monks whom the monastic superior had earlier stationed there prevented him from killing the child.[30]

Cassian pairs the man's wealth with his paternal stature and, in narrating his evolution into submission, crushes Patermutus' reputation and identity as an elite man and *paterfamilias*: "Thus, just as he knew that he was no longer a rich man (*divitem*), so he might also know that he was not a father (*patrem*)." Patermutus' complete obedience to John extinguishes his prior masculine identities as elite man and *pater*. In one reading, Patermutus might be seen as an example sine qua non of a monasticism that begins, in the words of Goodrich, "with a true, self-immolating renunciation."[31] But does Cassian really erase Patermutus' manhood? In foregrounding the monk's obedience and relinquishment of paternal rights, Cassian masks his own appropriation of traditional views of legal fatherhood in the service of monastic fatherhood. The abba of the monastery takes on the rights and privileges of *paterfamilias* for the community, including the welfare and discipline of children as well as the control of property. And Patermutus, as a son in complete obedience and submission to his father, renounces his son as kin and heir but in doing so secures his *own* position as heir. He, Patermutus, becomes the next monastic father, with the monastery as his *familia* and *domus*.

---

[29] Cassian, *Institutes* 4.27, in Petschenig, *De institutis*, 65–66; trans. Ramsey, *Institutes*, 92.
[30] Cassian, *Institutes* 4.27, in Petschenig, *De institutis*, 66–67; trans. Ramsey, *Institutes*, 92–93.
[31] Goodrich, *Contextualizing Cassian*, 151.

Sonship

At the same time coenobitic monasticism was reconstituting the notions of paternity around abbas as monastic *fathers*, an understanding of coenobitism as the family of God, in which abbas are simultaneously sons, was developing. All monks, whether father or son, are also sons of God, with all the rights the status of "son" conveys.

At Shenoute's monastery, while the monks are bound together as spiritual children of one spiritual father – their abba – they are also the offspring of one divine father, God. In a passage on discipline in *Canons*, Volume 3, Shenoute writes of monks as simultaneously enslaved people and higher status than enslaved people – as children: "And they shall say that this is the way that God did it for us, because we are his slaves, and the Lord disciplines us mercifully, and he chastises us mercifully, because we are his children, and he is our father."[32] Shenoute's language here, and its slippage from enslaved person to child, recalls the letters of Paul, both Galatians 4:7 ("So you are no longer a slave but a child, and if a child then also an heir, through God") and Romans 8:15–17 ("When we cry, 'Abba! Father!' it is that very Spirit bearing witness with our spirit that we are children of God, and if children, then heirs, heirs of God and joint heirs with Christ"). Unlike Paul, however, Shenoute draws no direct distinction between children and the enslaved, and therefore between *heirs* and the enslaved; the monks are simultaneously enslaved people and children, emphasizing their complete subordination to the father while also marking them as descendants.

This language is more than metaphor and more than a reconfiguration of *social* ties within the monastery: it is theological, eschatological, and economic. Shenoute continues by reminding them of the identities of their authentic parents: as long as they maintain their monastic community, they are "children of a single man, who is God," and "children of a single woman, who is Jerusalem" (Gal. 4:26). In the next line, he collapses both parenting roles into the person of Jesus: "Are our father and our mother, who begot us and who nourished us according to the flesh, more chosen than our Lord Jesus, our father and true mother? This one who begot us in his holy blood."[33] God (as Jesus) and Jerusalem have begotten the monastery as a divinely conceived *familia*. The "holy blood" of Jesus' sacrifice replaces the

---

[32] Shenoute, *A22*, *Canons*, vol. 3, MONB.ZC 305, in Leipoldt, *Vita et Opera Omnia*, vol. 4, 206.
[33] Shenoute, *A22*, *Canons*, vol. 3, MONB.YA 428, in Leipoldt, *Vita et Opera Omnia*, vol. 4, 129.

blood and placenta of childbirth, and from it emerges a familial line of monks.

In the letter to women monks known as *Abraham Our Father* (also in Volume 3 of *Canons*), this holy union of Christ and Jerusalem has spawned an entire family tree, linking the monks of the present with biblical "ancestors" both male and female ("*heneiote … eite hoout eite shime*"), whom he names as "the prophets and apostles, who were 'father' (*eiōt*) to a great many people with God's help."[34] Shenoute threads a needle in his use of the gendered noun "father" (*eiōt*), which I translate at times literally as "father" but also as "ancestor" or "parent." He explicitly qualifies "father" in this text as someone who can be either male or female. Shenoute's qualification ("whether male or female") is technically unnecessary, since the Coptic word (*eiōt*) can mean "parent." Shenoute's specificity suggests that he (and perhaps his audience) typically associate the word with masculinity and fatherhood. Here, in a letter addressed primarily to women, he attempts to ensure that these women see themselves in their biblical forebears. He goes on to specifically name the female ancestors/"fathers"/"patriarchs" Deborah, Huldah, and Anna, who are all biblical prophetesses.[35]

Imitating the prophets and apostles is not the mimesis of an "other" imagined as "self," no longer an act of reaching out across vast swaths of time and space in an effort to embody even one bit of the holiness of biblical exemplars. The prophets and apostles provide what Shenoute elsewhere in *Abraham Our Father* calls a "likeness" or a "pattern" (*smot*), to be replicated and repeated time after time by those who come after.[36] Mimesis thus becomes a generative act, enacted by asexual reproduction, in which the monk takes his rightful place in a position his forebears once occupied, as a recognized, authorized descendant of the prophets and apostles.

In their obedience to a monastic father and to each other, the monks also perform a sublime submission in imitation of the son Jesus' submission. In this letter – one originally composed for the women of the monastery but read or heard by all – Shenoute berates the women for their disobedience to

---

[34] Shenoute, *A22, Canons*, vol. 3, MONB.YA 527, in Leipoldt, *Vita et Opera Omnia*, vol. 4, 28. On "father," see Bentley Layton's Glossary in *Coptic Grammar*, 454; in contrast to Crum, who does not mention "parent" in his entry for the term in *Coptic Dictionary*, 86–87.

[35] Shenoute, *A22, Canons*, vol. 3, MONB.YA 527–28, in Leipoldt, *Vita et Opera Omnia*, vol. 4, 28.

[36] Shenoute, *Abraham Our Father*, MONB.ZH fragment 1, in Leipoldt, *Vita et Opera Omnia*, vol. 4, 32; trans. and edition also in Krawiec et al., ed., "Abraham, ZH Frg 1a–d," trans. Krawiec and Behlmer, urn:cts:copticLit:shenoute.abraham.monbzh:18–22, Coptic SCRIPTORIUM.

his commands, including their refusal to perform labor and to serve each other. He cites not only biblical figures but also Jesus as a model for submission and servitude:

> What is the work of God and our Lord Jesus but manual labor? It was his manual labor that formed us and created us. . . . [Jesus] remained steadfast on the cross for all our salvation, because he is our savior, our Lord and our father. . . . But let us be slaves (*hmhal*) to one another, like Jesus, who took the form of a slave for us, and like Paul, the slave of Jesus, and like all the apostles and prophets who were slaves to the Lord and his Christ.[37]

Shenoute's Christology here is high. The Christ on the cross is not the Jesus of the Gospel of Mark, demanding to know why he has been forsaken by *his* father. Shenoute's Christ is fully Son and Father. His typology for monastic childhood and fatherhood therefore is messy, with the monk as son/daughter as Jesus as father as God as Abba. But perhaps that is as it should be, for the son indeed becomes the father. Be he the divine Christ the Logos – the word who is with God, who is God in John 1 – or be he the heir who assumes his father's throne, property, position, and name, the son is ultimately the father. Shenoute's gender politics here are also messy. In Egypt, women and girls could be heirs.[38] They could not, however, become abbas, supreme monastic "fathers" of the monastic federation, despite his inclusion of women (Deborah, Huldah, Anna) among the biblical "parents" that provided models and ancestral heritage in *Abraham Our Father*.[39] His gender inclusivity is strategic, made possible by the use of the masculine words for "son" and "father" as the gender-neutral words for "child" and "parent." Whether he speaks of male sons or male and female children, he writes of the *šēre* and his *eiōt*. And except when strategically cajoling the women to respect his authority, which he claims is authorized by scripture, women take a back seat to a monastic-prophetic genealogy constructed almost exclusively around men – fathers and sons.

Shenoute's discourse on "fatherhood" as an eternal lineage stretching from the Bible to the present and beyond appears in his writings beyond this letter to women, even in other volumes of the *Canons* for monks.

---

37 Shenoute, *Abraham Our Father*, MONB.YA 536, in Leipoldt, *Vita et Opera Omnia*, vol. 4, 33; trans. (mod.) and edition also in Krawiec et al., ed., "Abraham, YA 535–540," trans. Krawiec and Behlmer, urn:cts:copticLit:shenoute.abraham.monbya:21–27, Coptic SCRIPTORIUM.

38 The legal and economic situation, however, was complex. Egyptian women who were Roman citizens were governed by the Augustan marriage legislation, prohibiting inheritance to women without progeny; however, since not all Egyptian women were citizens, the circumstances on the ground were varied. See Rowlandson, *Women and Society*, 174–77, specifically on the Augustan laws, and throughout for more on women's economic and legal status.

39 Krawiec, "Role of the Female Elder."

Typically this monastic-prophetic genealogy is exclusively masculine.[40] In Volume 4 of the *Canons*, Shenoute links the monks' identity as children of their monastic fathers (he and his predecessors) to their identity as children of Abraham. In this text, he is defending a disciplinary action he took against an accusation by other monks that he implemented an excessive or inappropriate punishment. (Here, I translate *šēre* as "son," emphasizing the masculine father-son lineage.) He uses the reputation of earlier monastic leaders and the biblical patriarch Abraham to justify his actions:

> And those people say these things because they did not intend to understand that if we were the sons of our first father, we would do his works, as it is written, "If you were the sons of Abraham, you would do the works of Abraham" [John 8:39]. And as for our fathers, their abomination is everyone who is disobedient toward their teachings and everyone who is disobedient toward what is prescribed for them in their houses and what is prescribed for them in all their works according to the regulations of the holy ones. Therefore, if it is fitting for us to be ashamed before our fathers who have died and to submit in the congregation when we anger those who live with us, then even more so it is fitting for us to be ashamed before our fathers who have died and flee from every enmity and hatred that we have toward those who live with us now.[41]

The monks must answer to their ancestors, their current monastic father, and their fellow monks. In describing submission in the community, Shenoute seems to describe a public ritual of humiliation, which he justifies by an appeal both to the monastic fathers and to the monks' heritage as children of the biblical patriarchs.

The paintings in the sanctuary of the Red Monastery represent a later artistic expression of this monastic theology.[42] The church was constructed circa 475–550, and several layers of paintings survive in the sanctuary.[43] Most of the visible art dates to the fourth phase of painting in the church's

---

[40] In addition to the passages examined in this chapter, see also Shenoute, *God Is Holy, Canons*, vol. 7, MONB.XG 176–77, in Wesseley, *Griechische und koptische Texte theologischen Inhalts*, vol. 1, 86–87. On continuing the genealogy with future monastic sons, see Shenoute, *Canons*, vol. 9, MONB.FM 173–74, in Leipoldt, *Vita et Opera Omnia*, vol. 4, 110.

[41] Shenoute, *Why Oh Lord, Canons*, vol. 4, MONB.BZ 5–6, in Leipoldt, *Vita et Opera Omnia*, vol. 3, 118–19.

[42] I am indebted to Elizabeth Bolman for hosting me during a visit to the Red Monastery in December 2012 with David Brakke, Gene Rogers, and Malcolm Choat, and for providing permission for me to take and publish these photographs; Bolman and William Lyster both provided detailed descriptions and analyses of the paintings; in addition to the publications cited, I draw on Bolman's and Lyster's remarks, and on site discussions with them, Brakke, Rogers, Choat, and Agnes Szymańska.

[43] See the comprehensive account of the church, its wall paintings, and their conservation in Bolman, *Red Monastery Church*.

history, with the figural paintings discussed here likely dating to circa the sixth century during Phases 2 and 3.[44] The sanctuary is redolent with figurative and nonfigurative art in bright colors and with a variety of patterns as borders and accents.[45] Multiple theologically symbolic programs adorn the space (which is structured as a triconch sanctuary, similar to the White Monastery church). Among them is a monastic genealogy.

Each of the three lobes of the triconch sanctuary contains three registers: a row of niches on the lowest level, another row of niches in the middle level, and a semi-dome at the top. Christ the Logos, holding the Bible and flanked by the four Gospels (personified as their authors), sits in the southern semi-dome (Figure 6). Across the sanctuary is a procession of monastic fathers in the northern lobe, facing into the sanctuary. The monks Pshoi, Pcol, Shenoute, and Besa each gaze out from decorative niches on the register just below the semi-dome, with its painting of the Nursing Virgin (Figure 7).[46]

The Red Monastery was founded by Pshoi and likely later joined with the monastery to the south (the White Monastery), possibly during the lives of both founders. A medieval text about the much earlier origins of the monastery asserts that after the union of the two communities, the father of the northern monastery became subordinate to the father of the southern monastery. Then, probably during Shenoute's tenure, the federation became consolidated with three residences: the main one for men (at the site of what is now the "White" Monastery), another for men (at the "Red" Monastery), and finally one for women to the south in the village of Atripe. In the basilica of the Red Monastery, in the northern lobe of the triconch sanctuary, we see painted this genealogy of fathers. Pshoi stands at the right hand of God. He is positioned in the first niche of the northern lobe, right next to the central (eastern) lobe, which contains an image of the second coming of Christ in its semi-dome (see niche on far right in Figure 8). Next, in the niche to the left of Pshoi, appears Pcol (first father of the White Monastery and likely first leader of the combined "federation"). Thus, Pcol, second in the gallery, is second in the lineage of monastic fathers for the Red Monastery. Third (left of Pshoi), we find Shenoute and last (in the far left niche), Besa, Shenoute's successor. (Notably erased from this genealogy is the second leader of the White Monastery, Ebonh, who was almost erased from history entirely until Stephen Emmel's research in the 1990s uncovered references to him in Shenoute's letters.)[47] Thus, the Fathers of the Red Monastery gaze

---

[44] Bolman, "Iconography of Salvation," 131–49; Bolman, "Figural Styles," 156–59.
[45] Bolman, "Staggering Spectacle."   [46] Bolman and Szymańska, "Ascetic Ancestors."
[47] Emmel, "Shenoute the Monk"; Emmel, *Shenoute's Literary Corpus*, vol. 2, 558–64.

Figure 6 Southern apse of the triconch sanctuary of the Red Monastery basilica.
Christ enthroned, flanked by figures representing the Gospels (Gospel authors).
Niche portraits important church officials. Photograph by Caroline T. Schroeder.

upon their Father Jesus, the Logos, the Father made flesh, in eternal mimesis.
Again, monk as father as Son as Jesus as Logos as God as Father.

In Gaul, Cassian's monks too live an eternal life of love, regeneration,
and submission in *imitatio Christi*. As we saw in the previous chapter,
Cassian in his *Conferences* exhorts the men to follow the asceticized
instruction of Matthew 19:29, to leave their household, family, and property for Jesus and receive eternal life.[48] In Cassian's *Conferences*, monks

---

[48] Cassian, *Conferences* 24.26, in Petschenig, *Collationes*, 704–05; trans. Ramsey, *Conferences*, 847.

Figure 7 Northern apse of the triconch sanctuary of the Red Monastery basilica. Nursing virgin. Figures in niches beneath are the "fathers" of the Red and White Monasteries, from right to left: Pcol, Pshoi, Shenoute, Besa. Photograph by Caroline T. Schroeder.

who renounce family and property – all the trappings of Roman legacy – will receive two rewards: a divine inheritance as God's true heirs but also, in this life, the experience of a love so sublime and so sweet, it surpasses any a familial bond could confer. The "delights" of monasticism are one hundred times greater than the "brief and uncertain pleasure" of sex with just one woman.[49] The bonds of love between monastic brethren are stronger, sweeter, more permanent – even eternal.

---

[49] Cassian, *Conferences* 24.26, in Petschenig, *Collationes*, 705–06; trans. Ramsey, *Conferences*, 847–48; on reading, scripture, and sublimity, see Krawiec, "Monastic Literacy," 785–94.

Figure 8 Northern apse of the triconch sanctuary of the Red Monastery basilica. Niches below the Nursing Virgin. Figures in niches (from right to left): Pcol, Pshoi, Shenoute, Besa (not pictured). Photograph by Caroline T. Schroeder.

Comparing the fruits of the asexual ascetic life to the fruits of marriage, Cassian insists that his hundred-fold love is also increasingly generative, producing an endless succession of monastic offspring: "For whoever has despised the love of a father or a mother or a child for the sake of Christ's name and has gone over to the most sincere love of all, those who serve Christ will receive a hundred brothers and parents. That is, in place of one he will begin to have that many fathers and brothers, bound to him by a more fervent and excellent affection."[50] These fathers and brothers are also sons, who, like Patermutus, secured their rightful inheritance through submission to the abba.

Cassian writes more than once that a monk imitates Jesus, who subjected himself in obedience to the Father unto death. In the *Conferences*, he explains why the revered Egyptian monk John (the subject of Book 19), has quit the life of a desert solitary for life in a coenobium by placing these words in John's mouth: "And subject to an abba until death, I shall seem to a certain degree to imitate him of whom it is said: 'He humbled himself, having become obedient until death' (Phil 2:8). And I shall deserve to say humbly in his own words, 'I have not come to do my own will but the will of him who sent me, the Father' (John 6:38)."[51] Submission becomes the highest calling of the monk, with forfeiting one's will to the will of the monastic father as the highest form of renunciation. Coenobitism becomes the most perfect imitation of the most perfect son.

Then again, in Book 24 on mortification, near the end of the *Conferences*, Cassian returns to the primacy of filial obedience by citing Jesus in the Gospels as a "pattern" for monks ("I have not come to do my own will but the will of him who sent me" [John 6:38]; "Not as I will but as you do" [Matt. 26:39, Mark 14:36, Luke 22:42]). He continues: "Those who dwell in coenobia and are ruled by the command of an elder, who never follow their own judgment but whose will depends on the will of an abba, are the ones who exercise this virtue in particular."[52]

Surrender to the will of the father is a fundamental act of collective monasticism for Cassian. This submission goes hand in hand with prayer. Contemplation of the divine trinity is one of the most sacred aspects of monastic prayer; it "charts a deepening encounter with Christ" himself, "drawing the monk into the very center of the 'indissoluble love'" between

---

[50] Cassian, *Conferences* 24.26, in Petschenig, *Collationes*, 707; trans. Ramsey, *Conferences*, 849.
[51] Cassian, *Conferences* 19.6, in Petschenig, *Collationes*, 541; trans. Ramsey, *Conferences*, 674.
[52] Cassian, *Conferences* 24.26, in Petschenig, *Collationes*, 709–10; trans. Ramsey, *Conferences*, 851.

Father and Son."[53] The monk imitates Christ and experiences God – both Son and Father.

Like Jesus, whose submission on the cross ensured his resurrection and ascension to a reunion with the Godhead, the submissive monk will receive his inheritance. In Book 11 of the *Conferences*, the New Testament parable of the prodigal son becomes an allegory for the imitation of Christ. The biblical son's status ranks higher than a laborer or enslaved person, with accompanying expectations for an inheritance. Cassian applies this tale to monastic sons, who likewise may expect a holy inheritance. He concludes, "Hence we also, mounting by the indissoluble grace of love to the third degree of sons, who believe that everything which belongs to their father is theirs, must strive to be worthy of receiving the image and likeness of the heavenly Father and of being able to proclaim in imitation of the true Son: 'All that the Father has is mine' (John 16:15)."[54] Book 11 broadly concerns perfection, here couched in terms of monastic mimesis, imitating the perfect son, Jesus. Cassian, like the scriptures he cites, and like most ancient people, links family or household with property. As he says in Book 24, quoting Mark 10:29, "There is no one who has left house or brothers or sisters or mother or children or fields who will not receive a hundredfold."[55] The *domus* of the *familia*, with its attendant property, is exchanged for the greater *domus* of the monastic *familia*, with its attendant and superior property.

The monk's bequest takes the form of family, property, and legacy. "Many" fathers and brothers replace the one father or brother. The monk who renounces his house "will possess innumerable dwellings as his own in monasteries everywhere in the world, and they will be his own houses as if by right."[56] In reputation and authority, such an ascetic will resemble the Egyptian monk John of Lycopolis: "Although born of an obscure family, he became so admired by nearly the whole human race on account of the name of Christ that the very lords of things present, who hold the government of this world and of the Empire and who are awesome even to all powers and kings, venerate him as their lord."[57] John exemplifies Cassian's ideal sublime submission. In perfecting the practice of *imitatio Christi*, he has become, like Christ, not lord of an earthly *domus* but lord of all. This exhortation to monastic sonship and its transformative power comes at the

[53] Stewart, *Cassian the Monk*, 108–09, citing *Conferences* 10.6–7.
[54] Cassian, *Conferences* 11.7, in Petschenig, *Collationes*, 319; trans. Ramsey, *Conferences*, 413.
[55] Cassian, *Conferences* 24.26, in Petschenig, *Collationes*, 707; trans. Ramsey, *Conferences*, 849.
[56] Cassian, *Conferences* 24.26, in Petschenig, *Collationes*, 707–08; trans. Ramsey, *Conferences*, 849.
[57] Cassian, *Conferences* 24.26, in Petschenig, *Collationes*, 710; trans. Ramsey, *Conferences*, 851.

end of the *Conferences*, as both a culmination and a promise. Cassian holds out John's ascetic *imitatio Christi* as a model for all monks, who, like their mimetic exemplars, come to hold dominion over much more than they have renounced. He then ends by revealing that his *Conferences* have been as much for the monastery's abba as for the monk, the abba who will nurture asceticism among the brethren. Cassian's penultimate sentence reads, "This is, rather, for the purpose of increasing your authority among your sons, if the precepts of the greatest and most ancient fathers confirm what you yourselves teach by your living example, not by the dead 'sound of words.'"[58] Cassian, in providing instructions for the perfect son, has cultivated the ideal father, a *pater monasterii* in place of a *paterfamilias*.

Eternal Genealogies

Both monastic leaders – one in Gaul, one in Middle Egypt – create monastic legacies constructed around timeless relationships between father and son; abba and monk in the coenobium imitate Father and Son in the heavens. For both authors, the father-monk relationship has temporal reach beyond each individual, particular pairing.

Shenoute creates a mimetic monastic-prophetic genealogy in which monastic children are descendants and imitators – spiritual spitting images – of their biblical forebears. This genealogy is eternal, reaching out from the pages of scripture into an endless line of spiritual progeny. In *Canons*, Volume 3:

> So that truly we may be like the sons (*šēre*) of Abraham and the sons (*šēre*) of all our ancient fathers, whom the Lord blessed because they not only loved their own sons (*šēre*) and daughters (*šeere*) and all their relatives, but they also loved everyone who believed in God and who kept God's commandments. And thus their offspring obtained as their inheritance everyone who is faithful and just, from the beginning until today and forever.[59]

The monastic community of Shenoute's time is just one generation in an old and venerable family – a family with a legacy and inheritance passed on from one generation to the next. Likewise, in *Canons*, Volume 6, echoing the Psalms and Ephesians, Shenoute likens the monastery to "the house

---

[58] Cassian, *Conferences* 24.26, in Petschenig, *Collationes*, 711; trans. Ramsey, *Conferences*, 852.

[59] Shenoute, *Abraham Our Father*, *Canons*, vol. 3, MONB.YA 547, in Young, "Five Leaves," 273–74; trans. 263–94, mod.; trans. and edition also in "Abraham, YA 547–550," ed. Krawiec et al., trans. Krawiec and Behlmer, urn:cts:copticLit:shenoute.abraham.monbya:37–42, Coptic SCRIPTORIUM.

that the fathers of your fathers built for them and the sons of the sons of their sons (*nšēre nnšēre nneušēre*) unto generations and unto all these forever."[60] The monasteries are houses with a heritage whose roots stretch deep into biblical histories. Their claim to tradition reaches further into the past than that of the most elite Roman *domus*. And it stretches "forever" into the future: the monastic-prophetic genealogy is both eternal and eschatological.[61] Moreover, it is textually, socially, and materially constructed – textually through Shenoute's writings, socially through raising children, and materially through the construction of the buildings and their art.

The purity of this monastic-prophetic genealogy is vulnerable to demonic corruption, requiring the monks to remain vigilant in their ascetic imitation of their forebears and to cut off from their family tree anyone who threatens its legacy. Satan can enter the monastery through monks who "desire fornication and fraud and deceit and every evil thing, whether male or female among us."[62] Just as our ancestors did, argues Shenoute, we monks too must prune our family tree, purge ourselves of those who sin, and embrace our children who are righteous:

> But if our ancient ancestors have disobedient and sinful children (*šēre*), they do not then turn their backs on their just children (*šēre*), and flee from them because of the amount of ignorance of the evil children (*šēre*), but they remove themselves from the sinful children (*šēre*) and remain with their just children (*šēre*) all the days of their lives. Therefore, just as many sinful children (*šēre*) cause grief to our ancient ancestors, so also many just children (*šēre*) bring them joy; and just as God often becomes angry and must destroy ancient tribes on account of the many sinful children (*šēre*) among them, so also God often restrains his anger from ancient tribes because of the just children (*šēre*) among them.[63]

The fertile soil of this monastic-prophetic family tree is the desert – the birthplace and homeland of both the biblical children of God and the monastic children of God. Merely descending from this genealogy does not ensure eternal salvation, neither does it guarantee permanent membership

---

[60] Shenoute, *Is It Not Written, Canons*, vol. 6, MONB.XM 182, in Leipoldt, *Vita et Opera Omnia*, vol. 3, 192. Citing Ps. 106:31, 146:10; Eph. 3:21.

[61] Much of my thinking on the eschatological dimensions of genealogies has been influenced by Chin.

[62] Shenoute, *You God the Eternal, Canons*, vol. 5, MONB.XS 387, in Leipoldt, *Vita et Opera Omnia*, vol. 4, 75.

[63] Shenoute, *Abraham Our Father, Canons*, vol. 3, MONB.YA 547–48, in Young, "Five Leaves," 274–75; trans. Young, mod.; edition and trans. also in Krawiec et al., ed., "Abraham, YA 547–550," trans. Krawiec and Behlmer, urn:cts:copticLit:shenoute.abraham.monbya:37–42, Coptic SCRIPTORIUM.

in a lineage of biblical fathers and sons. Like the Israelites in the desert, the monks in the desert face the destructive wrath of God when they break God their father's law:

> Look, oh wise ones, that just as the Lord destroyed all the cities that were filled with lawlessness and he struck down everyone who sinned from the first . . . this is the way also that he struck down everyone who sinned in the desert in every way; it is his people and they are his sons and his daughters, over whom he poured out his wrath so that he destroyed them.[64]

Membership in this genealogical tradition is thus a privilege and a responsibility.

The very same thing that binds biological family and kinship generations binds these monks each other, to their ancestors, and to their heirs: blood. Shenoute, as we saw earlier, interprets Christ's blood as the medium in which Jesus and the church gave birth to the monastic-prophetic genealogy. As David Biale has argued, Christians in late antiquity transformed "nonsacrificial practices into memorials of the original blood covenant," which Christians situated not only in Exodus 24 (when Moses sacrificed at the altar and threw half the blood onto the Jewish people) but also of course in the sacrificial death of Jesus.[65] Biale discusses this ritualization of the blood covenant in terms of practices such as the eucharist and baptism, and we see it also in the practices of ascetic renunciation. The monastic family is born of Jesus' blood and maintains its genealogical purity through the monastic practice of ascetic renunciation, which *includes* the double renunciation of biological family and sinful monastic family.

Shenoute, however, recognizes the danger of the power of this blood covenant in Volume 2 of the *Canons*. There, he writes to the women of the monastery, again condemning them for their sins:

> O foolish virgins and still more than you. But we never did that which the world does, be it in fornication, be it in honorable marriage, be it in a bed undefiled (Ps 108:16–18). The Lord bears witness! For we are not commending ourselves (Ps 108:20) saying these things to you, but I say these things to you and I tell you that I am innocent of your condemnation. Your blood shall be upon you and upon your head . . . [Here, Shenoute mentions that the prior fathers of the monastery also instructed them and continues] . . . Therefore, not only am I innocent of your judgment, but also my other holy and blessed fathers who have died are guiltless of your blood. And I have

---

[64] Shenoute, *Canons*, vol. 4, MONB.BZ 38, in Leipoldt, *Vita et Opera Omnia*, vol. 3, 132.
[65] Biale, *Blood and Belief*, 46–47.

come from them that your blood may be upon your head. And not only this that they are innocent of your judgment, but also [our] elder [father], Apa Pshoi, and all the elders are innocent of your judgment and they are guiltless of your blood. For he, for his part also, did not refrain from telling you the truth while coming to you many times. Shenoute also and Papnoute are innocent of your blood. Moreover, all the other holy elders, who are with us and who are of one mind with us, are guiltless of your blood, and your men and your siblings (lit. brothers, *snēu*) and your children (lit. sons, *šēre*) and all those who are with us from our least (*kouî*) to our greatest (*noc*), all are innocent of the reproach which will come upon you at the time of your need.[66]

Shenoute uses both the language of kinship and the language of blood to define the community. The men he cites are family of the women – fathers, sons, brothers, and husbands – relationships traditionally defined by law and/or blood. The passage's multiple scriptural allusions to blood covenants similarly define the relationships by bonds of blood and law. Shenoute quotes Acts 18:6, a turning point in the biblical book, when Paul has been rejected in multiple synagogues and finally declares that he will cease his ministry to the Jews and separate from them: "When they opposed and reviled him, in protest he shook the dust from his clothes and said to them, 'Your blood be on your own heads! I am innocent. From now on I will go to the Gentiles.'" Shenoute's passage is also, of course, an intertextual reference to the infamous blood curse of Matthew 27:24–25, in which the Jews of Jerusalem reportedly tell Pilate that Jesus' blood will be on their heads and the heads of their children. Blood is a biblical medium for shared responsibility, sin, and ultimately atonement. Paul's angry rejection in Acts is born of an original commitment to "save" the Jews; they were one community who could atone and be saved together, and now (according to Acts) they are no longer either. Additionally, the monastic text alludes to Exodus 24, in which (as mentioned earlier in this chapter) Moses throws the blood of the sacrifice upon the heads of the Israelites to bind the community in the atoning substance.

Finally, the genealogy in this passage is almost exclusively masculine. The people from whom Shenoute threatens to exile the women are fathers, sons, brothers, and husbands. The people Shenoute declares innocent are the previous "fathers" – Pcol, Ebonh, Pshoi, Papnoute, and Shenoute.

---

[66] Shenoute, *Canons*, vol. 2, MONB.XC 221, in Kuhn, *Letters and Sermons of Besa*, vol. 1, 117–18; trans. vol. 2, 113–14, mod. (This manuscript fragment was wrongly attributed to Besa.) In contrast to the dynamic described in my first book, *Monastic Bodies*, Shenoute lays the burden of sin and the onus of atonement on the individual, not the community; Shenoute, the men in the community, and all the "fathers" who came before him remain innocent and uncontaminated by the women's sins.

These are the monastic fathers, the men who led the community in previous years, but they are also linked scripturally to Paul, the Gospels, and Moses. This covenant Shenoute mentions – the covenant "from the beginning" – signifies both the beginning of the women's community in temporal history and the very beginning, the beginnings of humanity and the beginnings of the biblical covenant with the Lord.[67] Intertextually, Shenoute connects the monastic fathers to the biblical patriarchs and apostles to create a monastic-prophetic genealogy of father and sons.

Shenoute's monastery is not the only community in Egypt to construct its own biblical legacy. At the monastery of Jeremias in Saqqara, funerary inscriptions dating to three centuries later often invoke sacred figures: the Holy Spirit, the Archangel Gabriel, or Michael, Mary, and other saints, including prior monastic leaders. One inscription in particular bears the hallmarks of a sacred genealogy. The funerary prayer invokes a long list of figures, beginning with the Trinity and archangels, then Mary, a "celestial hierarchy" of twenty-four Elders and "powers of the Spirit," Adam, Eve, the Patriarchs, Prophets, Judges, Kings, Apostles, Evangelists, Archbishops, martyrs (listed by name), and then a long list of named monks ("founders of monasteries"), including Jeremias, Apollo, and Patermutus.[68] This part of the text ends with the name of the deceased. (Other prayers appear after the date of the inscription.) As an invocation, the list of figures is difficult to categorize, since it contains the ultimate divine power (God and the Trinity) as well as numerous biblical figures and sacred persons we might typically classify as intercessors (saints). The catalog of names does, however, resemble a genealogy. The inscription calls upon the powers of the deceased's "mothers" (only two in number: Mary and Ama Sibylla) and "fathers," who are named in a roughly chronological sequence going back to the eternal God the Father at the beginning of the lineage.[69]

We find this phenomenon elsewhere in Egypt as well. In Upper Egypt, south of Shenoute's monastery, Malcolm Choat has discovered a desert cave tomb repurposed as a monastic cell, in which a list of names rings the top of the monastic residence. It begins with biblical figures and then lists the names of monastic exemplars, constructing a prophetic-monastic

---

[67] On covenantal language in Shenoutean monasticism, see Schroeder, "Prophecy and Porneia," 87–91.

[68] Quibell and Thompson, *Excavations at Saqqara*, 59–60; trans. 60–61. See also no. 222 on 68 for a more abbreviated genealogy.

[69] Ama Sibylla is Sibyl (of the Sibyllene Oracles). Quibell and Thompson, *Excavations at Saqqara*, 48.

genealogy for the purposes of monastic prayer or mimesis right there in the individual monk's cell.[70]

Likewise, the literature from the Pachomian community deploys genealogical language to trace a lineage of authority from the scriptures to the monastery. First, the Bohairic *Life* constructs the monastery as a community of children of God whose founder, like the biblical prophets, establishes a "covenant" between God and the people. It likens Pachomius to Jeremiah, Paul, Abraham, Job, and other biblical "saints." Comparable to the scriptural fathers before him, Pachomius' special relationship with God marks him as a figure worthy of respect and veneration: "You see then, we have recounted for you from this multitude of witnesses from the holy Scriptures how all these saints exalt and glorify their fathers before them. Is it not right for us also to exalt and honor a just man and a prophet whom the Lord gave us, in order that through his holiness, we might come to know him?"[71] In the Pachomian community, authority then passes from father to son. The Greek *vita* frames this monastic succession as inheritance. Theodore proves himself a worthy "heir" of Pachomius through his obedience and imitation (especially imitation *of* obedience). An angel pronounces divine sanction of Theodore as one of Pachomius' successors: "Now, Pachomius, this man's father, by obeying God in all things became well-pleasing in his sight. And if this man too is steadfast after his likeness, then he will be his heir."[72] Philip Rousseau has argued that the Pachomian line of succession posits a direct relationship between the monastic present, the biblical past, and the eschatological future, transcending the vagaries or uncertainties about any individual monastic father and asserting a divinely authorized historical trajectory. "Thus a clearer line of descent was marked upon the historical chart of uncertain development and varying personal fortune; a line that passed from the Bible and the early church, through Pachomius, and on to the following generations."[73]

As both Derwas Chitty and Rousseau have argued, this genealogical authorization of power in Egyptian ascetic literature extended beyond the Pachomian community to the *History of the Monks of Egypt* and Egyptian monasticism more broadly. "Masters had to be themselves the disciples of

---

[70] Choat, "Narratives of Monastic Genealogy."

[71] *V. Pach. Bo* 194, in Lefort, *S. Pachomii Vita Bohairice Scripta*, 184; ed. and trans. Veilleux, *Pachomian Koinonia, Volume One*. See also Theodore, *Catechesis 3*, in Lefort, *Oeuvres de S. Pachôme*, vol. 1, 41; trans. vol. 2, 40–41.

[72] *V. Pach. G¹* 108, in Veilleux, *Pachomian Koinonia, Volume One*, 373. The Bohairic *vita* emphasizes Theodore's obedience more than the Greek (Rousseau, *Ascetics, Authority, and the Church*, 31n67).

[73] Rousseau, *Ascetics, Authority, and the Church*, 23.

holy men; and the links between one generation and another were traced with care. Only in this way, it was felt, could they preserve their 'heritage of power.'"[74] Shenoute's genealogical language is therefore distinctive but not idiosyncratic; it is part of a larger discourse constructing a scriptural lineage for a monastic heritage.

Shenoute's genealogy is quite biblical, invoking notions of covenant and tribe to reconfigure the House of Shenoute as a present-day House of Israel. But, placed in its material and geographical context, his writings also position the "house of Shenoute" as a late antique estate with familial legacies. These concepts of genealogy and legacy need to be tied to our earlier discussion of property and inheritance. In the essay "Apostles and Aristocrats," C. M. Chin argues that the interplay between human agents and late antique buildings and estates birthed "a variety of human genealogies . . . aristocratic families, past apostles, and future popes."[75]

In the *Life of Melania the Younger*, property itself – not merely the "abstraction" of "wealth" and "money" – exerts power as "inheritance," making "temporal and genealogical claims" alongside its "spatial and material claims." Being propertied was wrapped up in being a high-status household in the Roman political economy. "[T]he highly competitive and sometimes unpredictable process of becoming and remaining a senatorial family in late antiquity meant that the genealogical claims of property extended both backward in time and forward."[76] Likewise, the Constantinian basilica complex in Rome, with its extensive and richly adorned figural decorations of Jesus, angels, and apostles, exerted its own forceful history in the context of an apostolic genealogy *and* exerted its own forceful influence over its present and future caretakers. Properties, as Chin argues, have both histories and aspirations and deploy their own "genealogical ambitions" on human agents.[77]

During the fifth and sixth centuries, the monastic federation of Shenoute embarked on two ambitious building projects – the construction of the great church at the White Monastery (Figure 9) in the mid-fifth century, and the smaller church of the Red Monastery later in the fifth century (Figure 10). It is in this church of the Red Monastery, in paintings that date probably to the seventh century, that the figural monastic genealogy of the community adorns the wall.

---

[74] Rousseau, *Ascetics, Authority, and the Church*, 24; citing Chitty, *Desert a City*, 67, and the *Historia Monachorum* 15.2, 28.450.
[75] Chin, "Apostles and Aristocrats," 20.   [76] Chin, "Apostles and Aristocrats," 22.
[77] Chin, "Apostles and Aristocrats," 28.

Figure 9 Basilica (or great church) of the White Monastery, exterior, originally fifth century. Photograph by Caroline T. Schroeder.

Figure 10 Basilica of the Red Monastery, exterior, fifth century. Photograph by Caroline T. Schroeder.

These aspects of *traditio* and *legatio* are precisely what elite *familiae* in the late Roman Empire found threatening about asceticism. The Roman household also made eternal claims to society, economy, and culture – claims that monks like Shenoute and Cassian promised to abolish with their construction of communities (estates, dare we say?) predicated on the severing of family ties. As Goodrich concisely states, "The objections of family members grew out of the idea among the elite class that the aristocratic families must be continued at all costs."[78] The late antique coenobium threatened to end genealogical lines that the imperial Roman ruling class had been struggling to maintain ever since the Augustan marriage legislation in 18–17 BCE established incentives for wealthy families to procreate more bountifully.[79]

Conclusion

The centuries after Pachomius, Cassian, and Shenoute witnessed dramatic transformations of economy and power, in which the monastery as estate proved a player. In Egypt, monasteries became landed estates, with taxes due, economic staff, and servants.[80] Coenobia briefly became monastic aristocracy in Egypt, with genealogies authorizing their heritage and their legacies, and future generations of monks as their progeny. In Gaul, increasing numbers of church officials came from the ranks of monastics, prominent leaders donated wealth and land to establish or support monasteries, and papal and episcopal privileges were extended to them.[81] As the late antique villa in Gaul shrank, the monastic estate grew.[82] Goodrich argues that Cassian's coenobia began as an effort to undermine this very aspect of the developing political economy; in contrast to other ascetic communities with estate servants (or lower-class monks assigned to those tasks), Cassian's monastery, he contends, required a complete status reversal of the male citizen, and implicitly challenged a trend espoused by

---

[78] Goodrich, *Contextualizing Cassian*, 161–62.

[79] Among the numerous books on this subject, see Dixon, *Roman Family*; Rawson, *Family in Ancient Rome*; Rawson and Weaver, *Roman Family in Italy*; Severy, *Augustus and the Family*.

[80] Regarding the White Monastery Federation, see *P.Mich.Inv.* 6898 in Alcock and Sijpesteijn, "Early 7th Cent. Coptic Contract"; trans. MacCoull, *Coptic Legal Documents*, 11–17; on dating also see Bagnall and Worp, "Dating the Coptic Legal Documents from Aphrodite."

[81] The literature on the intersections of politics, economic development, and the church in early medieval Gaul is extensive. See Fouracre and Gerberding, *Late Merovingian France*; Hen, *Culture and Religion*; Shanzer and Mathisen, *Society and Culture*; Jones, *Social Mobility*; Klingshirn, *Caesarius of Arles*; Wood, *Merovingian Kingdoms*, 20–32, 71–87, and esp. 181–98.

[82] On the abandonment and contraction of villas in fifth- and sixth-century Gaul, see Wickham, *Framing the Early Middle Ages*, 44, 178–81, 201–3, 442–518.

Paulinus, Sulpicius Severus, and others, in which the elite male citizen was not required to give up his privileged status (and especially his wealth). At Cassian's monastery, Goodrich writes, "the free man would take on the role of a slave" in performing manual labor and exercised humility in doing so.[83] This chapter has complicated the monastic narrative about wealth, property, and status even further. When I began my research on monks and their children several years ago, I started with the premise that the coenobia of the late fourth and fifth centuries were an entirely different animal than the estates of the late sixth and seventh centuries. Yet now I posit that the literature from early phases in the monastic movement laid the seeds for what was to come. As early as the fourth and fifth centuries, the monastery may have stripped the individual man of certain rights and positions, but it positioned the monastery itself as a *domus*, a *familia* with the heritage, property, and power to exert its own claims on the social and political landscape of the late antique Mediterranean.

[83] Goodrich, *Contextualizing Cassian*, 191–97.

Bibliography

Unpublished Manuscripts

Bibliothèque nationale de France, Paris (FR-BN)

Copte 130² (online, https://gallica.bnf.fr/ark:/12148/btv1b10089625 k, accessed December 4, 2019)
Copte 130⁴ (online, https://gallica.bnf.fr/ark:/12148/btv1b10090479 w, accessed December 4, 2019)
Copte 130⁵ (online, https://gallica.bnf.fr/ark:/12148/btv1b100904808, accessed December 4, 2019)

British Library, London (GB-BL)

Or. 3581A

Papyri and Ostraca

All papyri and ostraca are cited using the sigla at http://papyri.info/docs/checklist, accessed April 13, 2020. Many are available at http://papyri.info/ or www .trismegistos.org/, accessed April 13, 2020.

Publications

Primary Sources

Alcock, Anthony, and Pieter J. Sijpesteijn. "Early 7th Cent. Coptic Contract from Aphrodito (P. Mich. inv. 6898)." *Enchoria* 26 (2000): 1–19.
Ambrose. *Ambrose: De Officiis*. Edited and translated by Ivor J. Davidson. 2 vols. Oxford: Oxford University Press, 2002.
Amélineau, Émile. *Contes et romans de l'Égypte chrétienne*. Paris: E. Leroux, 1888.
Apophthegmata.Patrum Corpus. Edited by Mitchell Abrams, David Brakke, Elizabeth Davidson, Saskia Franck, Marina Ghaly, J. Gregory Given, Rebecca

Krawiec, Christine Luckritz Marquis, Paul Lufter, Lauren McDermott, Tobias Paul, Elizabeth Platte, Jennifer Quigley, Dana Robinson, Caroline T. Schroeder, Laura Slaughter, David Sriboonreuang, Janet Timbie, Alexander Turtureanu, Amir Zeldes, and Gianna Zipp. Translated by Mitchell Abrams, Elizabeth Davidson, Saskia Franck, Marina Ghaly, Rebecca Krawiec, Christine Luckritz Marquis, Paul Lufter, Tobias Paul, Elizabeth Platte, Dana Robinson, Caroline T. Schroeder, Laura Slaughter, Alexander Turtureanu, and Amir Zeldes. Coptic SCRIPTORIUM. v. 2.7.0, May 31, 2019. http://data.copticscriptorium.org/urn:cts:copticLit:ap.

Athanasius. *Athanasius: The Life of Antony and the Letter to Marcellinus*. Translated by Robert C. Gregg. Classics of Western Spirituality. Mahwah, NJ: Paulist Press, 1980.

Athanasius. *S. Athanase. Lettres festales et pastorales en copte*. Edited by L. Théophile Lefort. CSCO 150, SC 19. Louvain: L. Durbecq, 1955.

Augustine. *Augustine: The City of God against the Pagans*. Edited and translated by R. W. Dyson. Cambridge Texts in the History of Political Thought. Cambridge: Cambridge University Press, 1998.

Augustine. *De civitate dei: Libri I–X*. Edited by Bernhard Dombart and Alfons Kalb. CCSL 47. Turnhout: Brepols, 2014.

Augustine. *Confessions*. Edited by James J. O'Donnell. 3 vols. Oxford: Clarendon, 1992.

Augustine. *Confessions*. Translated by Henry Chadwick. Oxford: Oxford University Press, 1991.

Augustine. *Sancti Aurelii Augustini Quaestionum in Heptateuchum, libri VII, Locutionum in Heptateuchum, libri VII, De octo quaestionibus ex veteri Testamento*. Edited by Donatien de Bruyne and J. Fraipont. CCSL 33. Turnhout: Brepols, 1958.

Aurelius, Marcus, and Marcus Cornelius Fronto. *Marcus Aurelius in Love*. Translated by Amy Richlin. Repr. ed. Chicago: University of Chicago Press, 2016.

Bagnall, Roger S., and Raffaella Cribiore. *Women's Letters from Ancient Egypt, 300 BC–AD 800*. Ann Arbor: University of Michigan Press, 2006.

Bell, Harold Idris. *Jews and Christians in Egypt: The Jewish Troubles in Alexandria and the Athanasian Controversy*. Westport, CT: Greenwood, 1972.

Besa. *Besa: The Life of Shenoute*. Translated by David N. Bell. Kalamazoo, MI: Cistercian, 1983.

Besa. "Besa, to Aphthonia." Edited by So Miyagawa, Caroline T. Schroeder, David Sriboonreuang, and Amir Zeldes. Translated by So Miyagawa and Amir Zeldes. Coptic SCRIPTORIUM. v. 2.7.0, May 15, 2019. http://data.copticscriptorium.org/urn:cts:copticLit:besa.aphthonia.monbba.

Besa. *Letters and Sermons of Besa*. Edited and translated by K. H. Kuhn. 2 vols. CSCO 157–58, SC 21–22. Louvain: L. Durbecq, 1956.

Boon, Amand. *Pachomiana Latina: Règle et épîtres de S. Pachôme, épître de S. Théodore et "liber" de S. Orsiesius. Texte latin de S. Jérôme*. Bibliothèque de la Revue d'histoire ecclésiastique 7. Louvain: Bureaux de la Revue, 1932.

Cassian, John. *Iohannis Cassiani Collationes XXIII*. Edited by Michael Petschenig. CSEL 13. Vindobonae: Geroldi, 1886.

Cassian, John. *Iohannis Cassiani De institutis coenobiorum et de octo principalium vitiorum remediis libri XII*. Edited by Michael Petschenig. CSEL 17. Vindobonae: F. Tempsky, 1888.

Cassian, John. *John Cassian: The Conferences*. Translated by Boniface Ramsey. Ancient Christian Writers 57. New York: Paulist Press, 1997.

Cassian, John. *John Cassian: The Institutes*. Translated by Boniface Ramsey. Ancient Christian Writers 58. New York: Newman Press, 2000.

Chaîne, Marius, ed. *Le manuscrit de la version copte en dialecte sahidique des Apophthegmata Patrum*. Cairo: Institut français d'archéologie orientale, 1960.

Corrigan, Kevin, trans. "Saint Macrina: The Hidden Face behind the Tradition." *Vox Benedictina: A Journal of Translations from Monastic Sources* 5, no. 1 (1988): 13–43.

Crum, Walter E., and H. G. Evelyn-White, eds. *The Monastery of Epiphanius at Thebes, Part II: Coptic Ostraca and Papyri; Greek Ostraca and Papyri*. Repr. Arno Press, 1973. New York: Metropolitan Museum, 1926.

Crum, Walter E., and Georg Steindorff. *Koptische Rechtsurkunden des achten Jahrhunderts aus Djême (Theben), Bd. 1: Texte und Indices*. Leipzig: J. C. Hinrichs, 1912.

Cyprian. *St. Cyprian: Treatises*. Translated by Roy J. Deferrari, Angela Elizabeth Keenan, Mary Hannan Mahoney, and George Edward Conway. FC 36. Washington, DC: Catholic University of America Press, 1958.

Delattre, Alain. *Papyrus coptes et grecs du monastère d'apa Apollô de Baouît conservés aux Musées royaux d'Art et d'Histoire de Bruxelles*. Brussels: Académie royale de Belgique, 2007.

Drescher, James, ed. and trans. *Three Coptic Legends. Hilaria [Transcribed from Pierpont Morgan MS. M. 583], Archellites [Transcribed from Pierpont Morgan MS. 579], the Seven Sleepers [Transcribed from Pierpont Morgan MS. M. 633]*. Supplément aux Annales du Service des Antiquités de l'Égypte 4. Cairo: Institut français d'archéologie orientale, 1947.

Ephrem. *Ephrem the Syrian: Hymns*. Translated by Kathleen E. McVey. Classics of Western Spirituality. Mahwah, NJ: Paulist Press, 1989.

Ephrem. *Des heiligen Ephraem des Syrers Hymnen de Virginitate*. Edited by Edmund Beck. Vol. 94. CSCO 223, Scriptores Syri. Louvain: Secrétariat du Corpus SCO, 1962.

Epictetus. *The Works of Epictetus: His Discourses, in Four Books, the Enchiridion, and Fragments*. Translated by Thomas Wentworth Higginson. New York: Thomas Nelson and Sons, 1890. Online. http://data.perseus.org/texts/urn:cts:greekLit:tlg0557.tlg001.

Gardner, Iain, Anthony Alcock, and Wolf-Peter Funk, eds. *Coptic Documentary Texts from Kellis, Volume 1: P. Kell. V (P. Kell. Copt. 10–52; O. Kell. Copt. 1–2)*. Dakhleh Oasis Project Monograph 9. Oxford: Oxbow Books, 1999.

Gregory of Nyssa. "The Life of Macrina, by Gregory Bishop of Nyssa." Translated by Kevin Corrigan. Monastic Matrix. https://monasticmatrix.osu.edu/cartular ium/life-macrina-gregory-bishop-nyssa.

Gregory of Nyssa. *The Life of Saint Macrina by Gregory Bishop of Nyssa.* Translated by Kevin Corrigan. Eugene, OR: Wipf & Stock, 2005.

Hall, H. R., ed. *Coptic and Greek Texts of the Christian Period from Ostraka, Stelae, Etc. in the British Museum.* London: British Museum, 1905.

Hodak, Suzana, Tonio Sebastian Richter, and Frank Steinmann, eds. *Coptica: koptische Ostraka und Papyri, koptische und griechische Grabstelen aus Ägypten und Nubien, spätantike Bauplastik, Textilien und Keramik.* Katalog Ägyptischer Sammlungen in Leipzig 3. Berlin: Manetho Verlag, 2013.

Horner, George William, ed. *The Coptic Version of the New Testament in the Northern Dialect Otherwise Called Memphitic and Bohairic.* Oxford: Clarendon, 1898.

Isaac the Presbyter. *The Life of Samuel of Kalamun.* Edited and translated by Anthony Alcock. Warminster, England: Aris & Phillips, 1983.

Jerome. *Letters and Select Works.* In vol. 6 of *The Nicene and Post-Nicene Fathers,* Series 2. Edited by Philip Schaff and Henry Wace. Translated by W. H. Freemantle, G. Lewis, and W. G. Marley, revised and edited by Kevin Knight for *New Advent.* www.newadvent.org/fathers/3001039.htm.

Jerome. *The Letters of Jerome: Asceticism, Biblical Exegesis, and the Construction of Christian Authority in Late Antiquity.* Edited by Andrew Cain. Oxford Early Christian Studies. Oxford: Oxford University Press, 2009.

Jerome. *Sancti Eusebii Hieronymi Epistulae, Pars I: Epistulae 1–70.* Edited by Isidorus Hilberg. CSEL 54. Vindobonae and Leipzig: F. Tempsky and G. Freytag, 1910.

Jerome. *Sancti Eusebii Hieronymi Epistulae, Pars II: Epistulae 71–120.* Edited by Isidorus Hilberg. CSEL 55. Vindobonae and Leipzig: F. Tempsky and G. Freytag, 1912.

Jerome. *Sancti Eusebii Hieronymi Epistulae, Pars III: Epistulae 121–154.* Edited by Isidorus Hilberg. CSEL 56. Vindobonae and Leipzig: F. Tempsky and G. Freytag, 1918.

Jerome. *Select Letters.* Translated by F. A. Wright. LCL 262. Cambridge, MA: Harvard University Press, 1933.

The Lives of the Desert Fathers: Historia Monachorum in Aegypto. Translated by Norman Russell. Cistercian Studies Series 34. Kalamazoo, MI: Cistercian, 1981.

Lucchesi, Enzo. "Deux feuillets coptes inédits de Shenouté (Paris, Copte 130², ff. 115, 122 et 131." *Mus* 91 (1978): 171–78.

MacCoull, Leslie S. B. "The Bawit Contracts: Texts and Translations." *Bulletin of the American Society of Papyrologists* 31, no. 3/4 (1994): 141–58.

Mitteis, Ludwig, ed. *Griechische Urkunden der Papyrussammlung zu Leipzig.* Repr. Milan: La Goiardica, 1970. Leipzig: B. G. Teubner, 1906.

Munier, Henri. *Manuscrits coptes: Catalogue général des antiquités égyptiennes du Musée du Caire.* Cairo: Institut français d'archéologie orientale, 1916.

Pachomian Koinonia, Volume One: The Life of Saint Pachomius and His Disciples. Edited and translated by Armand Veilleux. Cistercian Studies Series 45. Kalamazoo, MI: Cistercian, 1980.

Pachomian Koinonia, Volume Two: Pachomian Chronicles and Rules. Edited and translated by Armand Veilleux. Cistercian Studies Series 46. Kalamazoo, MI: Cistercian, 1981.

Pachomius. *Oeuvres de S. Pachôme et de ses disciples.* Edited by L. Théophile Lefort. CSCO 159–160, SC 23–24. Louvain: L. Durbecq, 1956.

Pachomius. *S. Pachomii Vita Bohairice Scripta.* Edited by L. Théophile Lefort. CSCO 107, SC 7. Paris, 1925.

Pachomius. *S. Pachomii Vitae Sahidice Scriptae.* Edited by L. Théophile Lefort. CSCO 99, SC 9. Louvain: L. Durbecq, 1952.

Regnault, Lucien, ed. *Les sentences des Pères du désert: Troisième recueil et tables.* Solesmes: Abbaye Saint-Pierre de Solesmes, 1976.

Rowlandson, Jane, trans. *Women and Society in Greek and Roman Egypt: A Sourcebook.* Cambridge: Cambridge University Press, 1998.

Sahidic.OT (Old Testament) Corpus. Edited by Frank Feder, So Miyagawa, Elizabeth Platte, Caroline T. Schroeder, and Amir Zeldes. Coptic SCRIPTORIUM. v. 2.6.0, November 15, 2018. http://data.copticscriptorium .org/urn:cts:copticLit:ot.deut.

Sancti Pachomii Vitae Graecae. Subsidia Hagiographia 19. Edited by François Halkin. Brussels: Société des Bollandistes, 1932.

Schroeder, Caroline T., Amir Zeldes, et al. *Coptic SCRIPTORIUM.* 2013–2019. http://copticscriptorium.org.

Shenoute. *Le canon 8 de Chénouté (d'après le manuscrit Ifao Copte 2 et les fragments complémentaires): Introduction, édition critique, traduction.* Edited by Anne Boud'hors. 2 vols. Bibliothèque d'études Coptes 21. Cairo: Institut français d'archéologie orientale, 2013.

Shenoute. *Coptic Manuscripts from the White Monastery: Works of Shenute.* Edited by Dwight W. Young. 2 vols. Mitteilungen aus der Papyrussammlung der Österreichischen Nationalbibliothek (Papyrus Erzherzog Rainer). Neue Serie 22. Vienna: Hollinek, 1993.

Shenoute. "An Early Monastic Rule Fragment from the Monastery of Shenoute." Edited and translated by Caroline T. Schroeder. *Mus* 127, no. 1–2 (2014): 19–39.

Shenoute. *Oeuvres de Schenoudi: Texte copte et traduction française.* 2 vols. Edited by Émile Amélineau. Paris: E. Leroux, 1907.

Shenoute. *Le quatrième livre des entretiens et épîtres de Shenouti.* Edited by Émile Chassinat. Mémoires publiés par l'Institut français d'archéologie orien- tale du Caire 23. Cairo: Institut français d'archéologie orientale, 1911.

Shenoute. *Selected Discourses of Shenoute the Great: Community, Theology, and Social Conflict in Late Antique Egypt.* Translated by David Brakke and Andrew Crislip. New York: Cambridge University Press, 2015.

Shenoute. "Shenoute, Abraham Our Father, YA 535–540." Edited by Rebecca Krawiec, Caroline T. Schroeder, Amir Zeldes, and David Sriboonreuang. Translated by Rebecca Krawiec and Heike Behlmer. Coptic SCRIPTORIUM. v. 2.6.0, November 15, 2018. http://data.scriptorium.org/urn:cts:copticLit:she noute.abraham.monbya:21–27.

Shenoute. "Shenoute, Abraham Our Father, YA 547–550." Edited by Rebecca Krawiec, Caroline T. Schroeder, Amir Zeldes, and David Sriboonreuang. Translated by Rebecca Krawiec and Heike Behlmer. Coptic SCRIPTORIUM. v. 2.6.0, November 15, 2018. http://data.scriptorium.org/urn:cts:copticLit:shenoute.abraham.monbya:37–42.

Shenoute. "Shenoute, Abraham Our Father, ZH Fragments 1a-D." Edited by Rebecca Krawiec, Caroline T. Schroeder, Amir Zeldes, and David Sriboonreuang. Translated by Rebecca Krawiec and Heike Behlmer. Coptic SCRIPTORIUM. v. 2.6.0, November 15, 2018. http://data.scriptorium.org/urn:cts:copticLit:shenoute.abraham.monbzh:18–22.

Shenoute. *Sinuthii Archimandritae: Vita et Opera Omnia*. Edited by Johannes Leipoldt. 3 vols. CSCO 41, 42, 73. Paris: Imprimerie Nationale, 1906.

Theodoret. *Histoire des moines de Syrie*. Edited by Pierre Canivet and Alice Leroy-Molinghen. 2 vols. Sources chrétiennes 257. Paris: Éditions du Cerf, 1979.

Theodoret. *A History of the Monks of Syria*. Translated by R. M. Price. Kalamazoo, MI: Cistercian, 1985.

Till, Walter C. "Eine koptische Alimentenforderung." *BSAC* 4 (1938): 71–78.

Till, Walter C. *Die koptischen Rechtsurkunden aus Theben*. Sitzungsberichte der Österreichischen Akademie der Wissenschaften, phil.-hist. Klasse 244/3. Vienna: Österreichische Akademie der Wissenschaften, 1964.

Timbie, Janet A., and Jason R. Zaborowski. "Shenoute's Sermon *The Lord Thundered*: An Introduction and Translation." *Oriens Christianus* 90 (2006): 91–123.

"Vie de Sainte Marine: IV Texte Copte." Translated by Henri Hyvernat. *Revue de l'Orient chrétien* 7 (1902): 136–52.

Vita Danielis Scet. Saint Daniel of Sketis: A Group of Hagiographic Texts, Edited with Introduction, Translation, and Commentary. Edited by Britt Dahlman. Acta Universitatis Upsaliensis 10. Uppsala: Acta Universitatis Upsaliensis, 2007.

Ward, Benedicta, trans. *The Desert Fathers: Sayings of the Early Christian Monks*. London: Penguin Books, 2003.

Ward, Benedicta, trans. *The Sayings of the Desert Fathers: The Alphabetical Collection*. Cistercian Studies Series 59. Kalamazoo, MI: Cistercian, 1975.

Ward, Benedicta, trans. *The Wisdom of the Desert Fathers: Apophthegmata Patrum from the Anonymous Series*. Fairacres and Oxford: SLG Press and Convent of the Incarnation, 1975.

Wesseley, Carl, ed. *Griechische und koptische Texte theologischen Inhalts*. 5 vols. Studien zur Palaeographie und Papyruskunde 9, 11, 12, 15, 18. Leipzig: H. Haessel Hachfolger, 1909.

Winlock, Herbert E., and Walter E. Crum. *The Monastery of Epiphanius at Thebes, Part I: The Archaeological Material, the Literary Material*. Repr. Arno Press, 1973. New York: Metropolitan Museum, 1926.

Worp, Klaas Anthony. *Greek Papyri from Kellis: I: (P.Kell.G.) Nos 1–90*. Dakhleh Oasis Project Monograph 3, Oxbow Monograph 54. Oxford: Oxbow Books, 1995.

Wortley, John, ed. *The Anonymous Sayings of the Desert Fathers: A Select Edition and Complete English Translation*. Cambridge: Cambridge University Press, 2013.

Secondary Sources

Anderson, Graham. *The Second Sophistic: A Cultural Phenomenon in the Roman Empire*. London: Routledge, 2009.

Ariès, Philippe. *Centuries of Childhood: A Social History of Family Life*. Translated by Robert Baldick. New York: Vintage, 1965.

Arnett, Jeffrey Jensen. "Emerging Adulthood: A Theory of Development from the Late Teens through the Twenties." *American Psychologist* 55, no. 5 (2000): 469–80.

Arnett, Jeffrey Jensen, Marion Kloep, Leo B. Hendry, and Jennifer L. Tanner. *Debating Emerging Adulthood: Stage or Process?* Oxford: Oxford University Press, 2011.

Bagnall, Roger S. *Egypt in Late Antiquity*. Princeton, NJ: Princeton University Press, 1993.

Bagnall, Roger S., and Klaas A. Worp. "Dating the Coptic Legal Documents from Aphrodite." *Zeitschrift für Papyrologie und Epigraphik* 148 (2004): 247–52.

Baker, Cynthia. "Pseudo-Philo and the Transformation of Jephthah's Daughter." In *Anti-covenant: Counter-reading Women's Lives in the Hebrew Bible*, edited by Mieke Bal, 195–209. Bible and Literature 22. Sheffield: Sheffield Academic, 1989.

Basset, René, ed. "Arabic Synaxarion." In *Patrologia orientalis* 1.3, 3.3, 11.5, 16.2, 17.3, 20.5. Paris: Firmin-Didot, 1907–29.

Bauks, Michaela. "The Theological Implications of Child Sacrifice in and beyond the Biblical Context in Relation to Genesis 22 and Judges 11." In *Human Sacrifice in Jewish and Christian Tradition*, edited by Karin Finsterbusch, Armin Lange, and Diethard Römheld, 65–86. Numen Book Series: Studies in the History of Religion 112. Leiden: Brill, 2007.

Beaumont, Lesley A. *Childhood in Ancient Athens: Iconography and Social History*. London: Routledge, 2015.

Beaumont, Lesley A. "Shifting Gender: Age and Social Status As Modifiers of Childhood Gender in Ancient Athens." In *The Oxford Handbook of Childhood and Education in the Classical World*, edited by Judith Evans Grubbs, Tim Parkin, and Roslynne Bell, 195–206. Oxford: Oxford University Press, 2013.

Behlmer, Heike. "Koptische Quellen zu (männlicher) 'Homosexualität.'" *Studien zur altägyptischen Kultur* 28 (2000): 27–53.

Behlmer, Heike. "'Our Disobedience Will Punish Us ... ': The Use of Authoritative Quotations in the Writings of Besa." In *Texte, Theben, Tonfragmente: Festschrift für Günter Burkard*, 37–54. Ägypten und Altes Testament 76. Wiesbaden: Harrassowitz, 2009.

Biale, David. *Blood and Belief: The Circulation of a Symbol between Jews and Christians.* Berkeley: University of California Press, 2008.

Boles, John, and the Dictionary of Virginia Biography. "Dabney, Robert Lewis (1820–1898)." www.encyclopediavirginia.org/Dabney_Robert_Lewis_1820–1898.

Bolman, Elizabeth S. "Figural Styles, Egypt, and the Early Byzantine World." In *The Red Monastery Church: Beauty and Asceticism in Upper Egypt,* edited by Elizabeth S. Bolman, 151–63. New Haven, CT: Yale University Press, 2016.

Bolman, Elizabeth S. "The Iconography of Salvation." In *The Red Monastery Church: Beauty and Asceticism in Upper Egypt,* edited by Elizabeth S. Bolman, 129–49. New Haven, CT: Yale University Press, 2016.

Bolman, Elizabeth S. "Joining the Community of Saints: Monastic Paintings and Ascetic Practice in Early Christian Egypt." In *Shaping Community: The Art and Archaeology of Monasticism: Papers from a Symposium Held at the Frederick R. Weisman Museum, University of Minnesota, March 10–12,* edited by Sheila McNally, 41–49. British Archaeological Reports International Series 941. Oxford: Archaeopress, 2001.

Bolman, Elizabeth S. "The Medieval Paintings in the Cave Church, Phase One: Continuity." In *The Cave Church of Paul the Hermit: At the Monastery of St. Paul in Egypt,* edited by William Lyster, 163–77. New Haven, CT: Yale University Press, 2008.

Bolman, Elizabeth S. *The Red Monastery Church: Beauty and Asceticism in Upper Egypt.* New Haven, CT: Yale University Press, 2016.

Bolman, Elizabeth S. "A Staggering Spectacle: Early Byzantine Aesthetics in the Triconch." In *The Red Monastery Church: Beauty and Asceticism in Upper Egypt,* edited by Elizabeth S. Bolman, 119–27. New Haven, CT: Yale University Press, 2016.

Bolman, Elizabeth S. "Theodore, 'The Writer of Life,' and the Program of 1232/1233." In *Monastic Visions: Wall Paintings in the Monastery of St. Antony at the Red Sea,* edited by Elizabeth S. Bolman, photography by Patrick Godeau, 37–76. New Haven, CT: Yale University Press, 2002.

Bolman, Elizabeth S. "Theodore's Program in Context: Egypt and the Mediterranean Region." In *Monastic Visions: Wall Paintings in the Monastery of St. Antony at the Red Sea,* edited by Elizabeth S. Bolman, photography by Patrick Godeau, 91–102. New Haven, CT: Yale University Press, 2002.

Bolman, Elizabeth S. "Veiling Sanctity in Christian Egypt: Visual and Spatial Solutions." In *Thresholds of the Sacred: Architectural, Art Historical, Liturgical, and Theological Perspectives on Religious Screens, East and West,* edited by Sharon E. J. Gerstel, 73–104. Washington, DC: Dumbarton Oaks, 2006.

Bolman, Elizabeth S., and Agnieszka Szymańska. "Ascetic Ancestors: Identity and Genealogy." In *The Red Monastery Church: Beauty and Asceticism in Upper Egypt,* edited by Elizabeth S. Bolman, 165–73. New Haven, CT: Yale University Press, 2016.

Boswell, John. *The Kindness of Strangers: The Abandonment of Children in Western Europe from Late Antiquity to the Renaissance.* New York: Pantheon Books, 1988.

Brakke, David. *Athanasius and Asceticism.* Baltimore, MD: Johns Hopkins University Press, 1998.

Brakke, David. *Demons and the Making of the Monk: Spiritual Combat in Early Christianity.* Cambridge, MA: Harvard University Press, 2006.

Brakke, David. "Shenoute, Weber, and the Monastic Prophet: Ancient and Modern Articulations of Ascetic Authority." In *Foundations of Power and Conflicts of Authority in Late-Antique Monasticism: Proceedings of the International Seminar in Turin, December 2–4,2004,* edited by Alberto Camplani and Giovanni Filoramo, 47–74. OLA 157. Louvain: Peeters, 2007.

Breydy, Michel. "Appendice. La version des *Règles et préceptes de St. Antoine* vérifiée sur les manuscrits arabes." In *Études sur le christianisme dans l'Égypte de l'antiquité tardive,* edited by Ewa Wipszycka, 395–403. Studia Ephemeridis Augustinianum 52. Rome: Institutum Patristicum Augustinianum, 1996.

Brooten, Bernadette J. *Love between Women: Early Christian Responses to Female Homoeroticism.* Chicago: University of Chicago Press, 2009.

Brown, Peter. *The Body and Society: Men, Women, and Sexual Renunciation in Early Christianity.* New York: Columbia University Press, 1988.

Brunt, P. A. "Morality and Social Convention in Stoic Thought." In *Studies in Stoicism,* edited by Miriam Griffin and Alison Samuels, 108–50. Oxford: Oxford University Press, 2013.

Burkert, Walter. *Homo Necans: The Anthropology of Ancient Greek Sacrificial Ritual and Myth.* Berkeley: University of California Press, 1986.

Burkert, Walter. "Sacrifice, Offerings, and Votives: Introduction." In *Religions of the Ancient World: A Guide,* edited by Sarah Iles Johnston, 325–48. Cambridge, MA: Harvard University Press, 2004.

Burrus, Virginia. "Reading Agnes: The Rhetoric of Gender in Ambrose and Prudentius." *JECS* 3, no. 1 (1995): 25–46.

Burrus, Virginia. *The Sex Lives of Saints: An Erotics of Ancient Hagiography.* Divinations: Rereading Late Ancient Religion. Philadelphia: University of Pennsylvania Press, 2004.

Burton-Christie, Douglas. *The Word in the Desert: Scripture and the Quest for Holiness in Early Christian Monasticism.* Oxford: Oxford University Press, 1993.

Bynum, Caroline Walker. *Wonderful Blood: Theology and Practice in Late Medieval Northern Germany and Beyond.* Philadelphia: University of Pennsylvania Press, 2007.

Cain, Andrew, ed. *Jerome's Epitaph on Paula: A Commentary on the Epitaphium Sanctae Paulae.* Oxford Early Christian Texts. Oxford: Oxford University Press, 2013.

Caldwell, Lauren. *Roman Girlhood and the Fashioning of Femininity.* Cambridge: Cambridge University Press, 2014.

Caseau, Béatrice Chevallier. "Childhood in Byzantine Saints' Lives." In *Becoming Byzantine: Children and Childhood in Byzantium,* edited by Arietta Papaconstantinou and Alice-Mary Maffry Talbot, 127–66.

Dumbarton Oaks Symposia and Colloquia. Washington, DC: Dumbarton Oaks, 2009.

Castelli, Elizabeth. "Researching and Responding to Violence, Ten Years On." *AJR*, March 16, 2016. www.ancientjewreview.com/articles/2016/3/16/research ing-and-responding-to-violence-ten-years-on.

Chin, C. M. "Apostles and Aristocrats." In *Melania: Early Christianity through the Life of One Family*, edited by C. M. Chin and Caroline T. Schroeder, 19–33. Christianity in Late Antiquity 3. Oakland: University of California Press, 2016.

Chin, C. M. *Grammar and Christianity in the Late Roman World*. Divinations: Rereading Late Ancient Religion. Philadelphia: University of Pennsylvania Press, 2011.

Chitty, Derwas. *The Desert a City: An Introduction to the Study of Egyptian and Palestinian Monasticism under the Christian Empire*. Crestwood, NY: St. Vladimir's Seminary Press, 1966.

Choat, Malcolm. "Monastic Letters on Papyrus from Late Antique Egypt." In *Writing and Communication in Early Egyptian Monasticism*, edited by Malcolm Choat and Mariachiara Giorda, 17–72. Texts and Studies in Eastern Christianity 9. Leiden: Brill, 2017.

Choat, Malcolm. "Narratives of Monastic Genealogy in Coptic Inscriptions." *Religion in the Roman Empire* 1, no. 3 (2015): 403–30.

Clackson, Sarah J. *"It Is Our Father Who Writes": Orders from the Monastery of Apollo at Bawit*. American Studies in Papyrology 43. Cincinnati, OH: American Society of Papyrologists, 2008.

Clark, Elizabeth A. "Ascetic Renunciation and Feminine Advancement: A Paradox of Late Ancient Christianity." *Anglican Theological Review* 63 (1981): 240–57.

Clark, Elizabeth A. "Foucault, the Fathers, and Sex." *Journal of the American Academy of Religion* 56, no. 4 (1988): 619–41.

Clark, Elizabeth A. *Jerome, Chrysostom, and Friends: Essays and Translations*. 2nd ed. Studies in Women and Religion 2. New York: Mellen, 1982.

Clark, Elizabeth A. *The Origenist Controversy: The Cultural Construction of an Early Christian Debate*. Princeton, NJ: Princeton University Press, 1992.

Clark, Elizabeth A. *Reading Renunciation: Asceticism and Scripture in Early Christianity*. Princeton, NJ: Princeton University Press, 1999.

Clark, Kenneth Willis. *Checklist of Manuscripts in St. Catherine's Monastery, Mount Sinai*. Washington, DC: Library of Congress, 1952.

Clédat, M. Jean. *Le monastère de la nécropole de Baouît, Fascicule 2, Mémoires publiés par les membres de l'Institut français d'archéologie orientale du Caire sous la direction de M. É. Chassinat*. MIFAO 12. Cairo: Institut français d'archéologie orientale, 1906.

Colish, Marcia L. *The Stoic Tradition from Antiquity to the Early Middle Ages*. 2 vols. Studies in the History of Christian Thought 34–35. Leiden: Brill, 1985.

Cooper, Kate. *The Fall of the Roman Household*. Cambridge: Cambridge University Press, 2011.

Cooper, Kate. "The Household and the Desert: Monastic and Biological Communities in the Lives of Melania the Younger." In *Household, Women, and Christianities in Late Antiquity and the Middle Ages*, edited by Anneke B. Mulder-Bakker and Jocelyn Wogan-Browne, 11–35. Turnhout: Brepols, 2005.

Cooper, Kate, and Conrad Leyser. "The Gender of Grace: Impotence, Servitude, and Manliness in the Fifth-Century West." *Gender & History* 12, no. 3 (2000): 536–51.

Cribiore, Raffaella. *Gymnastics of the Mind: Greek Education in Hellenistic and Roman Egypt*. Princeton, NJ: Princeton University Press, 2001.

Crislip, Andrew T. "Care for the Sick in Shenoute's Monasteries." In *Christianity and Monasticism in Upper Egypt: Volume 1, Akhmim and Sohag*, edited by Gawdat Gabra and Hany N. Takla, 21–30. Cairo: American University in Cairo Press, 2008.

Crislip, Andrew T. "Emotion Words in Coptic: Reflections on Evidence from Shenoute the Great." *Journal of the Canadian Society for Coptic Studies*, no. 10 (2018): 45–56.

Crislip, Andrew T. *From Monastery to Hospital: Christian Monasticism and the Transformation of Health Care in Late Antiquity*. Ann Arbor: University of Michigan Press, 2005.

Cromwell, Jennifer. "An Abandoned Wife and Unpaid Alimony." *Papyrus Stories* (blog), May 12, 2018. www.papyrus-stories.com/2018/05/12/an-abandoned-wife -and-unpaid-alimony/, accessed April 13, 2020.

Cromwell, Jennifer. "From Village to Monastery: Finding Children in the Coptic Record from Egypt." In *Handbook of Children in Antiquity*, edited by Leslie Beaumont, Matthew Dillon, and Nicola Harrington. London: Routledge, 2020.

Cromwell, Jennifer. "Potential Paternity Problem." *Papyrus Stories* (blog), June 8, 2018. www.papyrus-stories.com/2018/06/08/potential-paternity-pro blem/, accessed April 13, 2020.

Cromwell, Jennifer. "A Runaway Child Bride." *Papyrus Stories* (blog), May 29, 2018. www.papyrus-stories.com/2018/05/29/a-runaway-child-bride/, accessed April 13, 2020.

Crum, Walter E. *Catalogue of the Coptic Manuscripts in the British Museum*. London: British Museum, 1905.

Crum, Walter E. *A Coptic Dictionary*. Oxford: Clarendon, 1939.

Cunningham, Miranda J., and Marcelo Diversi. "Aging Out: Youths' Perspectives on Foster Care and the Transition to Independence." *Qualitative Social Work* 12, no. 5 (2013): 587–602.

Czaja-Szewczak, Barbara. "Tunics from Naqlun." In *Christianity and Monasticism in the Fayoum Oasis*, edited by Gawdat Gabra, 133–42. Cairo: American University in Cairo Press, 2005.

Dabney, Robert Lewis. *Life and Compaigns of Lieut.-Gen. Thomas J. Jackson*. New York: Blelock, 1866.

Darling Young, Robin. "A Life in Letters." In *Melania: Early Christianity through the Life of Own Family*, edited by C. M. Chin and Caroline T. Schroeder,

153–70. Christianity in Late Antiquity 3. Oakland: University of California Press, 2016.

Davis, Stephen J. *Coptic Christology in Practice: Incarnation and Divine Participation in Late Antique and Medieval Egypt.* Oxford Early Christian Studies. Oxford: Oxford University Press, 2008.

Davis, Stephen J. "Crossed Texts, Crossed Sex: Intertextuality and Gender in Early Christian Legends of Holy Women Disguised As Men." *JECS* 10, no. 1 (2002): 1–36.

De Bruyn, Theodore S. "Philosophical Counsel versus Customary Lament in Fourth-Century Christian Responses to Death." In *Rhetoric and Reality in Early Christianities*, edited by Willi Braun, 161–86. Studies in Christianity and Judaism 16. Waterloo, ON: Wilfrid Laurier University Press, 2005.

De Jong, Mayke. *In Samuel's Image: Child Oblation in the Early Medieval West.* Studies in Intellectual History 12. Leiden: Brill, 1996.

Dekker, Renate. "A Relative Chronology of the *Topos* of Epiphanius: The Identification of Its Leaders." In *Coptic Society, Literature and Religion from Late Antiquity to Modern Times*, vol. 1, edited by Paola Buzi, Alberto Camplani, and Federico Contardi, 755–67. OLA 27. Louvain: Peeters, 2016.

Delattre, Alain. "La traduction des institutions administratives dans les monastères égyptiens (VIIe–VIIIe siècles)." In *Interpretatio: Traduire l'altérité culturelle dans les civilisations de l'Antiquité*, edited by Frédéric Colin, Olivier Huck, and Sylvie Vanséveren, 213–28. Études d'archéologie et d'histoire ancienne. Paris: Éditions de Boccard, 2015.

Denzey, Nicola. "Facing the Beast: Justin, Christian Martyrdom, and Freedom of the Will." In *Stoicism in Early Christianity*, edited by Tuomas Rasimus, Troels Engberg-Pedersen, and Ismo Dunderberg, 176–98. Peabody, MA: Hendrickson, 2010.

Depauw, Mark, and Tom Gheldof. "Trismegistos. An Interdisciplinary Platform for Ancient World Texts and Related Information." In *Theory and Practice of Digital Libraries – TPDL 2013 Selected Workshops*, edited by Łukasz Bolikowski, Vittore Casarosa, Paula Goodale, Nikos Houssos, Paolo Manghi, Jochen Schirrwagen, 40–52. Communications in Computer and Information Science 416. Cham: Springer, 2014.

Depuydt, Leo. *Catalogue of Coptic Manuscripts in the Pierpont Morgan Library.* Louvain: Peeters, 1993.

Derda, Tomasz. *Deir El-Naqlun: The Greek Papyri (P. Naqlun I).* Studia Antiqua 11, *Journal of Juristic Papyrology Supplement* 9. Warsaw: Warsaw University, 1995.

Derda, Tomasz. "Polish Excavations at Deir El-Naqlun 1986–1991: Interdependence of Archaeology and Papyrology." In *Proceedings of the 20th International Congress of Papyrology, Copenhagen, 23–29 August, 1992*, edited by Adam Bülow-Jacobsen, 124–30. Copenhagen: Museum Tusculanum Press, 1994.

Dijkstra, Jitse H. F. "Blemmyes, Noubades and the Eastern Desert in Late Antiquity: Reassessing the Written Sources." In *The History of the Peoples of the Eastern Desert*, edited by Hans Barnard and Kim Duistermaat, 238–47. Cotsen Institute of Archaeology Press Monographs 73. Los Angeles: Cotsen Institute of Archaeology Press, 2012.

Dilley, Paul C. "Inscribed Identities: Prosopography of the Red and White Monasteries in the Early Byzantine and Medieval Periods." In *The Red Monastery Church: Beauty and Asceticism in Upper Egypt*, edited by Elizabeth S. Bolman, 217–29. New Haven, CT: Yale University Press, 2016.

Dilley, Paul C. *Monasteries and the Care of Souls in Late Antique Christianity: Cognition and Discipline*. Cambridge: Cambridge University Press, 2017.

Dixon, Suzanne. *The Roman Family*. Baltimore, MD: Johns Hopkins University Press, 1992.

Doerfler, Maria. "Holy Households." In *Melania: Early Christianity through the Life of Own Family*, edited by C. M. Chin and Caroline T. Schroeder, 71–85. Christianity in Late Antiquity 3. Oakland: University of California Press, 2016.

Doerfler, Maria. "The Infant, the Monk and the Martyr: The Death of Children in Eastern Patristic Thought." *Mus* 124 (2011): 243–58.

Doerfler, Maria E. *Jephthah's Daughter, Sarah's Son: The Death of Children in Late Antiquity*. Christianity in Late Antiquity 8. Oakland: University of California Press, 2020.

Draycott, Jane Louise. "Approaches to Healing in Roman Egypt." PhD diss., University of Nottingham, 2011.

Dworsky, Amy, and Mark E. Courtney. "Homelessness and the Transition from Foster Care to Adulthood." *Child Welfare* 88, no. 4 (2009): 23–56.

Elm, Susanna. *Sons of Hellenism, Fathers of the Church: Emperor Julian, Gregory of Nazianzus, and the Vision of Rome*. Transformation of the Classical Heritage 49. Berkeley: University of California Press, 2012.

Elm, Susanna. *"Virgins of God": The Making of Asceticism in Late Antiquity*. Oxford Early Christian Studies. Oxford: Oxford University Press, 1994.

Emmel, Stephen. "The Historical Circumstances of Shenute's Sermon 'God Is Blessed.'" In *Themelia: Spätantike und koptologische Studien: Peter Grossmann zum 65. Geburtstag*, edited by Martin Krause and Sofia Schaten, 81–96. Sprachen und Kulturen des christlichen Orients 3. Wiesbaden: Reichert, 1998.

Emmel, Stephen. *Shenoute's Literary Corpus*. 2 vols. CSCO 599–600. Louvain: Peeters, 2004.

Emmel, Stephen. "Shenoute the Monk: The Early Monastic Career of Shenoute the Archimandrite." In *Il monachesimo tra eredità e aperture: atti del simposio "Testi e temi nella tradizione del monachesimo cristiano" per il 50e anniversario dell'istituto monastico di Sant'Anselmo, Roma, 28 maggio–1e giugno 2002*, edited by Maciej Bielawski and Daniël Hombergen, 151–74. Rome: Pontificio ateneo S. Anselmo, 2004.

Enmarch, Roland. "Mortuary and Literary Laments: A Comparison." In *Ancient Egyptian Literature: Theory and Practice*, edited by Roland Enmarch and Verena M. Lepper, 83–100. Proceedings of the British Academy 188. Oxford: Oxford University Press for the British Academy, 2013.

Equiano, Olaudah. *The Interesting Narrative and Other Writings: Revised Edition.* Edited by Vincent Carretta. New York: Penguin, 2003.

Festugière, André Jean, ed. *Historia Monachorum in Aegypto.* Subsidia Hagiographia 53. Brussels: Société des Bollandistes, 1971.

Finsterbusch, Karin. "The First-Born between Sacrifice and Redemption in the Hebrew Bible." In *Human Sacrifice in Jewish and Christian Tradition*, edited by Karin Finsterbusch, Armin Lange, and Diethard Römheld, 87–108. Numen Book Series: Studies in the History of Religions 112. Leiden: Brill, 2007.

Foreman, P. Gabrielle, et al. "Writing about 'Slavery'? This Might Help." https://docs.google.com/document/d/1A4TEdDgYslX-hlKezLodMIM71My3KTNozx RvoIQTOQs, accessed August 19, 2019.

Forrer, Robert. *Die Graeber- und Textilfunde von Achmim-Panopolis.* Strassburg: E. Birkhäuser, 1891.

Foucault, Michel. *The History of Sexuality, Vol. 2: The Use of Pleasure.* Translated by Robert Hurley. Reissue edition. New York: Vintage Books, 1990.

Fouracre, Paul, and Richard A. Gerberding. *Late Merovingian France: History and Hagiography, 640–720.* Manchester Medieval Sources Series. Manchester: Manchester University Press, 1996.

Frank, Georgia. *The Memory of the Eyes: Pilgrims to Living Saints in Christian Late Antiquity.* Transformation of the Classical Heritage 30. Berkeley: University of California Press, 2000.

Frankfurter, David. "Egyptian Religion and the Problem of the Category 'Sacrifice.'" In *Ancient Mediterranean Sacrifice*, edited by Jennifer Wright Knust and Zsuzsanna Varhelyi, 75–93. New York: Oxford University Press, 2011.

Frankfurter, David. "Illuminating the Cult of Kothos: The *Panegyric on Macarius* and Local Religion in Fifth-Century Egypt." In *The World of Early Egyptian Christianity: Language, Literature, and Social Context*, edited by James E. Goehring and Janet A. Timbie, 176–88. CUA Studies in Early Christianity. Washington, DC: Catholic University of America Press, 2007.

Frankfurter, David. "The Perils of Love: Magic and Countermagic in Coptic Egypt." *Journal of the History of Sexuality* 10, no. 3/4 (2001): 480–500.

Funk, Wolf-Peter. "A Work Concordance to Shenoute's Canons." Unpublished. 2007.

Gabra, Gawdat. *Coptic Monasteries: Egypt's Monastic Art and Architecture.* Cairo: American University in Cairo Press, 2002.

Gabra, Gawdat. "Perspectives on the Monastery of St. Antony: Medieval and Later Inhabitants and Visitors." In *Monastic Visions: Wall Paintings in the Monastery of St. Antony at the Red Sea*, edited by Elizabeth S. Bolman, photography by Patrick Godeau, 173–84. New Haven, CT: Yale University Press, 2002.

Gaca, Kathy L. *The Making of Fornication: Eros, Ethics, and Political Reform in Greek Philosophy and Early Christianity.* Hellenistic Culture and Society. Berkeley: University of California Press, 2003.

Gardner, Iain. "A Letter from the Teacher: Some Comments on Letter-Writing and the Manichaean Community of IVth Century Egypt." In

Coptica-Gnostica-Manichaica: Mélanges offerts à Wolf-Peter Funk, edited by Louis Painchaud and Paul-Hubert Poirier, 317–23. Bibliothèque Copte de Nag Hammadi 7. Louvain: Peeters, 2006.

Gleason, Maud. "Visiting and News: Gossip and Reputation Management in the Desert." *JECS* 6, no. 3 (1998): 501–21.

Godlewski, Włodzimierz. "Excavating the Ancient Monastery at Naqlun." In *Christianity and Monasticism in the Fayoum Oasis*, edited by Gawdat Gabra, 155–71. Cairo: American University in Cairo Press, 2005.

Godlewski, Włodzimierz. *Le monastère de St. Phoibammon.* Deir el-Bahari 5. Warsaw: PWN, Editions scientifique de Pologne, 1986.

Goehring, James E. "The Dark Side of Landscape: Ideology and Power in the Christian Myth of the Desert." In *The Cultural Turn in Late Ancient Studies: Gender, Asceticism, and Historiography*, edited by Dale B. Martin and Patricia Cox Miller, 136–49. Durham, NC: Duke University Press, 2005.

Goehring, James E. "The Encroaching Desert: Literary Production and Ascetic Space in Early Christian Egypt." In *Ascetics, Society, and the Desert: Studies in Early Egyptian Monasticism*, 73–88. SAC. Harrisburg, PA: Trinity Press International, 1999.

Goehring, James E. *The Letter of Ammon and Pachomian Monasticism.* Patristische Texte und Studien 27. Berlin: de Gruyter, 1986.

Goehring, James E. "Monastic Diversity and Ideological Boundaries in Fourth-Century Christian Egypt." In *Ascetics, Society, and the Desert: Studies in Early Egyptian Monasticism*, 196–218. SAC. Harrisburg, PA: Trinity Press International, 1999.

Goehring, James E. "New Frontiers in Pachomian Studies." In *Ascetics, Society, and the Desert: Studies in Early Egyptian Monasticism*, 162–86. SAC. Harrisburg, PA: Trinity Press International, 1999.

Goehring, James E. "The Origins of Monasticism." In *Ascetics, Society, and the Desert: Studies in Early Egyptian Monasticism*, 13–35. SAC. Harrisburg, PA: Trinity Press International, 1999.

Goehring, James E. "Pachomius's Vision of Heresy: The Development of a Pachomian Tradition." In *Ascetics, Society, and the Desert: Studies in Early Egyptian Christianity*, 137–61. SAC. Harrisburg, PA: Trinity Press International, 1999.

Goehring, James E. "The World Engaged: The Social and Economic World of Early Egyptian Monasticism." In *Ascetics, Society, and the Desert: Studies in Early Egyptian Monasticism*, 39–52. SAC. Harrisburg, PA: Trinity Press International, 1999.

Golden, Mark. "Did the Ancients Care When Their Children Died?" *Greece & Rome* 35, no. 2 (1988): 152–63.

Goode, Leslie. "'Creating Descent' after Nancy Jay: A Reappraisal of Sacrifice and Social Reproduction." *Method & Theory in the Study of Religion* 21, no. 4 (2009): 383–401.

Goodrich, Richard J. *Contextualizing Cassian: Aristocrats, Asceticism, and Reformation in Fifth-Century Gaul.* Oxford Early Christian Studies. Oxford: Oxford University Press, 2007.

Gould, Graham. *The Desert Fathers on Monastic Community*. Oxford: Clarendon, 1993.

Graver, Margaret R. *Stoicism and Emotion*. Chicago: University of Chicago Press, 2007.

Greenfield, Richard. "Children in Byzantine Monasteries: Innocent Hearts or Vessels in the Harbor of the Devil?" In *Becoming Byzantine: Children and Childhood in Byzantium*, edited by Arietta Papaconstantinou and Alice-Mary Maffry Talbot, 253–82. Dumbarton Oaks Symposia and Colloquia. Washington, DC: Dumbarton Oaks, 2009.

Grossmann, Peter. "Zur Stiftung und Bauzeit der großen Kirche des Schenuteklosters bei Sūhāğ (Oberägypten)." *BZ* 101, no. 1 (2008): 35–54.

Grubbs, Judith Evans. "Church, State and Children: Christian and Imperial Attitudes toward Infant Exposure in Late Antiquity." In *The Power of Religion in Late Antiquity*, edited by Noel Lenski and Andrew Cain, 119–31. Farnham, Surrey: Ashgate, 2010.

Grubbs, Judith Evans. "Infant Exposure and Infanticide." In *The Oxford Handbook of Childhood and Education in the Classical World*, edited by Judith Evans Grubbs, Tim Parkin, and Roslynne Bell, 83–107. Oxford: Oxford University Press, 2013.

Grubbs, Judith Evans. *Law and Family in Late Antiquity: The Emperor Constantine's Marriage Legislation*. Oxford: Oxford University Press, 1995.

Grubbs, Judith Evans. *Women and the Law in the Roman Empire: A Sourcebook on Marriage, Divorce and Widowhood*. London: Routledge, 2002.

Grubbs, Judith Evans, Tim Parkin, and Roslynne Bell, eds. *The Oxford Handbook of Childhood and Education in the Classical World*. Oxford: Oxford University Press, 2013.

Gunderson, Erik. *Staging Masculinity: The Rhetoric of Performance in the Roman World*. The Body, in Theory. Ann Arbor: University of Michigan Press, 2000.

Haines-Eitzen, Kim. "'Girls Trained in Beautiful Writing': Female Scribes in Roman Antiquity and Early Christianity." *JECS* 6, no. 4 (1998): 629–46.

Halperin, David M. *One Hundred Years of Homosexuality: And Other Essays on Greek Love*. New York: Routledge, 1989.

Harmless, William. *Desert Christians: An Introduction to the Literature of Early Monasticism*. New York: Oxford University Press, 2004.

Hedrick, Charles W. "A Monastic Exorcism Text." *Journal of Coptic Studies* 7 (2005): 17–21.

Hedstrom, Darlene Brooks. *The Monastic Landscape of Late Antique Egypt*. Cambridge: Cambridge University Press, 2017.

Hen, Yitzhak. *Culture and Religion in Merovingian Gaul: A.D. 481–751*. Cultures, Beliefs, and Traditions 1. Leiden: Brill, 1995.

Hengstenberg, Wilhelm. Review of *Ten Coptic Legal Texts*, by Arthur A. Schiller. *BZ* 34 (1934): 78–95.

Heywood, Colin. *A History of Childhood: Children and Childhood in the West from Medieval to Modern Times*. Malden, MA: Wiley-Blackwell, 2001.

Hickey, Todd Michael. *Wine, Wealth, and the State in Late Antique Egypt: The House of Apion at Oxyrhynchus.* New Texts from Ancient Cultures. Ann Arbor: University of Michigan Press, 2012.

Hillner, Julia. "Monks and Children: Corporal Punishment in Late Antiquity." *European Review of History* 16, no. 6 (2009): 773–91.

Holman, Susan R. "Martyr-Saints and the Demon of Infant Mortality: Folk Healing in Early Christian Pediatric Medicine." In *Children and Family in Late Antiquity: Life, Death and Interaction,* edited by Christian Laes, Katariina Mustakallio, and Ville Vuolanto, 235–56. Interdisciplinary Studies in Ancient Culture and Religion 15. Louvain: Peeters, 2015.

Holman, Susan R. "Sick Children and Healing Saints: Medical Treatment of the Child in Christian Antiquity." In *Children in Late Ancient Christianity,* edited by Cornelia B. Horn and Robert R. Phenix, 145–70. Studien und Texte zu Antike und Christentum 58. Tübingen: Mohr Siebeck, 2009.

Horn, Cornelia B., and John W. Martens. *"Let the Little Children Come to Me": Childhood and Children in Early Christianity.* Washington, DC: Catholic University of America Press, 2009.

Horn, Cornelia B., and Robert R. Phenix, eds. *Children in Late Ancient Christianity.* Studien und Texte zu Antike und Christentum 58. Tübingen: Mohr Siebeck, 2009.

Huebner, Sabine R. "Adoption and Fosterage in the Ancient Eastern Mediterranean." In *The Oxford Handbook of Childhood and Education in the Classical World,* edited by Judith Evans Grubbs, Tim Parkin, and Roslynne Bell, 510–31. Oxford: Oxford University Press, 2013.

Huebner, Sabine R. *The Family in Roman Egypt: A Comparative Approach to Intergenerational Solidarity and Conflict.* Cambridge: Cambridge University Press, 2013.

Jacobs, Andrew S. "'Let Him Guard Pietas': Early Christian Exegesis and the Ascetic Family." *JECS* 11, no. 3 (2003): 265–81.

Jacobs, Andrew S., and Rebecca Krawiec. "Fathers Know Best? Christian Families in the Age of Asceticism." *JECS* 11, no. 3 (2003): 257–63.

Jay, Nancy. *Throughout Your Generations Forever: Sacrifice, Religion, and Paternity.* Chicago: University of Chicago Press, 1991.

Jones, Allen E. *Social Mobility in Late Antique Gaul: Strategies and Opportunities for the Non-elite.* Cambridge: Cambridge University Press, 2009.

Junior, Nyasha. *An Introduction to Womanist Biblical Interpretation.* Louisville, KY: Westminster John Knox, 2015.

Kāmil, Murād. *Catalogue of All Manuscripts in the Monastery of St. Catherine on Mount Sinai.* Wiesbaden: Harrassowitz, 1970.

Katz, Phyllis B. "Educating Paula: A Proposed Curriculum for Raising a 4th-Century Christian Infant." In *Constructions of Childhood in Ancient Greece and Italy,* edited by Ada Cohen and Jeremy B. Rutter, 115–27. Hesperia Supplement 41. Princeton, NJ: American School of Classical Studies at Athens, 2007.

Klingshirn, William E. *Caesarius of Arles: The Making of a Christian Community in Late Antique Gaul.* Cambridge Studies in Medieval Life and Thought, 4th Series 22. Cambridge: Cambridge University Press, 1994.

Konstan, David. *The Emotions of the Ancient Greeks: Studies in Aristotle and Classical Literature.* Toronto: University of Toronto Press, 2007.

Koziol, Geoffrey. Review of *Emotional Communities in the Early Middle Ages*, by Barbara H. Rosenwein. *Medieval Review* (2008, January 4). www .scholarworks.iu.edu/journals/index.php/tmr/article/view/16508.

Krawiec, Rebecca. "'From the Womb of the Church': Monastic Families." *JECS* 11, no. 3 (2003): 283–307.

Krawiec, Rebecca. "'Garments of Salvation': Representations of Monastic Clothing in Late Antiquity." *JECS* 17, no. 1 (2009): 125–50.

Krawiec, Rebecca. "Monastic Literacy in John Cassian: Toward a New Sublimity." *Church History* 81, no. 4 (2012): 765–95.

Krawiec, Rebecca. "The Role of the Female Elder in Shenoute's White Monastery." In *Christianity and Monasticism in Upper Egypt: Volume 1, Akhmim and Sohag*, edited by Gawdat Gabra and Hany N. Takla, 59–71. Cairo: American University in Cairo Press, 2008.

Krawiec, Rebecca. *Shenoute and the Women of the White Monastery.* New York: Oxford University Press, 2002.

Kuper, Laura E., Laurel Wright, and Brian Mustanski. "Gender Identity Development among Transgender and Gender Nonconforming Emerging Adults: An Intersectional Approach." *International Journal of Transgenderism* (2018): 1–20.

Kuryłowicz, Marek. "Adoption on the Evidence of Papyri." *JJP* 19 (1983): 61–75.

Laes, Christian. *Children in the Roman Empire: Outsiders Within.* Cambridge: Cambridge University Press, 2011.

Laes, Christian, and Johan Strubbe. *Youth in the Roman Empire: The Young and the Restless Years?* Cambridge: Cambridge University Press, 2014.

Laes, Christian, and Ville Vuolanto, eds. *Children and Everyday Life in the Roman and Late Antique World.* London: Routledge, 2016.

Lampe, Geoffrey W. H., ed. *A Patristic Greek Lexicon.* Oxford: Oxford University Press, 1969.

Lange, Armin. "'They Burn Their Sons and Daughters – That Was No Command of Mine' (Jer 7:31): Child Sacrifice in the Hebrew Bible and in the Deuteronomistic Jeremiah Redaction." In *Human Sacrifice in Jewish and Christian Tradition*, edited by Karin Finsterbusch, Armin Lange, and K. F. Diethard Römheld, in association with Lance Lazar, 109–32. Numen Book Series: Studies in the History of Religions 112. Leiden: Brill, 2007.

Larsen, Lillian I. "The *Apophthegmata Patrum*: Rustic Rumination or Rhetorical Recitation." *Meddelanden* 23 (2008): 21–30.

Larsen, Lillian I. "On Learning a New Alphabet: The Sayings of the Desert Fathers and the Monostichs of Menander." In *Studia Patristica. Vol. LV: Papers Presented at the Sixteenth International Conference on Patristic Studies Held in Oxford 2011. Volume 3: Early Monasticism and Classical Paideia*, edited by Markus Vinzent and Samuel Rubenson, 59–77. Studia Patristica 55. Louvain: Peeters, 2013.

Layton, Bentley. *The Canons of Our Fathers: Monastic Rules of Shenoute.* Oxford: Oxford University Press, 2014.

Layton, Bentley. *A Coptic Grammar.* 3rd ed., rev. Porta Linguarum Orientalium Neue Serie 20. Wiesbaden: Harrassowitz, 2011.

Layton, Bentley. "Rules, Patterns, and the Exercise of Power in Shenoute's Monastery: The Problem of World Replacement and Identity Maintenance." *JECS* 15, no. 1 (2007): 45–73.

Layton, Bentley. "Social Structure and Food Consumption in an Early Christian Monastery." *Mus* 115 (2002): 25–55.

Layton, Bentley. "Some Observations on Shenoute's Sources: Who Are Our Fathers?" *Journal of Coptic Studies* 11 (2009): 45–59.

Lear, Andrew, and Eva Cantarella. *Images of Ancient Greek Pederasty: Boys Were Their Gods.* London: Routledge, 2009.

Lee, Joann S., Mark E. Courtney, and Jennifer L. Hook. "Formal Bonds during the Transition to Adulthood: Extended Foster Care Support and Criminal/Legal Involvement." *Journal of Public Child Welfare* 6, no. 3 (2012): 255–79.

Legras, Bernard. "Mallokouria et mallocourètes. Un rite de passage dans l'Égypte romaine." *Cahiers du Centre Gustave Glotz* 4 (1993): 113–27.

LeVine, Robert A. "Human Variations: A Population Perspective on Psychological Processes." In *Psychological Anthropology*, edited by Robert A. LeVine, 55–59. Malden, MA: Wiley-Blackwell, 2010.

Leyerle, Blake. "Appealing to Children." *JECS* 5, no. 2 (1997): 243–70.

Leyerle, Blake. "Children and 'the Child' in Early Christianity." In *The Oxford Handbook of Childhood and Education in the Classical World*, edited by Judith Evans Grubbs, Tim Parkin, and Roslynne Bell, 559–79. Oxford: Oxford University Press, 2013.

Leyerle, Blake. "Children and Disease in a Sixth Century Monastery." In *What Athens Has to Do with Jerusalem: Essays on Classical, Jewish, and Early Christian Art and Archaeology in Honor of Gideon Förster*, edited by Leonard Rutgers, 345–68. Louvain: Peeters, 2002.

Leyser, Conrad. "*Lectio Divina, Oratio Pura*: Rhetoric and the Techniques of Asceticism in the *Conferences* of John Cassian." In *Modelli di santità e modelli di comportamento: Contrasti, intersezioni, complementarità*, 79–105. Turin: Rosenberg and Sellier, 1994.

Liddell, Henry George, and Robert Scott. *A Greek-English Lexicon.* Perseus Digital Library. www.perseus.tufts.edu.

Limberis, Vasiliki M. *Architects of Piety: The Cappadocian Fathers and the Cult of the Martyrs.* New York: Oxford University Press, 2011.

Logan, Alice. "Rehabilitating Jephthah." *Journal of Biblical Literature* 128 (2009): 665–86.

López, Ariel G. *Shenoute of Atripe and the Uses of Poverty.* Transformation of the Classical Heritage 50. Berkeley: University of California Press, 2013.

Lösch, Sandra, Estelle Hower-Tilmann, and Albert Zink. "Mummies and Skeletons from the Coptic Monastery Complex Deir El-Bachit in Thebes-West, Egypt." *Anthropologischer Anzeiger* 70, no. 1 (2013): 27–41.

Lubomierski, Nina. "The Coptic Life of Shenoute." In *Christianity and Monasticism in Upper Egypt: Volume 1, Akhmim and Sohag*, edited by Gawdat Gabra and Hany N. Takla, 91–98. Cairo: American University in Cairo Press, 2008.

Lubomierski, Nina. *Die Vita Sinuthii: Form- und Überlieferungsgeschichte der hagiographischen Texte über Schenute den Archimandriten*. Tübingen: Mohr Siebeck, 2007.

Lubomierski, Nina. "The *Vita Sinuthii* (The Life of Shenoute): Panegyric or Biography?" In *Studia Patristica vol. XXXIX: Papers Presented at the Fourteenth International Conference on Patristic Studies Held in Oxford 2003: Historica; Biblica; Ascetica et hagiographica*, edited by Frances Margaret Young, Mark J. Edwards, and Paul M. Parvis, 417–22. Louvain: Peeters, 2006.

Luckritz Marquis, Christine. "Namesake and Inheritance." In *Melania: Early Christianity through the Life of Own Family*, edited by C. M. Chin and Caroline T. Schroeder, 34–49. Christianity in Late Antiquity 3. Oakland: University of California Press, 2016.

Luckritz Marquis, Timothy. "Perfection Perfected." *Novum Testamentum* 57, no. 2 (2015): 187–205.

Luijendijk, AnneMarie. *Greetings in the Lord: Early Christians and the Oxyrhynchus Papyri*. Harvard Theological Studies 60. Cambridge, MA: Harvard University Press, 2008.

Lundhaug, Hugo, and Lance Jenott. *The Monastic Origins of the Nag Hammadi Codices*. Studien und Texte zu Antike und Christentum 97. Tübingen: Mohr Siebeck, 2015.

Lyster, William. "Reviving a Lost Tradition: The Eighteenth-Century Paintings in the Cave Church, Context and Iconography." In *The Cave Church of Paul the Hermit: At the Monastery of St. Paul in Egypt*, edited by William Lyster, 209–32. New Haven, CT: Yale University Press, 2008.

MacCormack, Sabine. *The Shadows of Poetry: Vergil in the Mind of Augustine*. Transformation of the Classical Heritage 26. Berkeley: University of California Press, 1998.

MacCoull, Leslie S. B. "Child Donations and Child Saints in Coptic Egypt." *East European Quarterly* 13 (1979): 409–15.

MacCoull, Leslie S. B. *Coptic Legal Documents: Law As Vernacular Text and Experience in Late Antique Egypt*. Medieval and Renaissance Texts and Studies 377. Tempe: Arizona Center for Medieval and Renaissance Studies, 2009.

Martin, Dale B. *The Corinthian Body*. New Haven, CT: Yale University Press, 1995.

Martin, Dale B. *Slavery As Salvation: The Metaphor of Slavery in Pauline Christianity*. New Haven, CT: Yale University Press, 1990.

Maspero, Jean. *Fouilles exécutées à Baouît*. MIFAO 59. Cairo: Imprimerie de l'Institut français d'archéologie orientale, 1931.

Mauss, Marcel. *The Gift: Forms and Functions of Exchange in Archaic Societies*. Translated by W. D. Halls. London: Routledge, 1990.

McClymond, Kathryn. *Beyond Sacred Violence: A Comparative Study of Sacrifice.* Baltimore, MD: Johns Hopkins University Press, 2008.

Miller, Patricia Cox. "Visceral Seeing: The Holy Body in Late Ancient Christianity." *JECS* 12, no. 4 (2004): 391–411.

Miller, Timothy S. "Charitable Institutions." In *The Oxford Handbook of Byzantine Studies,* edited by Elizabeth Jeffreys, John F. Haldon, and Robin Cormack, 621–30. Oxford: Oxford University Press, 2008.

Miller, Timothy S. *The Orphans of Byzantium: Child Welfare in the Christian Empire.* Washington, DC: Catholic University of America Press, 2003.

Moussa, Mark R. "Abba Moses of Abydos." MA Thesis, Catholic University of America, 1998.

Moussa, Mark R. "I Have Been Reading the Holy Gospels by Shenoute of Atripe (Discourses 8, Work 1): Coptic Text, Translation, and Commentary." PhD diss., Catholic University of America, 2010.

Nasrallah, Laura. "What Violence Does: Representing Bia in Antiquity." *AJR,* March 9, 2016. www.ancientjewreview.com/articles/2016/3/8/what-violence-does-representing-bia-in-antiquity.

Nau, François. "Histoires des solitaires égyptiens." *Revue de l'Orient chrétien* 12 (1907): 43–69, 171–89; 13 (1908): 47–66, 266–97; 14 (1909): 357–79; 17 (1912): 201–11, 294–301; 18 (1913): 137–46.

Nussbaum, Martha Craven. *The Therapy of Desire: Theory and Practice in Hellenistic Ethics.* Rev. ed. Princeton, NJ: Princeton University Press, 2009.

Nussbaum, Martha Craven. *Upheavals of Thought: The Intelligence of Emotions.* Cambridge: Cambridge University Press, 2001.

O'Connell, Elisabeth R. "Transforming Monumental Landscapes in Late Antique Egypt: Monastic Dwellings in Legal Documents from Western Thebes." *JECS* 15, no. 2 (2007): 239–73.

Orlandi, Tito. "The Library of the Monastery of Saint Shenute at Atripe." In *Perspectives on Panopolis: An Egyptian Town from Alexander the Great to the Arab Conquest,* edited by A. Egberts, B. P. Muhs, and J. van der Vliet, 211–31. Leiden: Brill, 2002.

Papaconstantinou, Arietta. "Notes sur les actes de donation d'enfant au monastère thébain de Saint-Phoibammon." *JJP* 32 (2002): 83–105.

Parca, Maryline. "The Wet Nurses of Ptolemaic and Roman Egypt." *Illinois Classical Studies* 42, no. 1 (2017): 203–26.

Patlagean, Evelyne. "L'histoire de la femme déguisée en moine et l'évolution de la sainteté féminine à Byzance." *Studi medievali* 17 (1976): 598–623.

Pearson, Birger A. "The Coptic Inscriptions in the Church of St. Antony." In *Monastic Visions: Wall Paintings in the Monastery of St. Antony at the Red Sea,* edited by Elizabeth S. Bolman, photography by Patrick Godeau, 217–39. New Haven, CT: Yale University Press, 2002.

Penn, Michael. *Kissing Christians: Ritual and Community in the Late Ancient Church.* Divinations: Rereading Late Ancient Religion. Philadelphia: University of Pennsylvania Press, 2005.

Piasecki, Karol. "The Skulls from Naqlun." *Polish Archaeology in the Mediterranean* 12 (2000): 173–80.

Pierpont Morgan Library. "MS M.583 Curatorial Description." http://corsair .themorgan.org/msdescr/BBM0583a.pdf, accessed April 13, 2020.

Prinzing, Günter. "Observations on the Legal Status of Children and the Stages of Childhood in Byzantium." In *Becoming Byzantine: Children and Childhood in Byzantium*, edited by Arietta Papaconstantinou and Alice-Mary Maffry Talbot, 15–34. Dumbarton Oaks Symposia and Colloquia. Washington, DC: Dumbarton Oaks, 2009.

Pudsey, April. "Children in Roman Egypt." In *The Oxford Handbook of Childhood and Education in the Classical World*, edited by Judith Evans Grubbs, Tim Parkin, and Roslynne Bell, 484–509. Oxford: Oxford University Press, 2013.

Pudsey, April. "Nuptiality and the Demographic Life Cycle of the Family in Roman Egypt." In *Demography and the Graeco-Roman World*, edited by Claire Holleran and April Pudsey, 60–98. Cambridge: Cambridge University Press, 2011.

Quibell, James E., and Herbert Thompson. *Excavations at Saqqara (1908–09, 1909–10): The Monastery of Apa Jeremias*. Cairo: Institut français d'archéologie orientale, 1912.

Rasimus, Tuomas, Troels Engberg-Pedersen, and Ismo Dunderberg, eds. *Stoicism in Early Christianity*. Peabody, MA: Hendrickson Publishers, 2010.

Rawson, Beryl. *The Family in Ancient Rome: New Perspectives*. Ithaca, NY: Cornell University Press, 1987.

Rawson, Beryl, and Paul Weaver. *The Roman Family in Italy: Status, Sentiment, Space*. Humanities Research Centre of the Australian National University Series. Oxford: Oxford University Press, 1999.

Reddy, William M. *The Navigation of Feeling: A Framework for the History of Emotions*. Cambridge: Cambridge University Press, 2001.

Richlin, Amy. "Not before Homosexuality: The Materiality of the Cinaedus and the Roman Law against Love between Men." *Journal of the History of Sexuality* 3, no. 4 (1993): 523–73.

Richlin, Amy. Review of *One Hundred Years of Homosexuality: And Other Essays on Greek Love*, by David M. Halperin. *BMCR*, 1991. https://bmcr.brynmawr.edu /1991/1991.01.08, accessed April 13, 2020.

Richter, Tonio Sebastian. " ' . . . Jealously We Looked at All the Sound Children Who Are Their Parents' Comfort . . . ' Pleasant and Unpleasant Emotions in Coptic Legal Documents." Paper presented at the 26th International Congress of Papyrology, Geneva, Switzerland, August 16–21, 2010.

Richter, Tonio Sebastian. "What's in a Story? Cultural Narratology and Coptic Child Donation Documents." *JJP* 35 (2005): 237–64.

Rosenwein, Barbara H. *Emotional Communities in the Early Middle Ages*. Ithaca, NY: Cornell University Press, 2007.

Rosenwein, Barbara H. "Worrying about Emotions in History." *American Historical Review* 107, no. 3 (2002): 821–45.

Rousseau, Philip. *Ascetics, Authority, and the Church in the Age of Jerome and Cassian.* 2nd ed. Notre Dame, IN: University of Notre Dame Press, 2010.

Rousseau, Philip. *Pachomius: The Making of a Community in Fourth-Century Egypt.* Rev. ed. Berkeley: University of California Press, 1999.

Ruddick, Sue. "The Politics of Aging: Globalization and the Restructuring of Youth and Childhood." *Antipode* 35, no. 2 (2003): 334–62.

Ruffini, Giovanni. *Life in an Egyptian Village in Late Antiquity: Aphrodito before and after the Islamic Conquest.* Cambridge: Cambridge University Press, 2018.

Scannapieco, Maria, Kelli Connell-Carrick, and Kirstin Painter. "In Their Own Words: Challenges Facing Youth Aging Out of Foster Care." *Child & Adolescent Social Work Journal* 24, no. 5 (2007): 423–35.

Schenke, Gesa. "The Healing Shrines of St. Phoibammon: Evidence of Cult Activity in Coptic Legal Documents." *Zeitschrift für Antikes Christentum* 20, no. 3 (2016): 496–523.

Schenke, Gesa. "Kinderschenkungen an das Kloster des Apa Thoma(s)?" *JJP* 37 (2007): 177–83.

Schiller, A. Arthur. *Ten Coptic Legal Texts.* New York: Metropolitan Museum of Art, 1932.

Schroeder, Caroline T. "Child Sacrifice in Egyptian Monastic Culture: From Familial Renunciation to Jephthah's Lost Daughter." *JECS* 20, no. 2 (2012): 269–302.

Schroeder, Caroline T. "Children in Early Egyptian Monasticism." In *Children in Late Ancient Christianity,* edited by Cornelia B. Horn and Robert R. Phenix, 317–38. Studien und Texte zu Antike und Christentum 58. Tübingen: Mohr Siebeck, 2009.

Schroeder, Caroline T. "Exemplary Women." In *Melania: Early Christianity through the Life of One Family,* edited by C. M. Chin and Caroline T. Schroeder, 50–66. Christianity in Late Antiquity 3. Oakland: University of California Press, 2016.

Schroeder, Caroline T. "In the Footsteps of Shenoute." *Marginalia Review of Books,* October 13, 2015. http://marginalia.lareviewofbooks.org/in-the-footsteps -of-shenoute-caroline-t-schroeder/.

Schroeder, Caroline T. *Monastic Bodies: Discipline and Salvation in Shenoute of Atripe.* Divinations. Philadelphia: University of Pennsylvania Press, 2007.

Schroeder, Caroline T. "Monastic Family Values: The Healing of Children in Late Antique Egypt," *Coptica* 10 (2011): 21–28.

Schroeder, Caroline T. "The Perfect Monk: Ideals of Masculinity in the Monastery of Shenoute." In *Copts in Context: Negotiating Identity, Tradition, and Modernity,* edited by Nelly van Doorn-Harder, 181–93. Columbia: University of South Carolina Press, 2017.

Schroeder, Caroline T. "Prophecy and Porneia in Shenoute's Letters: The Rhetoric of Sexuality in a Late Antique Egyptian Monastery." *Journal of Near Eastern Studies* 65, no. 2 (2006): 81–97.

Seibert, Peter. *Die Charakteristik: Untersuchungen zu einer altägyptischen Sprechsitte und ihren Ausprägungen in Folklore und Literatur.* Aegyptologische Abhandlungen 17. Wiesbaden: Harrassowitz, 1967.

Sessa, Kristina. *The Formation of Papal Authority in Late Antique Italy: Roman Bishops and the Domestic Sphere.* New York: Cambridge University Press, 2012.

Severy, Beth. *Augustus and the Family at the Birth of the Roman Empire.* New York: Routledge, 2003.

Shanzer, Danuta, and Ralph W. Mathisen. *Society and Culture in Late Antique Gaul: Revisiting the Sources.* Aldershot, Hants: Ashgate, 2001.

Sigismund-Nielsen, Hanne. "Slave and Lower-Class Roman Children." In *The Oxford Handbook of Childhood and Education in the Classical World,* edited by Judith Evans Grubbs, Tim Parkin, and Roslynne Bell, 286–301. Oxford: Oxford University Press, 2013.

Silvas, Anna M. *The Asketikon of St Basil the Great.* Oxford Early Christian Studies. Oxford: Oxford University Press, 2005.

Sontag, Susan. *Regarding the Pain of Others.* New York: Farrar, Straus, and Giroux, 2003.

Stewart, Columba. *Cassian the Monk.* Oxford Studies in Historical Theology. New York: Oxford University Press, 1998.

Stott, Tonia. "Placement Instability and Risky Behaviors of Youth Aging Out of Foster Care." *Child & Adolescent Social Work Journal* 29, no. 1 (February 2012): 61–83.

Tanner, Jennifer Lynn. "Recentering during Emerging Adulthood: A Critical Turning Point in Life Span Human Development." In *Emerging Adults in America: Coming of Age in the 21st Century,* edited by Jeffrey Jensen Arnett and Jennifer Lynn Tanner, 21–55. Washington, DC: American Psychological Association, 2006.

Thomas, John Philip, and Angela Constantinides Hero. *Byzantine Monastic Foundation Documents: A Complete Translation of the Surviving Founders' Typika and Testaments.* With the assistance of Giles Constable. 5 vols. Dumbarton Oaks Studies 35. Washington, DC: Dumbarton Oaks, 2000.

Thompson, Herbert. "Dioscorus and Shenoute." In *Recueil d'études égyptologiques dédiées à la mémoire de Jean-François Champollion: à l'occasion du centenaire de la lettre à M. Dacier, relative à l'alphabet des hiéroglyphes phonétiques, lue à l'Académie des Inscriptions et belles-lettres le 27 septembre 1822,* 367–76. Paris: E. Champion, 1923.

Thompson, John Lee. *Writing the Wrongs: Women of the Old Testament among Biblical Commentators from Philo through the Reformation.* Oxford Studies in Historical Theology. Oxford: Oxford University Press, 2001.

Thorsteinsson, Runar M. "Stoicism As a Key to Pauline Ethics in Romans." In *Stoicism in Early Christianity,* edited by Tuomas Rasimus, Troels Engberg-Pedersen, and Ismo Dunderberg, 15–38. Peabody, MA: Hendrickson Publishers, 2010.

Timbie, Janet A. "Writing Rules and Quoting Scripture in Early Coptic Monastic Texts." In *Ascetic Culture: Essays in Honor of Philip Rousseau,* edited by

Blake Leyerle and Robin Young, 29–49. Notre Dame: University of Notre Dame Press, 2013.

Van Dam, Raymond. *Leadership and Community in Late Antique Gaul.* Transformation of the Classical Heritage 8. Berkeley: University of California Press, 1985.

Van Loon, Gertrud J. M. *The Gate of Heaven: Wall Paintings with Old Testament Scenes in the Altar Room and the Hūrus of Coptic Churches.* Publications de l'Institut historique-archeologique neerlandais de Stamboul 85. Leiden: Nederlands Instituut voor het Nabije Oosten, 1999.

Van Moorsel, Paul. "Jephthah? Or, an Iconographical Discussion Continued." In *Mélanges offerts à Jean Vercoutter*, edited by Francis Geus and Florence Thill, 273–78. Paris: Editions Recherche sur les civilizations, 1985.

Vaughn, Michael G., Jeffrey J. Shook, and J. Curtis McMillen. "Aging Out of Foster Care and Legal Involvement: Toward a Typology of Risk." *Social Service Review* 82, no. 3 (September 2008): 419–46.

Vogt, Kari. "'The Woman Monk': A Theme in Byzantine Hagiography." In *Greece and Gender*, edited by Brit Berggreen and Nanno Marinatos, 141–48. Papers from the Norwegian Institute at Athens 2. Bergen: Norwegian Institute at Athens, 1995.

Von Hefele, Karl Joseph. *Histoire des conciles d'après les documents originaux.* Paris: Letouzey, 1907.

Vuolanto, Ville. "Children and Asceticism: Strategies of Continuity in the Late Fourth and Early Fifth Centuries." In *Hoping for Continuity: Childhood, Education, and Death in Antiquity and the Middle Ages*, edited by Katariina Mustakallio, Jussi Hanska, Hanna-Leena Sainio, and Ville Vuolanto, 119–32. Rome: Institutum Romanum Finlandiae, 2005.

Vuolanto, Ville. *Children and Asceticism in Late Antiquity: Continuity, Family Dynamics and the Rise of Christianity.* Farnham, Surrey: Ashgate, 2015.

Vuolanto, Ville. "Choosing Asceticism: Children and Parents, Vows and Conflicts." In *Children in Late Ancient Christianity*, edited by Cornelia B. Horn and Robert R. Phenix, 255–91. Studien und Texte zu Antike und Christentum 58. Tübingen: Mohr Siebeck, 2009.

Vuolanto, Ville. "Early Christian Communities As Family Networks: Fertile Virgins and Celibate Fathers." In *De amicitia: Friendship and Social Networks in Antiquity and the Middle Ages*, edited by Katariina Mustakallio and Christian Krötzl, 97–113. Rome: Institutum Romanum Finlandiae, 2010.

Ward, Benedicta. *Harlots of the Desert: A Study of Repentance in Early Monastic Sources.* Cistercian Studies Series 106. Kalamazoo, MI: Cistercian, 1987.

Watts, Edward. *Riot in Alexandria: Tradition and Group Dynamics in Late Antique Pagan and Christian Communities.* Transformation of the Classical Heritage 46. Berkeley: University of California Press, 2010.

Weitzmann, Kurt. "The Jephthah Panel in the Bema of the Church of St. Catherine's Monastery on Mount Sinai." *DOP* 18 (1964): 341–52.

Wheaton, Nathaniel S. *A Discourse on St. Paul's Epistle to Philemon; Exhibiting the Duty of Citizens of the Northern States in Regard to the Institution of Slavery; Delivered in Christ Church, Hartford; Dec. 22, 1850*. Hartford, CT: Tiffany, 1851.

Wickham, Chris. *Framing the Early Middle Ages: Europe and the Mediterranean 400–800*. Oxford: Oxford University Press, 2005.

Wiedemann, Thomas E. J. *Adults and Children in the Roman Empire*. New Haven, CT: Yale University Press, 1989.

Wilfong, Terry G. "'Friendship and Physical Desire': The Discourse of Female Homoeroticism in Fifth-Century CE Egypt." In *Among Women: From the Homosocial to the Homoerotic in the Ancient World*, edited by Nancy Sorkin Rabinowitz and Lisa Auanger, 304–29. Austin: University of Texas Press, 2002.

Wilfong, Terry G. *Women of Jeme: Lives in a Coptic Town in Late Antique Egypt*. Ann Arbor: University of Michigan Press, 2002.

Wipszycka, Ewa. "Apports de l'archéologie à l'histoire du monachisme Égyptien." In *The Spirituality of Ancient Monasticism: Acts of the International Colloquium held in Cracow-Tyniec 16–19 November 1994*, edited by Marek Starowieyski, 68–70. Krakow: Tyniec Wydawnictwo Benedyktynów, 1995.

Wipszycka, Ewa. "Les aspects économiques de la vie de la communauté des Kellia." In *Études sur le christianisme dans l'Égypte de l'antiquité tardive*, by Ewa Wipszycka, 337–62. Studia Ephemeridis Augustinianum 52. Rome: Institutum Patristicum Augustinianum, 1996.

Wipszycka, Ewa. "Donation of Children." In *Coptic Encyclopedia*, vol. 3, edited by Aziz Atiya, 918–19. New York: MacMillan, 1991.

Wipszycka, Ewa. *Études sur le christianisme dans l'Égypte de l'antiquité tardive*. Studia Ephemeridis Augustinianum 52. Rome: Institutum Patristicum Augustinianum, 1996.

Wipszycka, Ewa. *Moines et communautés monastiques en Égypte (IVe–VIIIe Siècles)*. *Journal of Juristic Papyrology Supplement* 11. Warsaw: Warsaw University, 2009.

Wipszycka, Ewa. "Le monachisme égyptien et les villes." In *Études sur le christianisme dans l'Égypte de l'antiquité tardive*, by Ewa Wipszycka, 281–336. Studia Ephemeridis Augustinianum 52. Rome: Institutum Patristicum Augustinianum, 1996.

Wipszycka, Ewa. "Les rapports entre les monastères et les laures à la lumière des fouilles de Naqlun (Fayoum)." In *Études sur le christianisme dans l'Égypte de l'antiquité tardive*, 373–93. Studia Ephemeridis Augustinianum 52. Rome: Institutum Patristicum Augustinianum, 1996.

Wipszycka, Ewa. "Resources and Economic Activities of the Egyptian Monastic Communities (4th–8th Century)." *JJP* 41 (2011): 159–263.

Wipszycka, Ewa. "Les terres de la congrégation pachômienne dans une liste de payments pour les apora." In *Le monde grec: pensée, littérature, histoire, documents. Hommages à Claire Préaux*, edited by Jean Bingen, Guy Cambier, and Georges Nachtergael, 625–36. Brussels: Éditions de l'Université de Bruxelles, 1975.

Wood, Ian. *The Merovingian Kingdoms, 450–751*. London: Longman, 1994.

Young, Dwight W. "Five Leaves from a Copy of Shenute's *Third Canon*." *Mus* 113, no. 3–4 (2000): 263–94.

Young, Dwight W. "Two Leaves from a Copy of Shenute's Ninth Canon." *WZKM* 88 (1998): 281–301.

Young, Dwight W. "With Respect to the Fourth Work of Shenute's *Sixth Canon*." *Göttinger Miszellen* 179 (2000): 85–106.

Žižek, Slavoj. *Looking Awry: An Introduction to Jacques Lacan through Popular Culture*. October Books. Cambridge: Massachusetts Institute of Technology Press, 1991.

Index of Ancient Sources

Papyri and Ostraca

All papyri are cited using the sigla at http://papyri.info/docs/checklist.
Many are available at http://papyri.info/ or www.trismegistos.org/.

BGU III 822, 115.n7; IV 1104, 7.n38; VIII 1848,
116.n9

O.Brit.Mus.Copt. I XX/4, 23.n14, 16; I XX/1,
54.n11; I LXVI/1, 42.n100, 53.n7; I add.23,
40.n93
O.CrumST 360, 119.n24
O.Lips. 24, 9.n46, 138.n25
O.Mon.Epiph. 120, 24.n25, 119–120

P.CLT 1 and 2, 32.n63
P.Grenf. 1.61, 121.n30
P.Heid. III 237, 7.n36
P.Kell.Copt. V 12, 26.n37; V 20–29,
27.n39, 40, 41, 42, 43, 44, 45
P.Kell.G. I 12, 26.n37
P.KRU 67, 31.n61; 75, 23.n19; 78–114, 42.n103; 79,
142.n35, 143.n39, 152.n24, 153.n28; 80,
142.n36, 152.n24, 153.n28; 81, 152.n24;
81.21, 153.n27; 86.17–32, 43.n107, 120.n26;
88.7, 12, 43.n111; 91, 142.n35, 142; 91.23–
26, 43.n110, 152.n22; 91.5–13, 43.n109, 43;

91.7, 120.n27; 92.14, 153.n25; 93, 152.n24,
153.n28; 93.32, 153.n25; 93.32–34,
153.n25,27; 96, 152.n24, 153.n29; 99.13,
153.n27; 100.14–43, 43.n108; 100.59–61,
152.n23
P.Lips. 28, 30–31, 32, 38
P.Lond. III 951, 121.n30; V 1676, 7.n39; VI 1914,
28.n49,50; VI 1915, 29.n52; VI 1916,
29.n53; VI 1926, 119.n24
P.Lond.Copt. 1130, 24.n23
P.Mich. 3.202, 121.n30; Inv. 6898, 218.n80
P.Mon.Epiph. 297, 23.n18; 359, 23.n19, 54.n10,
63.n47
P.Oxy. L 355, 7.n40
P.Pisentius 17, 7.n35, 119
P.Tebt 2, 6.n34
P.Wisc. 1, 6.n33

SB 5.7743, 116.n10; 14.11585, 115.n7
SB Kopt. IV 1709, 7.n37

UPZ I.59, 116.n8

Literary Sources

Acts of the Apostles 18:6, 212
Ammon, *Epistula Ammonis* 2, 46.n124; 9,
45.n120, 49.n135; 30, 47.n128
Apophthegmata Patrum (Alphabetical
Collection): Apollo 2, 99.n43, 108.n67;
Carion 1–3, 8.n45, 33.n64, 72.n10; Daniel
7, 99.n41; Gelasios 3, 39.n92; Isaac of
Kellia 5, 1.n1, 69.n2, 69; John the Persian
1, 74.n14; Macarius the Great 5, 69.n1, 69;
15, 114.n4, 114–115; Olympius 2, 112.n1,

112; Poemen 7, 116–117, 117.n12;
Prologue, 82.n36; Sisoes 10, 84–85,
85.n3, 94.n30
Apophthegmata Patrum (Anonymous
Collection): 171, 33.n64, 34.n69; 173,
33.n64, 34.n70; 187, 33.n64; 295, 85.n3,
94.n31; 340, 34.n71; 341, 33.n64,
34.n71
Apophtegmata Patrum (Systematic Collection):
Humility 16–18, 57.n22, 57

247

Index of Names and Subjects

CPSIA information can be obtained
at www.ICGtesting.com
Printed in the USA
LVHW011651060621
689491LV00002B/109